To B
with v.

C000183273

Kenneth Ballantyne

All the Things You Are

Published by
Laundry Cottage Books
Laundry Cottage
Shawbirch Road
Admaston
Wellington
Shropshire
TF5 0AD

Tel: 01952 – 223931

Email: cenneach@westcoast13.wanadoo.co.uk

First published in Great Britain in 2012
by Laundry Cottage Books, Shawbirch Road,
Admaston, Wellington, Shropshire, TF5 0AD
ISBN 978-0-9550601-4-4

An environmentally friendly book, typeset, printed and bound in England
by www.printondemand-worldwide.com

This book is made entirely of chain-of-custody materials

Other Titles Published by Laundry Cottage Books

Another Dawn Another Dusk
by Kenneth Ballantyne

> The biography of Trevor Bowyer, DFC, ISM, a rear gunner in
> RAF Bomber Command during World War Two and survivor of
> fifty-nine missions
> ISBN 978-0-9550601-3-7

The Journey
by Kenneth Ballantyne

> [Title no longer available]

The D-Day Dodger
by Albert F Darlington

> The autobiography of an infantry soldier who fought his way
> through the Italian campaign during World War Two and was
> awarded the American Purple Heart
> ISBN 978-0-9550601-2-0

Acknowledgements

I am deeply grateful to all those people who have made the telling of these stories possible by kindly sharing their very personal memories and experiences with me. I am especially grateful to them for showing so much interest in this work and for giving me of their time and unreserved consent to use their own material and personal photographs.

I am indebted to Cornelius Ryan for his authoritative and documented work on Operation Market-Garden, *A Bridge Too Far*. I have found it an invaluable resource in following the experiences of Pier Nuke the British 1st Airborne paratrooper who fought at Arnhem [Chapter 12] and putting them into context as Pier related them to me almost seventy years after they had occurred.

My thanks are also due to Fred Henderson, the Super Moderator of the Ships Nostalgia Forum, who very kindly provided me with a great deal of factual information about the HMT *Laconia*, and to Susan Fry, who kindly interpreted the greeting from Karl Dönitz to Frank Parker [Chapter 7].

I would also like to thank all the people who have kindly made their photographs generally available by uploading them onto the internet for wider enjoyment and use.

Remaining photographs are from my own collection.

I am once more indebted to Sue Browning of Sue Browning, Editing and Proofreading for kindly correcting my literary waywardness and grammatical inexactitudes, and for guiding the flow of this story through the pitfalls of writing. I also add my apologies to Sue if I have dabbled with the manuscript after she returned it to me and in so doing take full responsibility for any consequential errors.

The fact that this book has become a reality from the original idea is in no small way due to the immeasurable help and support which my wife Elaine has given to me whilst I have been writing it. An integral part of the team, she never lost faith that this book is a worthy sequel to *Another Dawn Another Dusk*, which continues to enjoy great success. Thank you could never be adequate.

Kenneth Ballantyne

Dedication

This book is dedicated to all those who have so kindly and so generously shared their memories and experiences with me on behalf of the men and women of Britain who served this country, whether in the Services, on the land, in the factories and offices, in the voluntary services, in the hospitals or in the home during the dark and uncertain years of World War Two between 1939 and 1945 to keep our country free.

It is the duty of those of us who have come afterwards to ensure that they shall never be forgotten.

It should never be forgotten that victory, after almost six years of bloody and ruthless war, both in Europe and in the Far East, was only won through the courage of hundreds of thousands of ordinary men and women and with the lives of far too many.

On VE Day, 8th May 1945 and VJ Day, 15th August 1945, there were many people in Britain and across the world who did not feel like celebrating. Pleased and relieved though they were that the killing had stopped, for them it was time for reflection, for considering the cost of having lost someone close and dear to them. For some, the loss was of more than one and the pain was multiplied. To celebrate the end of the war was good and it was necessary, but let us not forget those who didn't see it and those that they left behind.

Contents

All the Things You Are

A collection of twelve true stories from World War Two
told by the women and men who lived them

by
Kenneth Ballantyne

All the Things You Are

"Let us therefore brace ourselves to our duty; so bear ourselves that if the British Empire and its Commonwealth lasts for a thousand years, men will still say, 'This, was their finest hour.'"

Winston Spencer Churchill
British Prime Minister. 18th June 1940

Whilst many books have been written about the Second World War, there are relatively few which tell the stories of the ordinary men and women of Britain to whom the chalice of war was passed by the government.

This book is not just a selection of stories from a few individuals, but is the embodiment of a generation which achieved what no generation of Britons had ever achieved before – the total defeat of an enemy who not only had the intention to invade this country, but one who had all the necessary means at his disposal to achieve that aim.

Unlike any previous war in the history of these islands, it was a war which affected and engulfed every man, woman and child alike. The bombs that indiscriminately rained down upon our cities made no distinction between young and old, sick and healthy, rich and poor, unknown and well known, or men and women; death or survival was in the gift of fate alone. For the first time, the entire population was totally embraced by and deeply involved in the war on a daily basis; bombing, rationing, evacuation, the threat of invasion, restrictions on movement and liberty, hunger, weariness, fear, worry, separation, and for so many, personal loss.

The Great War of 1914–1918 had involved the populace, but in a different way. Almost all families had husbands, sons and brothers away in the Army, the Navy or the Royal Flying Corps but, despite severe shortages and rationing, day-to-day life was not as fundamentally affected in the same way as it was twenty years later. There were two main differences; during the Second World War the civilian population were on the front line and were just as likely to be killed or injured as anyone else, and secondly, women were much more involved in the Armed Forces and the Home Front than their mothers had been.

The prosecution of the war saw fighting progressively undertaken on several fronts, but from the very first day until well after the end of hostilities, the Home Front represented a constant and unremitting battle and it was the women of Britain who were holding that front line. Women, some of whom had husbands away in the Services, including the Merchant Navy or as prisoners of war, still had to bring up a family, to work on the land and in the forests, in the factories, the brickworks, the railways, keeping the war supplies flowing, or to take in evacuees and help in the canteens, and at a time of intense rationing, when everything was either 'on points' or in short supply, they had to queue for hours, all too often in vain. With no supermarkets or fast-food outlets, hunger and hardship were about the only commodities not in short supply.

By the autumn of 1941, Britain had just two weeks' food supply left; where the Luftwaffe had failed to win the Battle of Britain, the U-boat wolf packs almost prevailed in the Battle of the Atlantic and their endeavour to starve the country into submission. The Women's Land Army became the engine which fed the nation.

Over half a million women joined the WRNS, the ATS, the WAAF and the military or civilian nursing services. Others engaged in factory work or joined the fire services, the Land Army, the Observer Corps and many other government schemes and organisations. For more than three years, across the length and breadth of Britain, as night after night the bombs relentlessly fell on our towns and cities, men and women stood out on roof tops in the open air on fire watch duty, engaged in a very close and personal battle with the incendiary bombs, which if left to burn would ignite raging fires, causing greater and more extensive damage than the high explosives. The destruction of Coventry still resonates in the British psyche.

In addition, some one million older women or those with young families worked tirelessly in the Women's Voluntary Service and other unpaid roles. The WVS did not just serve tea and sandwiches from the ubiquitous canteen on every major railway station and troop landing port, but also assisted the local authorities to re-unite, re-house and re-clothe families bombed out of their homes, and with the necessary but draining task of administering the makeshift mortuaries set up after the heavy bombing raids which razed great swathes of the cities from Portsmouth to Glasgow, from Hull to Liverpool. By the end of the war, more than six million women had served on the Home Front.

They worked, fought and sometimes died in almost every capacity in that generation's struggle for freedom against the tyranny that was the Nazi domination of Europe from the late 1930s to 1945. For a small, select group of women, that meant taking the fight to the enemy in occupied Europe: the Special Operations Executive agents. Recruited mainly from the WAAF and the FANY, the First Aid Nursing Yeomanry, they were parachuted into enemy-held territory to link up with the local Resistance groups and cause as much disruption to the German forces as possible. Trusting almost no-one helped personal survival, but even so, many were captured, brutally tortured and executed in concentration camps.

This book, written through the eyes of the individuals, tells some of the experiences of just a few of the ordinary men and women of that remarkable generation. Dazzling, exciting, funny, sobering, heart-warming, and incredible, theirs are stories of courage, resourcefulness, and resoluteness on the Home Front and on the battle front. They are each unique in their own way but collectively they are the embodiment of the spirit which saw Britain through its darkest time for a thousand years: this was indeed their finest hour.

Mary-Jane and Robert Brown.

Chapter One
Anne Shaw's great-grandmother, Mary-Jane Brown

> *"I'll tell you, shall I, something that I remember?*
> *Something that still means a great deal to me. It was*
> *long ago.*
> *A dusty road in summer I remember, a mountain, and*
> *an old house, and a tree that stood, you know..."*

> From 'It Was Long Ago'. *Eleanor Farjeon*

My charismatic great-grandmother was christened Mary-Jane Gilchrist, but has been known throughout the family as Granny Manie for as long as I can remember. She was born in 1867 in Wallsend-on-Tyne, married and lived there all her life until she passed away aged 87 in 1954, leaving many fond memories. Although it is now part of the Newcastle-upon-Tyne conurbation, Wallsend was originally an independent settlement which dates right back to Roman times, from where it gets its name. The fort of Segedunum stood at the eastern end of Hadrian's Wall, which was built between AD 122 and 129 to protect this part of the Roman Empire from the marauding northern tribes of Scots and Celts who caused the Empire so much harm, not least by annihilating its Ninth Legion. The wall started in the west at Bowness-on-Solway just outside modern-day Carlisle and ran across one of the narrowest parts of England. Today the 2,000-year-old wall is a World Heritage Site.

Before the 1800s had turned into the war-torn 20th century, before Edward VII had succeeded Queen Victoria to the throne of the British Empire, Granny Manie had given birth to eighteen children, fifteen girls and just three ill-fated boys, John, William and Robert. Not all the children survived beyond childhood as in those days infant mortality was very high. Life in Wallsend in the 19th century was hard for everyone, but it was particularly hard for the poor: it didn't get much better until after the Second World War and was a place of despair and destitution for many years during the great depression of the late 1920s and 1930s. Even now, in the comparative affluence of the 21st century, unemployment in the North East stubbornly remains higher than the national average.

My great-grandparents lived, with most of their nine surviving children in a first-floor flat at 26 Charlotte Street, Wallsend-on-Tyne. Their home had two rooms, plus a scullery and a back yard with privy. It had no sanitation, no electricity, gas only when there was money for the meter and a basic cold water supply. Washday really was a whole day's job, done by hand in a dolly tub with a washboard for scrubbing. Every drop of water had to be heated on the coal fire of the kitchen range and then carried to the scullery and poured into the tub. Drying it all, especially in winter, was another day's work, and then it had to be ironed with a solid smoothing iron heated on the fire plate. The kitchen was the heart of the home with the range bread oven in constant use, filling the house with the evocative smell of freshly baked bread, the ever present great cauldron of soup bubbling over the fire and suet puddings filled with whatever she could afford to buy.

Granny Manie, who was quite a small woman, was lucky in those days because her husband Robert was mostly in work, at least until the years of the great depression, which brought unemployment to her family as it did to almost every family in the North East at that time. Great-grandfather Robert was very good to Manie and he treated her well, but she did avoid many an argument with him by using her canny wits. One thing that he insisted upon was that his tea should be on the table when he got home from work or from the pub, whatever time that might be and he would moan and groan at her if it wasn't. As she got older, Granny Manie took less notice of what her husband wanted and tended to please herself much more; after all, she had borne him eighteen children. On one occasion, Manie had, as so often, been next door blethering with Mrs Marshall. Before she realised what time it was she heard my great-grandfather arrive home. As she came through the door he met her with a torrent of complaint for sitting next door when she should have been at home preparing his tea for him after he had been working hard all day.

Completely unconcerned by all his remonstrations, she prepared his tea and the next day she was back with Mrs Marshall again. Once more teatime arrived and there was no sign of Granny. However, this time Robert had been to the boozer for a couple of beers or so on his way home and whilst waiting for his wife to come back, he fell asleep in his chair. When she came in, Granny saw him there fast asleep and snoring quietly. Knowing that this time she might well be in for real trouble, she took some beef dripping from the cupboard and smeared it on his moustache; when he awoke and demanded his tea, she looked at him with innocent surprise and told him that he had already had it and that there was still dripping on his moustache.

In 1904, her eldest son, John, left home to work on the North East Railway. Ten years later, the Great War started and, at the age of forty-seven, Granny Manie saw her other two sons enlist into the army and go to war in France. But by 1920 her three sons were all dead. Robert, the youngest, was killed on the Western Front at Ypres in 1917, where he is buried. Her middle son, William, survived the horrors of the trenches and returned home, only to die in the influenza pandemic of 1919, and a year later her eldest son, John, too old to have gone to France, was electrocuted whilst working on the railway. Life can be very cruel, but death even more so.

By the end of the Great War her six daughters had all left home and were married, once more returning the little dwelling to the sole occupancy of my great-grandparents. Mr and Mrs Marshall still lived next door and the turbulent relationship Granny had with her closest neighbours continued. She had a family clock which she kept on a shelf in the kitchen facing the adjoining wall of the Marshall's flat. Whenever Mrs Marshall wanted to know what the time was, she would pull a loose brick out of the fireplace and look at the clock on the shelf across Granny's kitchen. From time to time, the two women would have a disagreement over something and nothing and the first thing that Granny would do was turn the clock around so that Mrs Marshall could not see it. Undeterred, the brick would be removed, even though she knew she would not be able to see the clock, and she would shout through the hole, "Hey, Brown, what time is it?", to which Granny would call back, "Time you bought yoursel' a bloody clock."

In 1927, Mr Marshall became the proud owner of an accordion which he played with great gusto. At times when relations were good between the two houses, Granny would bang on the wall and invite her neighbour to play the accordion by shouting, "Hey, Marshall, give us a tune on that thing."

My great-grandmother's prized possession was her candlewick bedspread. It seems inconceivable today when people have so much so easily, that such a simple possession could be so important. She had saved long and hard for this bedspread at 3d a week, which was a big commitment when wages were counted in shillings not pounds, and it was the only one in the street. She never used this bedspread as everyday bedding, it was far too valuable, but typical of the era when the bond of belonging bound communities tightly together through good and bad and people helped each other, she would lend her precious bedspread to anyone in the street who needed to call the doctor; in this way appearances were kept up and the pride of the community maintained. What great people they were then.

I also had an uncle, Jimmy, who was a bookies' runner, in the days when betting was only allowed on a race course or dog track. Every now and then, the police would have a clampdown and wait for Jimmy to have his pockets full of betting slips and the bookies' clock. When the police chased him, he would always run to Granny Manie's, where he would stash the evidence in the bread oven, whether it was in use or not, and when the constables came in he would be sitting having a cup of tea with his grandmother. They never did catch

Jimmy, even though the local bobby's name truly was Dick Barton!

September 1939 saw Britain once more at war with Germany. This time, though, the whole civilian population was involved in a way that was unprecedented. The bombing of civilian homes, factories and fishing boats brought a new dimension to modern warfare. The government provided an Anderson shelter kit to every home that had enough garden to accommodate one. A little later, Morrison shelters, named after Ernest Morrison the Minister of Supply, were developed, which were rugged steel-framed cages designed to be erected inside the house to help protect against the bombing, although a direct hit would still be fatal.

The Anderson shelters were often cold and damp as they were erected by digging a hole in the ground and then covering it with corrugated iron sheets. The soil from the hole was then piled on top of the sheets to provide stability and protection against blast. Inevitably, water seeped into most of these shelters and it was not unusual for families to sit for hours on end during an air raid with their feet in several inches of water. Some were able to make their shelter a little less uncomfortable by putting bricks or duckboards on the floor to keep their feet out of the water or building bunks to lie on. But on the whole they were rather uninviting and many people did not bother to go into them but preferred to stay in the house and take their chance.

Not everyone had a garden and those that didn't were not provided with an Anderson shelter by the government; instead, communal air-raid shelters were built in the streets. One night, as the air-raid siren sounded, my Auntie Betty gathered up her blankets and flask of hot tea and went down into the shelter which was opposite her house. Her parents, sisters and brother all stayed in the house because they were fed up with sitting for hours on end on the hard wooden planks that served as benches in the damp, smelly congestion of the public shelter.

In the gloom of the public shelter, Betty pulled her blanket more tightly around her body as she shivered with cold and the fear that gripped everyone during an air raid. Exhaustion from lack of sleep and the constant trauma of yet another raid added to her misery. She heard the drone of the engines becoming louder as the bombers got nearer, and then they were overhead. She felt the tremors through the ground under her feet, gently at first but soon more violently as the carpet of explosions crept inexorably closer with each passing aircraft. Suddenly, the whole shelter shook then lifted up, before the bricks settled back in place like a pack of shuffled cards. Someone screamed, children started crying; brick dust and earth silently trickled from the joints in the ceiling, the dim lighting spluttered then failed altogether, and in the darkness of that moment, Betty knew. She rushed outside and in the bright glow of the fires she saw the home she had left half an hour before, now just a pile of burning timber and rubble. She was completely numbed by the sight that confronted her; her entire family, parents, sisters and brother, gone. She couldn't take it in and was still standing staring vacantly at the burning house when the Air Raid Precaution [ARP] wardens arrived and guided her away to be cared for by the WVS. She was never the same again and she never forgot that terrible night.

The whole community shared the war. Telegrams, good or bad, were delivered by a GPO messenger boy on his bicycle, and whenever one of them turned into the road, everybody stopped what they were doing and held their breath. They watched the boy cycle slowly down the street to the address on the little brown envelope. The telegram boys knew what the message was and people got to know whether it was good or bad by the speed of the bicycle; the slower it was pedalled, the worse the news in the envelope. The telegram delivered, the boy would cycle away as fast as he could, unless, of course, it was particularly good news, in which case he would wait in case there was a tip on offer. The whole street would read the telegram and those who received the dreaded news of the loss of a son, a husband, or sometimes a daughter, were taken care of, together with any young children in the house. During the war, rich and poor alike, we really were all in it together, unlike now.

Manie's family were all strong Church of England Christians and even though they were very poor, they worshipped every Sunday, attending St. Peter's Church in Wallsend, which was built in 1807–09 to replace the mediaeval church of Holy Cross and was the very first church known to be built in Wallsend.

My own parents met in London during an air raid, when they were literally thrown together. The sirens were still sounding when the bombers arrived and unloaded the first wave of high explosives. My father, who was one of Manie's grandsons, was a soldier and whilst running for cover heard the whistle of the approaching bomb and instinctively knew that it was going to be a very close thing. Next to him and also running for shelter was a young woman. As the bomb screamed down towards them, at the last moment my father threw himself against the young women to protect her from the flying shards of glass that inflicted so many injuries to anyone caught by the blast. That particular young woman in time became my mother, so I suppose I have to be thankful for that bomb. I hope that it did not kill anyone, because it ultimately gave me life.

My mother's cousin was Bertie Stubbins, who lived in Whitley Bay and played football for Newcastle United in the days when footballers were real people and part of the communities in which they lived, not like the many over-paid, over-rated and over-indulged prima donnas in the game today. Bertie, like everyone else who played football at the highest level in those days, had a proper job in the week, trained in the evenings and played the matches on a Saturday afternoon in front of an enthusiastic, well-behaved family crowd. They also played with a leather football which when wet, doubled its weight. I doubt whether too many of today's footballers could perform at all if they had to use a leather football instead of the modern lightweight plastic ones.

In 1947, Newcastle had a good and very high-scoring run in the FA cup which took them all the way to the semi-finals. On 11th January their opponents were Crystal Palace. The game was played at Newcastle's home ground, St. James' Park. Bertie was playing that day and all the family gathered at Granny Manie's house to listen to the game on her new wireless set. Newcastle won the game 6–0 but when they scored their first goal, Auntie Maggie jumped up on the kitchen table and danced a jig, showing everyone her knickers in the process – an event she was not allowed to forget in a hurry. That might seem very tame now, but at the time it was simply not something a woman of her age would have normally done and demonstrates how excited we all were at Newcastle's success over a London club.

My great-grandmother was born before the Battle of Rorke's Drift in the South African Zulu wars; she lived through the Boer War then two world wars, and was ruled by four kings and two queens. She saw the invention of cars, aeroplanes, telephones, wireless and television, the discovery of penicillin, radiation and the double helix structure of DNA. She was of the generation who lived through the greatest fundamental changes that the world has ever seen, and she embraced it all.

Manie with her daughters and great-granddaughter Anne Shaw.

The memorial stone to the Home Front at the National Memorial Arboretum, Alrewas, Staffordshire.

Chapter Two
Nancy Salter

> *"The bombs have shattered my churches, have torn my streets apart,*
> *But they have not bent my spirit and they shall not break my heart.*
> *For my people's faith and courage are lights of London town*
> *which still would shine in legends though my last broad bridge were down."*
>
> *From* 'London Under Bombardment'. *Greta Briggs*

William Salter and I were married on Friday 1st September 1939 at about the same time that the German army was busy invading Poland. We had arranged our wedding back in the April, and whilst William, who worked at the Admiralty in London, told me that war with Germany was now inevitable, no-one knew just when it would come and we certainly didn't think that it would be quite so close to our wedding day. For our honeymoon, we had taken a room at the New Inn, Clovelly, on the north Devon coast. After our wedding at St. Barnabas' Church, Pimlico, we spent the night in London before travelling on Saturday by train to the West Country.

I was so excited to be going away on my honeymoon, but at the same time I was very apprehensive because all the railway stations were crowded with an odd mix of troops en route to wherever, and hundreds of children, each with a buff-coloured luggage label tied to their coat or jacket bearing their name on one side and destination on the other; they were evacuees from London. Later in our journey, Bristol Temple Meads Station was the same. William didn't say much, other than that the invasion of Poland could start the war. Surely not, I kept thinking, I've just got married; but I could tell that he was worried about it all.

Once out of Paddington Station, I tried not to think too much about the impending war, and as the proud steam engine sped the train westward leaving a trail of smoke and steam in its wake, I concentrated on enjoying the journey through the lush late summer countryside, of which there was a great deal more then than there is today.

Tired and a little grubby from our journey, we arrived at the New Inn in time for dinner on Saturday evening and then afterwards we walked hand in hand down the cobbled hill to the harbour. I gazed at the picture that was the evening sky, the boats and the cottages reflected in the flat peaceful sea that barely disturbed the little craft at their moorings, the water gently slapping against their boards whilst a lone seagull wheeled overhead, mournfully crying as it looked for a late supper. We stood for a long time, hardly speaking, just watching the glory of the fading sunset drifting away below the western horizon, each of us wrapped in our thoughts of what lay ahead. Finally, the flickering lights in the little cottages around the harbour told us that it was time to make our way back to the New Inn, and so we set off back up that well-trodden hill, resolved to enjoy whatever time we had here.

At breakfast the next morning, there was only one topic of conversation around the little dining room. Afterwards, we left and went to the morning service in the lovely 12th-century stone church of All Saints. It was a very short service as everyone wanted to be home to hear the Prime Minister speak. Just before 11.15, along with everyone else in the hotel, we gathered around the wireless set and heard Alvar Lidell introduce Neville Chamberlain:

> "*I am speaking to you from the Cabinet Room of 10, Downing Street. This morning the British Ambassador in Berlin handed the German Government a final note, stating that unless we heard from them by 11 o'clock that they were prepared at once to withdraw their troops from Poland, a state of war would exist between us. I have to tell you now that no such undertaking has been received and that consequently, this country is at war with Germany.*"

So that was that.

"What do we do now, William?" I asked.

"For the moment, nothing, although I expect I shall have to return to London rather sooner than I had hoped. I'm afraid I had to tell them where we were staying."

The telegram from the Admiralty arrived next day shortly after lunch. Our honeymoon was over and we were to return to London as soon as possible. I ordered two packed lunches for our journey and after breakfast on Tuesday morning, William settled our account and with much sadness set off for London, leaving the New Inn bathed in the warm September sunshine. Bloody Nazis! Didn't they know I had just got married; I was so angry.

At that time we had rented a house just south of the Thames, barely into the suburbs, which of course did not stretch anything like as far from the city centre as they do today, and once the Blitz started in September 1940, we were very heavily bombed. And then from summer 1944 onwards for the rest of the war we were in the main area for the V1s and V2s. Although many of Britain's cities had been bombed for several months already, London, on Hitler's strict orders, had been spared. Saturday 24th August 1940 changed all that.

Almost certainly by mistake, a number of Luftwaffe bombers unloaded their incendiaries and high explosives over the city. The next night, on Winston Churchill's orders, the RAF retaliated and bombed Berlin for the first time. For nearly a fortnight no more bombs fell on London, and then during the day on the 7th September a major raid hit the city. The fires started during the day acted as a beacon for the waves of bombers which came in that night. The Blitz had started in earnest for London, the East End and the docks in particular, and it continued for another seventy-five consecutive nights and then for a long time afterwards, with some of the worst bombing causing a firestorm on the night of 29th December 1940.

The end of the Battle of Britain saw an intensification of the mass bombing of all of Britain's major cities and ports. Inevitably London was the most consistently bombed city but immense damage was caused to every target area. Hull, at the mouth of the Humber River on the east coast of England, was one of the most devastated cities in Britain because of its easy access across the North Sea from the Luftwaffe airfields in France and Holland. Indeed, the devastation was so great in Hull, and also on Clydebank just outside Glasgow, that the government prevented any accurate reporting of the true extent of the damage in order not to undermine morale and give the enemy a propaganda fillip as well.

William was never at home during these air raids because he was also a member of the Auxiliary Fire Service, the AFS, and didn't get home until well after the raids were over. Sometimes he wouldn't get home at all and would go straight to his Admiralty work. Many times the crews of both the full-time London Fire Brigade and the AFS worked through most of the day after a big raid and they only had a little time to rest before the raids started again the next night. The Blitz had started and it was relentless, night after night. Sometimes we wondered if it would ever end.

Whenever he could, William would let me know that he was safe, but the raids very often disrupted the main services including the telephone network and so communications became very difficult. Even though we had a telephone because of William's work it would sometimes be two or three days before I saw or heard from him and I had no idea whether he was alive or not: I worried about him terribly. I knew that the fire services were out in the open, not just in London but in all our towns and cities whilst the bombs were falling, trying to contain the spread of the fires. William would tell me that putting the large fires out was not really possible; the effort on the fires caused by the incendiaries and by the high-explosive bombs was to stop the spread of the flames to other buildings. In the confines of a city, these raging fires destroyed more buildings and supplies than the actual bombs, which was of course the whole idea. They also acted as a marker for the bombers coming in the next night. The Home Defence strategy was to contain the fires by dousing the outside walls with water and so keep them as cool as possible to prevent the fire spreading.

The small incendiary bombs were dropped along with the high explosives so that they would cause a major fire if they were not put out very quickly with sand or water. Often this task fell to the very courageous people on fire watch duty on the main buildings. If they could cover these small sticks of phosphorous that fell in their thousands during a raid then it would prevent a much bigger fire starting. That's what the fire watchers were able to do so successfully to save St Paul's Cathedral.

At the beginning of the Blitz, the authorities closed the underground stations at dusk to stop people going into them during air raids, but they soon had to stop doing that as people simply went down early before the raids started, often during the late afternoon or even sooner, and just stayed there. After a very short time the whole thing was put on a more formal footing, tickets were issued and by mid to late September more than 150,000 people were sleeping in the underground every night. The children were put into bunks along the platforms or in hammocks slung between the rails and meals were cooked on portable kitchen stoves in the foyer areas. When the best parts along the platforms and passageways were full, people would just get what sleep they could by curling up on the treads of the stairs and escalators. It wasn't for everyone, though. My friend Violet would never go down there; she preferred to take her chance under the kitchen table with the eight other members of her family. They would all lie on the floor with their heads under the table and the rest of their bodies sticking out into the kitchen.

As soon as it started to drop dusk, which got earlier each day as the autumn turned to the winter of 1940, I would put up the blackout curtains. The Air Raid Precaution wardens, the ARPs, were very strict about making sure that no chink of light could be seen so as not to give any sort of clue to the German bombers. Of course, more often than not, the fires were still burning from the night before, lighting up the East End and the docks. London was an easy target as all the bomber pilots had to do was find the mouth of the Thames at the North Sea and then follow it west until they reached the city. However, London wasn't undefended as in addition to the anti-aircraft guns which were placed around the city, all along the river there were more anti-aircraft guns mounted onto barges. These could be easily moved if needed and were mainly away from the danger of collapsing buildings. There were also fire-fighting barges moving up and down the river, drawing water directly from the Thames and pumping it onto the burning dockside buildings. William told me that the Germans knew this and would watch the tide times carefully, launching their biggest raids to coincide with particularly low tides so that there was less water to draw and the barges couldn't get in so close to the fires.

We didn't have long to wait after dark before it started. The air-raid sirens would wail and then the bombing would go on for hours. Where we lived there weren't as many official air-raid shelters for people to go to as there were in the city centres. In any event, packing up a few night things and going off to a shelter wasn't really an option for me since I was heavily pregnant by that time. Like most people who had a small garden, we had an Anderson shelter in it, but it was cold and damp, especially as the night temperatures were dropping with the approach of winter. I really didn't want to go in there on my own and being pregnant it was all too much of a struggle; and anyway, if the shelter took a direct hit, it wouldn't save me, so I decided that I was as well off in the house. Consequently, I would take my dog, a pillow and some blankets and make up a bed on the floor under the stairs.

When the bombs started to fall the noise was terrible, it became almost unbearable, night after night. I was so frightened that I would hug my little dog tighter as I could hear the crump, crump of distant explosions. Then the house started to tremble and the windows began to rattle with each explosion as the bombs got nearer; so close now. Then I heard the whistle, that wailing portent of the bomb that was coming to get me; I really thought I was going to die at that moment and I screamed. The explosion was deafening; the whole house seemed to lift up and then settle back again; the glass in the windows shattered and blew in, despite the tape that was on them all. Even under the stairs, the air was sucked out of my lungs, but the unending noise of explosions, of glass shattering, of the bells ringing on the fire engines and ambulances just carried on without a break; it seemed endless.

I don't know how long I lay there with my arm wrapped tightly around my faithful dog Molly, trying to take in the fact that I was still alive. I knew that the bomb had fallen very close. As my brain started to work again, I realised that I needed to know whether the house was on fire. I pushed on the door of the cupboard but it wouldn't open; I was trapped under the stairs and had no idea whether the house was burning or had collapsed on top of us. Trying not to panic, I sat up with my back against the wall and pushed the door with my feet. There was very little headroom under the stairs and with the bulge of my baby inside me, it was so difficult to get any pressure behind my efforts. I felt the door begin to move and it gave me hope. I pushed harder and it moved some more. Finally, I managed to ease it wide enough for me to get my head out so that I could see what had happened.

The sight that greeted me did nothing to cheer me up. Our front door had been blown in and I could see the devastation across the street. There was little left of the house opposite and what there was, was on fire: the wailing bomb had hit Emily Fullerton's house instead of ours. I felt sick. Was she in her shelter or the house?

The raid seemed to be moving further away now, the explosions were sounding more distant, and I thought that perhaps the bombers had had enough and were going home. The door to the cupboard I was in was jammed by the front door and most of the hall ceiling which had fallen onto the floor. I scraped some of the plaster away and reached out to give the broken remains of the front door a good shove. It didn't move much, but enough; I could get out. In the glow from the fires, I looked around at the mess. The blackout curtains in the front room were hanging off the rails and all the glass had gone from the windows. I slipped the lead onto Molly's collar and went outside. The ARPs were at Mrs Fullerton's and an appliance from the AFS had arrived. I could feel the heat from the burning house and then an arm slipped around my shoulder and my friend Jenny Golding guided me towards her house. "They said Emily wouldn't have known anything about it, Nancy." The shock of just how close I had come to being killed suddenly hit me; I burst into tears and vomited violently at the same time. She was such a sweet old lady. She didn't deserve to die like that.

As the daylight filtered through the pall of smoke which hung over our neighbourhood, people began to pick their way through the rubble-strewn streets to go to work. If you weren't bombed out, you just got on with the daily routine and went to work or whatever else it was that each one did. That was very important to us; it was a way of showing defiance, of not being beaten, not giving in no matter what was thrown at us.

William managed to get back home later that morning and started to clear up the mess in the house. We had been lucky, the damage was only superficial, although it was a long time before we had a proper front door and glass in the windows again.

The bombers came over with a relentless, punishing predictability for seventy-six consecutive nights. After that there were more breaks, but even so, I thought that it would never end, that sooner or later they would get me. I was so tired; we all were. Sleep was impossible during the endless bombing and then afterwards there was still so much noise with the firefighters and the rescue parties. And then the clearing up began and another day started. Sometimes the bombing had been further away and there was nothing different to see, but at other times it had been much closer and wherever I went there were newly damaged or burnt-out buildings. By the end of the war, over 40,000 civilians in Britain would have been killed by the bombs, 20,000 of them in London alone.

Then one night, just before what turned out to be a particularly heavy raid, Jenny, who had three children of her own, had come into the house to keep me company for a while. As we sat in the kitchen having a cup of tea and talking, the air-raid sirens sounded their mournful wailing, warning us that another raid was about to start, earlier than usual this time. Once more my heart started pounding with the fear that had gripped my life each night since Emily Fullerton had been killed. Then suddenly my underwear felt very wet: I didn't know what was happening to me. Fortunately, Jenny realised that my waters had broken and my first baby was on his way. She used our telephone to ring our local cottage hospital and they managed to get an old Great War ambulance to our house and, with its bells ringing loudly, rushed me in just as the bombs started to fall.

I went into labour more or less straight away, with the sounds of droning aircraft engines, the crump of bombs exploding as they hit the ground and the thudding bark of the anti-aircraft guns from the recreation ground ringing in my ears. I knew that the bombs were falling very close and I thought of Emily Fullerton again. I was so frightened that I would be killed before my baby was born, and then one fell almost on top of the hospital. There was a huge flash and several explosions; the old hospital shook on its foundations and some of the windows in the little delivery room shattered against the blackout material. The noise was terrifying; I heard myself scream, whether with fear or pain, I don't know, but in that moment, in the middle of an air raid, my son Raymond arrived into this world.

William came to see us that morning before going back to the Admiralty. That was just before Christmas 1940 and we had another five months of bombing to endure. However, by mid-1941, the Luftwaffe's blitz campaign had run out of steam. The spirit of the British people had not been broken but the German bomber crew losses had become unsustainable as the RAF night fighter force became increasingly effective. Of course, the bombing didn't stop altogether, but it wasn't like the dark days of the autumn, winter and spring of 1940/41.

As the war progressed, we had strict rationing as almost everything became increasingly scarce; even lavatory paper was in short supply. Tea, sugar, butter, margarine, meat, sausages, eggs, flour, clothes, petrol and much more were all rationed. There were queues everywhere for everything. I spent hours queuing, often without success; everybody did. It was soul destroying but there was nothing else for it. We had to register with the local shops in order to be served and when the supplies had gone, that was it, whether you had got anything or not.

Of course, most shopkeepers would usually keep a bit of something 'under the counter' for their regular customers. This was not the same as the 'black market' as the under-the-counter food was sold at the same price as everything else, it was just that it would be the better cuts of meat or an extra cracked egg for a young mother like me. The prices which the shops charged were set by the government, so everyone paid the same and that way everyone had access to the same food, irrespective of wealth.

The black market was altogether different and items were sold to the highest bidder, but it was a serious criminal offence to buy or sell anything on the black market. It was dangerous, expensive and over-rated and William would have never forgiven me if I had ever bought anything on the black market, even if we could have afforded it.

Women queued in bombed-out streets, between piles of rubble, in the rain, the sunshine, and the snow for that matter; we had to queue, there was no alternative. Petrol was rationed straight away, but even by January 1940, basic foods were in such short supply that on the 8th, just a week into the New Year, wider rationing started with bacon, butter and sugar. By March, all meat was rationed. In July tea was added, followed, during 1941, by jam, cheese, clothes, eggs, and coal. By 1942 things were really desperate and most shops had little or nothing that wasn't rationed. That year rice, dried fruit, soap, tinned tomatoes and peas, gas and electricity, sweets and chocolate, biscuits and finally, in 1943 even sausages were added to the list, and goodness knows, there was precious little meat in them by then anyway. Fish was 'off ration' because as an island nation we had easy access to the sea in theory, but it was always in short supply as the dangers of putting to sea in wartime to catch any fish were all too obvious. Rumours of fresh fish would create an instant queue.

The ration books, issued by the Food Executive Office, contained points, sixteen to start with, although this was increased to twenty later in the war, which were exchanged, along with the cost of the items, for food and other goods. Everybody of five years and over had their own buff-coloured ration book, although, like all expectant mothers, when I was pregnant with Raymond and for a year afterwards, I had a green-coloured book because it contained more points so I could get extra rations especially of milk and orange juice.

Water too was rationed; we were only allowed one bath each week with no more than five inches of water in it. The reason for this was that the fuel used to heat the water was coal, either directly or through gas or electricity, and coal was rationed, so baths were, too. At other times there simply wasn't any water for long periods because of the damage caused to the water mains by the bombing.

At the height of the bombing, across London and most other cities there were communal cooking centres, run by the local council or one of the many voluntary services such as the WVS, the Red Cross or the Salvation Army. They would cook meals which were then sold at very low prices to people who had been bombed out or in areas where all the gas and electricity had been cut off. There were also communal mobile laundry centres, because with water and heating fuel being rationed, it was more economical to have a communal laundry. These facilities would set up in a street at a convenient point and people would bring their dirty laundry; it also helped to prevent the spread of disease and particularly lice, which would have been more likely if people were unable to wash their clothes and bedding for long periods.

Then, on 13th June 1944, the first doodlebug, Hitler's Vengeance weapon, fell close to the railway bridge at Grove Road, Mile End, killing eight civilians.

After that they started to rain down on England, mainly London and the south-east, causing 22,892 casualties, of which 6,184 were deaths. Croydon was the most heavily hit area. In a way, these were more terrifying than the blitz raids because there was little or no warning of them. The V1 flying bombs were just that, a bomb with an engine attached to it that would come across the Channel and over the Kent countryside until it reached London. The sound of the engine was unmistakeable and I can still hear it to this day. It sounded like an old motor cycle with a splutter. You were all right as long as the engine kept going, but once it stopped, there was only about ten seconds to run for cover as it fell to earth and exploded.

These rockets were just aimed in the general direction of London and very many fell on the residential areas of the city, killing hundreds of women and children. By 1944, some Spitfires and the Hawker Tempest fighters were fast enough to catch them and together with anti-aircraft fire and barrage balloons, 4,261 V1s were shot down. Rather than shoot at them, some of the pilots would get their wing tip under the wing of the V1 and upset the gyro setting. Nevertheless, many hundreds got through, both by day and night and we hated and dreaded the sound of that spluttering engine. The last V1 to fall on Britain was on 29th March 1945 at Datchworth in Hertfordshire. After that, all the launch sites had been captured by our troops in Europe.

The end of the war did not bring an end to rationing and many items remained on the list until June 1954. These were desperately hard times and I look around with horror today when I see the amount of perfectly good food that is just thrown away, or that people waste on their plates. They wouldn't behave like that if they had had to live through the rationing of the war. A typical week's ration for one adult was 4oz of butter or lard, 12 oz of sugar, 4 oz of raw bacon or ham, 2 eggs, and 3½ oz of cooked bacon or ham. Bread was always in short supply and, like the fish, a queue would quickly form if there was to be a delivery of bread at the bakers. Most shops only opened for two or three days in the week as they didn't have anything to sell on the other days. Of course, there was no Sunday opening in those days; people went to church.

I had an older brother and a younger sister. We had all left home by 1939; my brother, Albert, joined the army, my sister, Lily, became a nurse, and I married William.

Albert was sent out to the Far East and was taken prisoner by the Japanese at Singapore in 1942, then forced to work on the notorious Burma railway. He was beaten repeatedly and nearly starved to death. He saw prisoners being tied up and stretched out on the ground whilst the guards rode motor cycles over their legs to break them; and then they rode back over them again. He never forgot the screams of those men. Sometimes it was done as a punishment and sometimes just to relieve the boredom of the guards.

Cruelty, work, starvation and disease cost the lives of thousands of Allied prisoners at the hands of the Japanese, and the atomic bombs on Hiroshima and Nagasaki came just in time for Albert and for many others in the living hell of those prison camps. Only about 45% of Allied prisoners survived the

Japanese camps, whereas 95% of Japanese prisoners survived in Allied camps. It tells its own story of the treatment that each side received. The conditions in the concentration camps in Germany which were uncovered at the end of the war are widely and rightly documented. However, much less is known and told about the appalling cruelty which the Japanese inflicted upon their prisoners during those years.

After he got home and began to physically recover from his experiences, Albert got a job and finally married, but it was many years before he would talk about what happened to him in the prison camp and on the railway. The physical scars healed but he never lost the psychological scars. A few years ago, together with a friend, I visited the National Memorial Arboretum at Alrewas in Staffordshire and saw the Far East Prisoners of War memorial there which is housed in a replica camp hut and contains many visual and written testaments. I began to understand.

St Barnabas' Church, Pimlico, where Nancy Slater was married.

St. Michael's Cathedral, Coventry.

Chapter Three
John Oldham

> *"Guns from the sea open against us: the smoke rocks bodily in the casement and a yell of doom goes up, we count and bless each new, heavy concussion – captives awaiting rescue."*
>
> From 'Dawn Bombardment'. *Robert Graves*

Sitting at home, somewhat absently listening to the wireless set, I became conscious that the BBC presenter was announcing that today was the 70th anniversary of the devastating German bombing of Coventry which destroyed its cathedral. I didn't need to be reminded of that night, because I had been in the midst of it at the time and had experienced the destructive terror of the attack as it unfolded. I had been on fire watch duty on the roof of the Council House, just a few yards away from St. Michael's Cathedral.

In April 1939, when the government saw that war with Germany was inevitable, it passed the Military Training Act, which required all men aged twenty and twenty-one to register for six months' military training. The Act also made exemptions for those in the reserved occupations and listed them as farmers, scientists, merchant seamen, railway workers, utility workers [gas, water and electricity], miners and dockers. By October 1939, we were still a long way short of a million men in the Services and so the government introduced conscription for all men between eighteen and forty-one who were not in reserved occupations. Call-up was by age and started with men between twenty and twenty-three. In November 1940 I was nineteen and knew that all the young men between twenty-one and thirty-two had either volunteered or already been called up and that it would not be long before that little brown envelope addressed to me and headed On His Majesty's Service would drop through the letter box at home.

I had worked in the Treasurer's Department of Coventry City Council at its main offices in Earl Street since leaving school; now I was nineteen years of age and waiting to join up.

We had already become used to German bombing raids on the city, which was a major manufacturing centre in the Midlands making aircraft, tanks, munitions and many other essential war materials. Sometimes raids on Coventry were carried out by just a single aircraft or perhaps a small group of bombers, usually Heinkel 111s and Dornier 17s, both twin-engine aircraft which were the mainstay of the Luftwaffe bomber force for most of the war.

It had been in one of these earlier raids that my grandparents' house at Albert Street in the Hillfields part of the city had been damaged and so every night they came over to our house to sleep. I lived with my parents at 216 Walsgrave Road which stood on the corner of King's Crescent. My mother's sister, Lily, who at this time was desperately ill with cancer, lived next door at 214.

The fact that Coventry was a target was no surprise to us and bombing raids had become a regular feature of our daily, or more accurately our nightly, lives. We were also caught up with the bombing of targets west of us, Birmingham and Wolverhampton in particular, so there were not many nights when the air-raid sirens didn't sound, even if we were not always destined or planned to be on the receiving end. Whenever the sirens started their mournful wailing sound, which even to this day sends a shiver down my spine, my parents, grandparents, who had been bombed out of their own home, and I all crowded into the small space under the stairs, dutifully following the advice given to everyone by the Ministry of Information that the safest place in the house during an air raid was under the stairs as a precautionary measure against blast, flying glass and other debris. A direct hit, though, almost always brought certain death wherever you were.

I hated it. I felt constrained, restricted and frustrated and would take every chance, together with my father, to go outside and see what was going on, despite the anxious pleas from my mother for us both to return to the crowded confines of the under-stairs cupboard where she felt that we would be safer, if only from the falling shrapnel residue of exploding anti-aircraft shells. After all, what goes up must come down.

Friday 10th May 1940 had seen the start of an extraordinary year in British history. Winston Churchill had replaced Neville Chamberlain as Prime Minister; the Germans had launched their *Blitzkrieg* offensive through the Low Countries and into France, and within a month Britain stood alone against the military might of the Third Reich. The French army had collapsed and the British Expeditionary Force lay isolated and defeated across the English Channel, but by logistical brilliance, an armada of small boats and ships, and many acts of courage, over 338,000 BEF and French troops were rescued from the beaches of Dunkirk and the French Atlantic ports.

Almost immediately, the Battle of Britain began and raged over southern England and the English Channel from mid-July until 15th September, which, in the event, turned out to be the decisive day in the battle. For it was on that day, as Winston Churchill sat in the operations room at Bentley Priory in Hertfordshire, the headquarters of RAF Fighter Command, he was informed that every last serviceable aircraft and pilot which the Command possessed was engaged against the enemy. There were no reserves: this day was make or break in the battle and the survival of Britain as a free country.

The struggle for control of the air space over the Channel couldn't have been more finely balanced, but on that September day it swung in favour of the British. The Luftwaffe losses were unsustainable and added to its losses throughout the summer, it simply did not have the crews to keep up the pressure. Operation Sealion, the German plan for the invasion of Britain, had to be postponed and later abandoned altogether. Had the Luftwaffe not succumbed to RAF Fighter Command that day, the invasion of Britain would have begun within a week and the history of Europe would have been very different.

Three weeks earlier, on 24th August, a seemingly minor event occurred which changed the course of the Battle of Britain and ultimately the war. Luftwaffe bomber crews, somewhat off course but with the lead navigator believing London to be away to the east, released their high-explosive bombs and incendiaries over the capital. This was a very unfortunate mistake for the flight commander because Hitler had given strict orders not to bomb London. In retaliation, the following night RAF Wellington, Whitley and Hampden aircraft bombed Berlin. The Luftwaffe's Commander-in-Chief Herman Göring had boasted that not a single bomb would fall on Berlin and that if it did, he said, "You may call me Mier", a term of ridicule and disdain in Germany. The bombs did fall on Berlin, he was called Mier, although not to his face, and Hitler was so enraged by the raid that he threatened to bomb London into oblivion. And so, with Göring's increasing failure to secure air supremacy for an invasion, on 7th September, the London Blitz began, starting with seventy-six consecutive days and nights of bombing.

The German High Command's decision to change tactics to the concentrated bombing of British cities, including civilian areas, affected every major town and city in Britain, not just London. Indeed, Hull became the most heavily bombed city because of its proximity to the North Sea and the German bases in northern France and Norway. Clydebank on the west coast of Scotland, downstream from Glasgow was to suffer particularly devastating raids on the nights of 13th and 14th March 1941. All across Britain, night after night, great swathes of the population were being killed, injured or made homeless. That then was the atmosphere in which I was living and working in Coventry as the beautiful summer weather of 1940 turned into a bitter winter of death and destruction on the ground.

With this increase in bombing activity everywhere, it wasn't long before the City Council asked for volunteers to form a fire watch team at the Council House and I wasted no time in offering my services. Although motivated by a desire to 'do my bit', there were a couple of other incentives; no longer would I have to huddle under the stairs with my parents each time the air-raid sirens sounded, and it also gave me an opportunity to have a pint of beer, for which I had definitely acquired a taste, in the NALGO Club which was in Hay Lane, only some twenty yards from the Council House.

Some nights earlier, during one of the raids on the city, an oil bomb, which was a type of fire bomb designed to increase the spread and intensity of fires started by high explosives or incendiaries, had fallen into the front garden of the house directly opposite our own. Apart from covering the front of the house with a sticky black oil scorch mark, it hadn't done much damage at all. However, this was enough for my grandfather who, having now been bombed twice, insisted that he, my grandmother and my mother spend all future nights with his other daughter Marjorie and her family, who lived at 2 Grasmere Avenue on the Green Lane estate, which was three miles away on the far side of the city. It was to prove a decision of great significance to my family.

The fire watch team leader and organiser was Fred Worrall, a tough, well-built chap who, before the war, had been a Metropolitan police officer and was now the superintendent of the Council House, responsible for its maintenance and repair. He was also responsible for attending upon the Lord Mayor on formal occasions. Fred and his wife Ethel lived in a flat on the top floor of the building and this became the fire watchers' meeting place and source of innumerable cups of tea, for which Fred seemed to have an insatiable capacity, regularly drinking thirty to forty cups a day, despite it coming onto rationing in July. Ethel must have had a good supply of it somewhere.

The fire watch team was made up of about a dozen men and women including me and a life-long friend, Wally Knight, whom I had known from my school days. Apart from one full-time member, we were all volunteers and all young because the older members of staff, if not called up, were either Air Raid Precaution wardens or were looking after their own families. We were issued with steel helmets, a pair of overalls and given some very basic fire-fighting training, which mainly consisted of dealing with incendiary bombs. These were small magnesium-based bombs, about eighteen inches long, which would lodge on or penetrate the roof of a building where the magnesium would ignite within about thirty seconds, generating intense heat and start a fire. They were dropped in their hundreds and it was vital to quickly smother as many as possible to reduce the number of burning buildings and try to prevent a firestorm starting.

Incendiaries were extinguished either by spraying them with water from a hose and stirrup pump or by slowly applying sand to smother them. We worked in pairs and when spraying water onto the bomb, one of us would lie full length on the ground and direct the spray onto the bomb whilst the other one would stand behind and work the stirrup, pumping the water from a bucket through the hose. When putting sand onto the bomb, we would use a long-handled shovel to slowly cover the bomb. If they were covered too quickly, the burning magnesium would explode. Our main protection from an exploding incendiary bomb was a metal dustbin lid used like a warrior's shield!

We had to know every inch of the inside of the building and every nook and cranny on the great roof outside, so that during a raid we were constantly checking all the little places that an incendiary bomb could land and burn unseen, so starting a major fire. The Council House was a great Victorian sandstone building facing onto Earl Street and which accommodated many of the city's public services. Most of the council's offices were at the front, whilst the side facing Hill Street was the Central Police Station. The basement was in effect a large wide corridor which ran the length of the building and housed the fire watch team, the police central control room, the WVS canteen and the emergency generator to provide lighting and power.

Outside, high up on the Earl Street corner, the building had a small clock tower with a crenulated parapet of eighteen-inch-thick sandstone blocks which provided us with a wonderful look-out point over the roof of the offices, St. Mary's Hall, St. Michael's Cathedral and across the city in all directions. Access to it was via an internal metal staircase and vertical ladder.

The team fire-watched every night for months; we were constantly tired because as well as fire watching at night, we had our full-time jobs to do during the day. There were usually ten of us on at any one time. If there was no raid, we would do two hours watching and four hours sleeping on the stretcher-type beds we were given, with a thin mattress and a couple of blankets down in the basement. Whenever there was a raid or a warning, which seemed to be most nights, we were all on duty. The only allowance we had was that we finished our day's work half an hour early at 16.30 to have time to go home, have some tea and then return for duty at 18.30. In the morning we finished fire watch at around 07.00 and were back at our desks for 09.30.

By the autumn of 1940, food rationing was really beginning to bite hard and I was constantly hungry, especially with being out in the fresh air most nights. If I wasn't thinking about food, I was thinking about sleep, and when I wasn't thinking about either of those then I was thinking about one of the women fire watchers with whom I was becoming closely involved; but that is very definitely another story. Everyone was tired and hungry because everything was in short supply but nevertheless, unless people were killed, injured or bombed out, they were up each morning and making their way to work. It was so important not to be beaten into submission, not to weaken, not to give in; that's what kept us going.

In the weeks before that devastating night, the frequency of the raids increased and hardly a night went by that we weren't on duty. Gradually, the raids seemed to become heavier and the noise which accompanied them grew exponentially. From our vantage point on the clock tower we could hear the sound of the bombers approaching and the firing crack of the Bofors gun which was located on the top of the BTH factory in Gosford Street. The sky would become a latticework of searchlight beams, weaving backwards and forwards across the blackness, searching out the enemy aircraft; but they very rarely managed to latch on to one.

At this stage of the war, we had no radar-guided defences; we were entirely dependent upon visual contact by the spotters of the Royal Observer Corps and the gunners of the ack-ack batteries. If Britain did have radar-guided ack-ack in 1940, it certainly hadn't reached as far as Coventry. As each raid started, it felt as if the Dorniers and Heinkels were coming in lower than on the previous raid, and in all the nights that I was on fire watch duty I didn't see our gunners bring down a single bomber, even when the searchlights did pick one out. In the end, they were releasing their bomb loads just above the height of the barrage balloons and were so low that I could actually hear the metallic squeal of the bombs slipping out of the racks in the aircraft. They came down in sticks of six and we would count the explosions; one, two, three, four, five, six; each explosion bringing terror, death and destruction to lives and property across the city.

One night when there had been no air-raid warning by midnight, I returned home and was looking forward to sleeping in my own bed for a change. I had turned the light out and pulled back the blackout curtains so that I could see out. Even though it was pitch dark out there, I just wanted to feel the sense of space that the open windows gave to me; try to grasp a moment of normality before giving myself up to some much-needed sleep.

It was very faint at first, but unmistakeable; the sound of an aircraft engine, getting louder as each minute ticked by, coming nearer, but making a strange noise. I knew that it wasn't a German aircraft; I had heard too many of those over the last few weeks not to recognise their sound and the air-raid sirens had not started. I held my breath and listened carefully; I was certain that it was one of ours and it sounded in trouble.

It was very loud now, and coming in low. I leaned out of the open bedroom window in time to see the aircraft shoot past over the house, the roar of the screaming engines deafening in the quiet of the night. The pilot had his landing lights on, the beam shining forward, trying to find the ground. Then they hit it, diving into the openness of the square of the Coventry and North Warwickshire Cricket Club. There was a blinding flash that lit up the cricket ground and a sickening explosion from which there could be no survival. Two of the crew had managed to bale out but the Hampden had been too low and they had both hit the outbuildings of the Bull's Head pub on the Binley Road, their parachutes half-open stretched out behind them. They had been on a night flying training exercise and had passed over Coventry too low; a wing tip had struck the cable of a barrage balloon.

Because of the high loss rates amongst both the RAF and Luftwaffe aircraft from daylight raids, both sides introduced night bombing, but the RAF navigational technology for such operations lagged far behind the demands made upon the crews and amounted to little more than a sextant and map, both of which were useless in cloud. Central Europe was a vast darkened landscape and particularly in the early stages of the war, crews were trying to find, more often than not by dead reckoning, small specific targets, in the middle of a huge land mass in total darkness; it was soon shown to be totally impracticable. On one occasion a bomber crew became so lost in poor weather conditions at night that it bombed what it believed to be an enemy aerodrome in Holland; in fact they had bombed a fighter base in Cambridgeshire. Fortunately no-one was injured and the bomber returned home safely. The next day a couple of spirited Spitfire pilots, upon discovering the identity of the squadron concerned, flew over its base and dropped dummy German Iron Crosses, in a gesture of good humour.

A political policy of appeasement towards Germany and a refusal to recognise and prevent its re-arming during the 1930s had also stifled much government-funded military research and development in Britain before the war. Aircraft navigation equipment was one such neglected area and it would be another eighteen months before the technology and the tactics caught up with the demands made upon RAF Bomber Command crews.

Thursday 14th November 1940 not only changed Coventry forever, it impacted upon the developing strategy for the bombing of Germany. I had left my desk in the City Treasurer's Department at 16.30 and cycled home to have my tea then change into my fire watch overalls. Two hours later, with my gas mask, steel helmet and a sandwich my mother had made for me, I cycled back through the darkened streets into the city centre and went to the NALGO Club in Hay Lane. I propped my bicycle up at the back of the club, went through to the bar, bought a pint of beer, took a sip and picked up my snooker cue. At the very instant that I struck the white ball down the table, the air-raid sirens sounded. Almost simultaneously I could hear aircraft overhead and the first crumps of exploding bombs falling on the city centre. Along with the other few members in the club that night, I dived under the solid slate snooker table for shelter.

After the first stick of bombs had exploded, we grabbed our steel helmets and ran the twenty-five yards or so across the street to the Council House. Gathered in the basement, we knew straight away that this raid was different. We had become used to the bombers coming in at about 19.30 and starting with a shower of incendiaries, but these were high explosives that were falling. We took turns, in pairs, to go up on to the roof to see what was happening and then return to the basement to report to Fred Worrall.

When I got up to the roof the raid was already well under way. The noise around the Council House was not just deafening, it was terrifying. Overhead, the heavy drone of aircraft engines filled the air with a throbbing beat; around us, every few seconds bombs were exploding and buildings collapsing in a cascading fountain of sparks with the splintering rending of timbers and brickwork. The streets below me were filled with the sounds of people screaming, some still running for shelter having been caught out in the open by the early suddenness of the raid, others lying injured where they had been struck by the lethal flying debris; the ringing of bells on fire engines and ambulances came up to me on the clock tower from all angles. Even in earlier raids, I had never seen anything like this and from my look-out post the full scale of the horror of what was unfolding across the city was laid bare before me.

Back in the basement I reported what I had seen to Fred. However, we knew that several bombs had fallen very close to us and were not at all sure that one had not come through the roof, but not exploded. After about half an hour the raid seemed to come to an end and the whole team set about searching the Council House to find that bomb. The hole made by a bomb, even a 1,000 pounder, is quite small and since the only lighting we had was our own shaded torches, it was a difficult job. The entire time that we were searching the building, we were all too well aware that there could have been a delayed-action fuse on the bomb and that at any moment it could explode and take any one or more of us with it. In the event, we couldn't find either a bomb or any evidence that one had hit the building, though quite how we were not hit, I don't know, because so many fell on almost all the buildings around us.

Now that the raid seemed to have finished and we had searched the Council House, Wally and I went back outside and up onto the parapet of the clock tower to get a wider view of what had happened. There were fires burning as far as we could see; buildings, even some very close to us, had simply been blown apart, others were completely flattened, totally destroyed by the intensity of the bombing. Yet others still burned like so many blast furnaces, their insides a mass of flames whilst the regular and auxiliary fire brigades, fighting a losing battle with failing water pressure, tried to douse the brickwork to keep it cool. The sky over our heads was lit up across a vast area, a great orange glowing beacon reaching high up into the cold November air: a herald to the next, as yet undetected, wave of enemy bombers.

The noise levels had lessened a little now, although there were still bells ringing on the ambulances which we could see below us, trying to weave their way through the great mounds of fallen brickwork which had spilled across the roads like drifting snow, obstructing the routes to the hospital. As I stood there with Wally, trying to take in the scenes below us, I was shaken out of my trance by the wail of the sirens. They must be mistaken, surely; there can't be another raid so soon?

Any doubts I had were quickly dispelled. In a few moments it all started again. The searchlights were switched on, their beams weaving a criss-cross pattern in the now orange and black sky, struggling to penetrate the thick pall of smoke which was ballooning over the city and climbing high into the night from a hundred burning buildings. The ack-ack guns started firing, banging out their explosive shells, and then above our heads, the heavy drone of aircraft engines sounded once more over the noise from the guns. This time they were dropping fire-raising incendiary bombs. From the parapet, I could see a myriad of tiny specks of bright light appearing in every direction, like the sequins on a ball gown sparkling in the candlelight; but within a few seconds that perfidious beauty had turned each one into a brilliant white centre of glowing magnesium with flames flicking outwards; each one a new fire, each one the start of more destruction deep in the heart of our beautiful mediaeval city.

"Get down." Above the booming thunder of the anti-aircraft guns, we both shouted the warning at the same time and threw ourselves to the floor of the parapet. Like the roar of an approaching express train, we had heard the bomb hurtling towards us and I knew we were dead. Then, little more than a few yards from the clock tower there was a crashing explosion which shook the stonework, blocked my ears and hurt my brain, followed by the sounds of dozens of hissing incendiaries from the 'cocktail' cluster bomb, as they whizzed past us and fell onto the roofs of the Council House and other nearby buildings. The bomb, which had been set to detonate in the air just above rooftop level, must have been heading directly for the tower; another two or three seconds before detonation and we would both have been scattered over the roofs along with the incendiaries.

Gingerly, we looked out through the crenulated sides to see fires already starting to take hold on the buildings along Hill Street, at the top of Priory Street and, most serious of all, on the roof of the cathedral. But we couldn't stay up there any longer and ran down to help the others to put out the fires which had started on the Council House roof. Working in pairs, some were already easing sand over the burning magnesium from long-handled shovels. Others were using stirrup pumps to deal with the more advanced fires. Finally, when all the incendiaries had been dealt with and the roof checked and cleared, it was down onto the ground to see to the several which had fallen between the Council House and the rear of St. Mary's Hall.

Once we were satisfied that there were no more incendiaries for the time being, the team returned to the roof and were greeted by the sickening and tragic sight of the great crown of St. Michael's Cathedral ablaze. There were a few courageous fire watchers still on the roof trying to extinguish the flames, but we could see that it was already hopeless. There were too few of them and the fires had got a hold. Because we had been so close to the cluster bomb when it exploded, we missed most of the sticks, but the cathedral took the full force of it and was showered with incendiaries. Gradually the fire watchers, seeing the hopelessness of their task, gave up and left the cathedral roof, which was just as well in view of what was to follow.

There were more watchers on the roof of the nearby Trinity Church too, but, like us, they had managed to extinguish all the fires before they became too serious and ultimately the church survived. However, as I continued to look at the scene below us we seemed to be completely surrounded by blazing buildings. The shops on the other side of Earl Street were burning; the area around Broadgate and the Market was a mass of flames and all but a few shops in High Street were alight. Standing there looking at the devastation, to our utter disbelief we yet again heard the wail of the air-raid sirens. There must be a mistake; surely it can't be another raid? But it was, even though there seemed to be only a handful of buildings left to bomb, and the Council House was one of them.

Then, for the third time that night, the deafening noise of the bombers passing close by overhead pressed down upon us as the chaotic racket of air-raid sirens, ringing bells, shouts and burning buildings reached up to us from the city streets below: they were the sounds of a city being totally destroyed. Once more it was high explosives which poured out of the bomb bays as the aircraft passed over. The explosions seemed to be on every side of us, but still our luck held and the Council House was spared. The burning city was lit up from side to side and from end to end. The glow and even the explosions were seen as far as Madeley in Shropshire, well over fifty miles away to the west. With an inferno glowing like that, the returning bomber crews didn't need to navigate, they couldn't miss finding us. Through the chaos and noise I gradually realised that the ack-ack guns had, one by one, fallen silent; they had run out of ammunition or overheated and seized up, or both, from the near constant firing since half past six. The city was defenceless, the guns impotent, the searchlights pointless as they danced across the tortured sky above in a meaningless choreography.

As well as conventional bombs, the third wave also began to drop land mines, large containers two feet wide packed with high explosives which floated down beneath three parachutes. They were equipped with projecting detonators designed to explode the mine above the ground and so send the blast sideways, destroying anything within a hundred yards. From my look-out position, I could see them drifting down in the distance, the white of the parachutes lit up by the glow of the fires or caught in the beam of a searchlight, and then as one of the detonators struck an object, a great flash of light, followed a few moments later by the thundering noise and vibration of the explosion. A few became entangled in trees by their parachutes, the mine swaying beneath the branches, presenting an immensely dangerous and difficult job for the bomb-disposal teams of the Royal Engineers to tackle when daylight came.

There was nothing that we could do up on the clock tower any more so we turned away to go down the ladder and return to the basement. As we did so, I heard a loud explosion close by and then a terrible rending sound rose above the general clamour of the city centre. I turned to see our wonderful 14th-century cathedral completely engulfed in flames. It had taken a direct hit and the whole six-hundred-year-old roof had fallen in. My emotions boiled up inside me, but there was nothing I could do about it but thank God that the fire watchers had left the roof when they did.

When I got down into the basement, it was far more desperate than when I had last been in there. Knowing that we had a deep basement well underground, a few dozen people had found their way to us, either having been brought in by the police and ARPs from other shelters no longer considered safe, or simply having made their own way. Many were injured, some quite seriously, but were unable to get through to the hospitals. Bombs were still falling; roads were choked with collapsed and burning buildings, water pipes, telephone lines and electricity cables were cut, and several gas mains had already exploded.

The WVS volunteers were doing a wonderful job keeping the police, the ARPs, ourselves and everyone else down there supplied with cups of tea and a sandwich. Glad of the chance for a rest and relief from being out in the open amidst the falling bombs, I took my mug of tea and sat down on one of the stretcher beds. Across the corridor from where I was sitting, the storeroom door was wide open and on the far side of the room I could see the outer wall of the basement. As I sat there absently staring at the blank wall, there was a colossal explosion as a bomb landed outside in Earl Street, buried itself into the ground and then detonated. Directly in front of me, the bricks of the storeroom wall bulged inwards, hung there for a moment and then eased back into place. I was mesmerised by what I had seen and that moment has left an indelible impression upon me because I realised the great force unleashed by these bombs. Had we not been so far underground, the wall would have exploded inwards under the pressure and I have no doubt that I, and those around me, would have been seriously injured or killed by the brickwork which would have been hurled at us like so much shot from a cannon.

At the police end of the basement corridor, uniformed officers were coming and going all the time. Those that staggered in looked stunned; they were dirty and dusty, their uniforms a mess. They did the same as I had done, collected a mug of tea and, without speaking to anyone, sat down wherever they could, glad of the rest, the relief, unable to comprehend that they were witnessing the destruction of our ancient city.

When an officer was called by his number to return to the streets he simply stood up, nodded to the others and walked out in silence, putting on his helmet as he went. These officers were particularly courageous because earlier in the evening several of them had been unable to save three of their colleagues from a burning building a short distance away in Much Park Street. They had been condemned to stand on the road outside and listen to the terrible screams of agony from inside as their friends frantically cried out to them in their last moments as they were being burned alive, trapped in the inferno of the building. Despite that experience, these men got up from the safety of the basement and went back out into the streets and the intensity of the bombing to try to save the lives of other people still caught up in the horror of it all.

Having had a short rest and mug of tea, I returned to relieve Wally from the task of making sure that no sparks or embers drifted onto the Council House and started a fire. The whole city centre around us was ablaze and the intense heat from the fires rose up to me on the Council House rooftop, even in the cold of a November night. It was like standing in front of a blast furnace. From time to time, another wall or roof from a nearby shop or office would collapse and send an eruption of sparks hurtling skywards to be caught by the wind and scattered far and wide across the city, endangering the few buildings that weren't already on fire. In every direction, the lovely old city was burning like a scene from Dante's *Inferno*; it broke my heart. By this time, the 14th-century cathedral of St. Michael had taken several direct hits and was completely ablaze, engulfed by flames; I knew it was lost, along with all its treasures. We were so close to it and watched the tragedy of its destruction in close, graphic detail, unable to do anything but stand there, helpless.

We kept this watch up until nearly midnight, when, on the advice of the police, Fred withdrew us from keeping a permanent presence on the roof. Their concern was that the great spire of the cathedral would come crashing down and at less than seventy yards from it, the Council House roof was within range. In the event, the spire didn't fall, indeed it was unlikely to have done so because it had completely separate foundations, but we didn't know that at the time. However, we did keep checking on the roof throughout the night by making regular brief visits.

A little after midnight, the main concentration of the third raid had eased, but bombers were still coming over every few minutes in small groups dropping more high explosives, and it wasn't until after 02.00 on Friday morning, nearly eight hours after the first bombs fell, that we could see any appreciable lessening in the intensity. But it would still be another five hours before we could be sure that the last bombers had returned home to stay and it was finally over, and by then there would be precious little of the centre of the city left standing.

Incredibly, the Council House remained largely unscathed even though nearly every building around it had suffered some sort of damage. We may have missed the bombs so far, but we were in very real danger of being caught in a firestorm the like of which Hamburg and Dresden would experience later in the war. With so much hot material floating about in the dry, super-heated air, there was a very real risk that a fire could start in one of the many offices if any of those sparks or embers got past the blackout curtains. Although the curtains were treated to make them inflammable, the wind created by the fires was blowing them about and making openings for the flying sparks.

In the early hours we were told to go around every office and tear down the blackout curtains, pile them up in the corridors and then push all the desks and other furniture, waste-paper bins, and so on as far away from the windows as possible. We did have great fun tearing down the blackout curtains because it gave us an opportunity to let out all the adrenalin-driven emotions which had built up inside us since the start of the raid; fear, anger, excitement, sadness, they all came pouring out of us as we pulled those curtains down and threw them into the corridors. It had the desired effect; we felt much better and the building did not catch fire despite being showered in sparks and burning embers for hours on end from every direction.

Finally, at around seven o'clock, as daylight began to filter through the smoke and orange glow of fire, it became apparent that the raid was over. There was no 'All clear' sounded that morning; there was no electricity available to the city to power the sirens. Dazed and disbelieving at what lay before them, the people of Coventry slowly ventured out from their air-raid shelters into the drifting pall of smoke which hung through the streets filtering the murky half-light on that November morning. We learned afterwards that, knowing there were no night fighters and that the ack-ack had all but ceased, the Luftwaffe crews were returning to their bases in France, refuelling and bombing up again and again, then coming back to further pulverise the stricken and defenceless city as it lay burning beneath them, like foxes in a chicken pen.

When the raids were obviously over for the night and the daylight had crept in, the whole team seemed to breathe a collective sigh of relief; we were all safe. We went up to Fred and Ethel Worrall's flat, just to sit and drink a few cups of tea which Ethel made by boiling the water on a spirit stove in their little kitchen. For a while we sat and looked at each other, dirty, exhausted, and sweaty, blackened from head to foot from the smoke; but we were alive. We had survived what was to be the most devastating raid of the war upon the city. I remember thinking that whatever else the Germans threw at me in this war, it could not be any worse than the thirteen hours that I had just come through.

With weary bodies and numbed minds, one by one we slowly pulled ourselves off our various seats to go home. But that was just it, how were we going to get home? Which way could we go, and when we got there, would any of us have a home left standing or families left alive to greet us?

Our desperately tired little group stood together in Earl Street and took in the total devastation that surrounded us. It was even worse than it had looked from up on the roof. Whole streets were still burning or smouldering in every direction and the smell of cordite, burnt timber and what I later came to recognise as death, hung in the morning air. The fire brigades had, like everyone else that night, been completely overwhelmed by the scale and duration of the raids. There was nothing that they could do but to let most of these buildings burn away and collapse. The ancient and historic heart of Coventry had been ripped out in a single night and the still-burning ruins of the cathedral stood at the centre as if to symbolise the desecration visited upon it and the magnitude of the destruction around it.

St. Michael's Cathedral had been built during the 1300s. It is a rather poignant and sad reflection to ponder upon, that whatever the reasons those 14th-century pilgrims had for choosing that particular piece of ground on which to build the cathedral, had they chosen a plot of land a little way to one side, where the Council House now stood, that fine cathedral would still be standing today. But such is the hand of fate; there was to be no St. Paul's miracle for Coventry.

Whichever way we looked, fires still raged and the streets were strewn with burning timbers and fallen masonry. The only means of escape seemed to be Little Park Street and so together with Wally and the others, I set off in the hope of being able to get home and whatever that would bring. We weaved our way along the road, around and over the mounds of rubble from flattened, collapsed and badly damaged buildings, trying to avoid as best we could those that were still burning, many quite clearly on the point of falling down at any moment.

By now it was approaching 08.00. On a normal day, the streets would have been busy with people by this time, but this wasn't a normal day and there were just a few other people wandering around in the road, dazed bewilderment and disbelief written across their faces, unable to comprehend the scale of the destruction they were witnessing. We probably looked the same to them as we plodded along in silence, picking our way carefully through the debris. Eventually we made it to the Armstrong Siddeley factory, which had been badly damaged and was still smouldering, clouds of billowing smoke and steam rising from within its walls like the panting breath of a primordial beast.

The others left Wally and me here and made their way towards the Martyrs Memorial, the station and Earlsdon, whilst we headed for Walsgrave Road. We passed the Gulson Road Hospital and went down the hill towards Gosford Green.

There was less damage here than in the centre of the city, although it would have been hard to imagine what more damage would have looked like. Nevertheless, there were plenty of burning and flattened houses, together with others which had suffered various amounts of damage, from severe to slight.

We cut across the Gosford Green onto Walsgrave Road, but when we were on the far side of Ball Hill we met a chap with whom I had been at Stoke Junior School. We stopped for a moment to chat to him and he told me that he thought that our house had been on fire in the night. I felt sick. We quickly took our leave of him and hurried to Harefield Road from where I could see my father's Morris car parked at the end of the passage to the back gate of our house. It was such a relief as I realised that my parents had survived. Despite the weight of tiredness that made my limbs leaden, made every movement an effort, I ran the remaining few yards until I stood outside my home. At first I was unable to take in the horror of what I was seeing. My home was just a shell, completely burned out, whilst my Aunt Lily's house next door was virtually undamaged. It must have been an incendiary bomb. Everything my parents had worked and saved for was gone. Everything I had was gone. I had nothing except the dirty, sweaty, smoky clothes I stood up in.

Wally put his hand on my shoulder and said how sorry he was. What else could he say? He turned and hurried away to find out whether his own home beyond the church on the fairly new Poets' Corner estate had fared any better.

Slowly, I walked back to Harefield Road; back to my father's car. As I turned the corner, there standing beside the car were my parents, safe and sound. We embraced each other and all the emotions of the night tumbled out of us in our tears. They had seen the inferno that Coventry city centre had become and had been sure that I must have been killed; they had never expected to see me alive again.

Standing there in the road, beside his car, for the first and only time in my life I heard my father swear: "Bugger 'em. We are on our own now." No doubt these days seen as ordinary language, back in 1940 this outburst represented the extremes of profanity for my father and was a reflection of the anger, the relief, the happiness, the worry, the hate and the grief that was coursing through him all at the same time.

We had missed each other at the front of the house because they had been next door to see Aunt Lily, who was dying from cancer. She had spent the night on a stretcher in an air-raid shelter in Harefield Road, and was now safely back home and in bed. My mother had been at her sister's house in Grasmere Avenue when the raid started. Mother, Marjorie, her husband Tom, their two daughters Helen and Jill and my grandparents had all spent the night in an Anderson shelter in their back garden. Seven of them, all huddled in that cold, damp, dark Anderson shelter during a thirteen-hour air raid; I was glad that I had been on fire watch duty!

Towards the end of the raid there had been a terrific blast, the vibrations from which were felt inside their Anderson shelter. A land mine, dropped by one of the bombers in the third wave, had floated quietly down until it struck a house in a nearby avenue. The blast from the mine ripped off all the roof tiles and shattered most of the windows in Uncle Tom's house. Had the mine landed fifty yards nearer, my cousins would have been homeless too.

Because of his job at Lord Beaverbrook's factory in Castle Bromwich, where he was part of the team making Spitfires, my father had essential-user petrol ration coupons and on the morning of 14th November he had driven to work as usual. By the evening, the bombing had already started when he finished and set off to come home, but the closer to Coventry he got, the more concerned he became by what he could see. On the outskirts of the city he was stopped at a police roadblock and told that he could go no further because of the raid. Unable to do anything other than worry about his family, my father had watched the raid from that roadblock, despondent about the outcome as he witnessed the growing intensity of the bombing and the extent of the fires as the night progressed.

Finally, after the raids had finished he was allowed through, but only because his destination was Grasmere Avenue which was a side road off the Kempas Highway, part of the Coventry by-pass and not near the city centre.

Now reunited, the three of us climbed into Dad's Morris and, leaving the smouldering, sad ruins of our home behind us, drove to Biggin Hall Crescent to learn of the fate of my Uncle Will and Aunt Dorothy. Just as we approached their house, there was a loud explosion and a plume of smoke billowed from the ground little more than a hundred yards away. The car was showered with soil, small stones and an assortment of winter vegetables. A delayed-action bomb had gone off in the allotment gardens. Happily, there were no casualties, but the allotment holders were understandably very unhappy to see the fruits of their labours scattered far and wide, although there were quite a few people who benefited from this unexpected windfall and pots of home-made vegetable soup were soon on the boil.

Uncle Will, still wearing his ARP warden overalls, and Aunt Dorothy were standing at the front of their house, which fortunately was undamaged, although they had lost their car to an incendiary bomb which had gone through the lock-up garage roof.

The final member of the family to trace was my mother's other brother, Norman, who turned up later in the day. Having been caught by shrapnel and suffering a small head wound, he had been taken to Gulson Road Hospital where the wound was stitched and dressed, and then along with the rest of the walking wounded he had gone to an air-raid shelter somewhere out of town. As a family, we had been very lucky and had fared much better than many people.

We spent the next two nights at West Haddon, a small village to the east of Rugby, where we had been taken in as refugees, which is exactly what we were. We had nothing except the clothes we stood up in, but we were given a bed to sleep in and some food to eat. We were just three people, but there were hundreds like us, homeless and totally destitute. There were women with small children whose faces showed the blank expression of trauma; parts of families who had been split up; survivors from families, the rest of whom had not made it through. We were a pitiful collection but we at least were alive.

Two days after the raid, King George VI, in full military uniform, visited Coventry and walked through the devastated streets. I was very sorry that I was not there to see him. The royal family remained in London throughout the war. When the London bombing started, Queen Elizabeth had been implored to take the two princesses, Elizabeth and Margaret, to Canada or at very least to Balmoral, but she had refused, famously saying that they couldn't go without her and she couldn't go without the King and he would not leave his people. Buckingham Palace was bombed at least twice during the war, which added to the general feeling that the royal family were going through the same dangers as the rest of us. That visit to Coventry helped to forge a lasting bond between the King and his people during the fearful days of the German bombing campaign.

On the second night at the village reception centre, we heard the steady rhythmic drone of the bombers flying overhead. That night they were heading for Birmingham as we could see the gun flashes and bomb explosions lighting up the sky over the city. It was too much for some people, who thought that they were going to be attacked again. It had a different effect on me because, although I was very grateful to the kind people of West Haddon, I couldn't settle there. The countryside was far too quiet. I was a city boy and needed to go back to Coventry. We had been the first of Britain's provincial cities to be subjected to blitz bombing and were to be revisited again and again before the war was over.

Thinking back now, I must have been completely unbalanced, because I persuaded my parents to let me go back to fire watch duty on the Council House. So, armed with some replacement clothes, courtesy of the WVS, and some supplementary clothing coupons, I returned to work in the City Treasurer's Department and to fire watch duty at night. I didn't need anywhere to live because when not on duty I had my stretcher bed in the basement, used the washing facilities there and ate in the council canteen.

I maintained this all through the winter of 1940/41 until the following March when I volunteered and left to join the Royal Artillery. However, six weeks later whilst I was training as part of a twenty-five-pound field gun team at Bulford on Salisbury Plain, there were two more blitz attacks upon Coventry within a few days of each other. As the news of the first raid came through, the worry and anxiety over my family's safety was agonising, but there was nothing I could do. A few days later, I had news from home that everyone had survived again. I sat down and breathed a sigh of relief just as Alvar Lidell read the BBC lunchtime news and announced that there had been yet another heavy raid on Coventry the previous night. I was back to square one not knowing the fate of my family.

Several days passed without any news and I began to fear the worst, but then I heard from my parents that they had survived once more but sadly Aunt Lily had not. By now desperately ill with the cancer she had, Lily had twice been taken from her bed on a stretcher to the air-raid shelter. However, the constant moving had been too much for her, and two days after that last raid, she had died. I can't help thinking that it really must have been a merciful relief for her. What she needed was care and peace; what she was forced to endure in the last few days of her life were bombs, noise, disruption and privation. Although everything that could have been done for her was done, her last weeks of life would have been considerably more content had we not been at war.

Not long after my training was completed I transferred to 51 Highland Division but was soon transferred again to the Royal Ordnance Corps where I was sent on a radar course. Finally I moved to REME, the Royal Electrical and Mechanical Engineers or, as it is somewhat disingenuously referred to in the Services, Rough Engineering Made Easy. I later declined a commission because I was perfectly happy doing the job I was in.

Towards the very end of the war, whilst still with REME, I was travelling through Germany by train. It was a long and tedious trip because every few yards there was major work taking place to repair the damage caused by RAF Bomber Command where both the heavy bombers and Mosquitoes had almost destroyed the rail system to prevent the Germans from getting reinforcements and supplies through to their troops as the Allies advanced upon their borders.

Time and again we passed through places of total devastation where Bomber Command had visited and dropped tons of high explosives and incendiaries. But the scenes did not shock or appal me; they were too familiar for they reminded me of Coventry on the morning of 15th November 1940 after more than twelve hours of relentless bombing, when together with my friend Wally I had picked my way between the burning buildings and through the broken streets on my way to find my own home a smouldering shell.

Occasionally, the train stopped at stations along the route and at every one there were young German children who were quite clearly starving, begging for food. In the final months of the war, the conditions for the civilian population in Germany grew steadily worse as what little food there was, was directed to the front-line troops and even then there was precious little, which is why in the prison camps, for a long time the guards had been keeping for themselves the Red Cross parcels meant for Allied prisoners.

War doesn't just bring physical wreckage upon buildings, it destroys lives too, and in one town that we came to, the stench of rotting bodies hung heavily in the air. There simply were not the people to bury the dead. The population of the town was so weakened by starvation that their whole focus was on finding food and staying alive.

At about the same time that I joined the Royal Artillery, my friend Wally joined the Fleet Air Arm and became a pilot. He had a distinguished war and was Mentioned in Dispatches for his part in a raid off the Norwegian coast. At the end of the war in Europe, Wally was serving on an aircraft carrier in the Pacific, flying four and five missions a day against the Japanese as part of the Tiger Force preparing for the invasion of Japan. The dropping of the atom bombs on Hiroshima and Nagasaki prevented that invasion taking place and thankfully brought the Second World War to an end on 15th August 1945.

I was very pleased that Wally had survived the war. We had grown up together as school chums and had been through the night of the first Coventry Blitz as fire watchers on a building right in the heart of the city where bombs had quite literally fallen on every side of us. Despite everything that had happened to us, we had a lot to be thankful for.

The Coventry Blitz has become notorious because it was the first really intensive heavy night bombing raid of a provincial town and because of the destruction of that fine mediaeval cathedral, which shocked the nation. Although it was hailed a great achievement by the German High Command, in retrospect I doubt whether this was in fact the case. Although it certainly destroyed the commercial heart of my beloved city, including so many of the irreplaceable ancient historic buildings, it did not destroy the industrial heart of the city.

In this respect, it seems to me that the German strategy was flawed. With the city at their mercy, the Luftwaffe continued to concentrate on the centre instead of spreading their attack more widely into the outskirts where the damage, although serious, was less intense and where most of the large vital factories were located, such as the aircraft production at Whitley and Baginton, together with the shadow factories at Ryton. Consequently, it was only the Armstrong Siddeley complex that was severely damaged. By February 1941, these other factories were back in full production once their gas, electricity, water and sewage services were restored. It was because of the failure to capitalise upon the November raid that the city was heavily attacked with two further blitz raids within a week in April 1941.

As with the East Enders of London and the citizens of other towns and cities who were blitzed, it was the indomitable spirit of the British people at that time which shone through and it makes me very proud to say that I am British.

Fires still smouldering days afterwards.

Daily lives carry on amidst the wreckage of the city.

Joan Barlow with her own two books.

Chapter Four
Joan Barlow

> *"And did the Countenance Divine shine forth upon our clouded hills? And was Jerusalem builded here among these dark Satanic Mills?"*
>
> From 'Jerusalem'. *William Blake*

I was the eldest of my parents' four children and I arrived late one night in 1921. My mother had gone into a nursing home in Stockton-on-Tees, in what is now County Durham to give birth to me. My father was very disappointed that I was a girl because he wanted his first child to be a son, eligible to play cricket for Yorkshire. He got over it, though, and cared for me greatly.

My parents were desperately poor. There is no real poverty in Britain today, not like there was in the days before the Second World War. Father worked as a riveter in the shipyards of the North East, mainly at Swan Hunter & Wigham Richardson on Tyneside and at Head Wrightson, where my young brother went on to become a director of the company in the 1950s, on Teesside. The work was very insecure because after the Great War, orders for new ships were few and far between. The government ordered a handful of smaller vessels to replace some of the losses of the war, but the competition for any order was very intense between the North East, Clydeside and Belfast. Trade around the world had virtually ground to a halt as countries became obsessed with protectionism and so little merchant shipping was being built. Consequently, Dad was out of work more than he was in it.

After I was born, Mother went to live with her parents at Norton-on-Tees and Dad took lodgings in South Wales to be able to get whatever work was available. As soon as I was old enough, I went to the Board School in Norton, where my form master Mr Fisher, was very strict. He did, though, introduce me to the world of books and literature and taught me how to write a composition, a skill which would be instrumental in shaping my future. The headmaster there was Mr Whittaker, and my lasting memory of him was that he taught me the meaning of the word 'indispensable' by telling me on one occasion that I was. However, I don't remember why or what it was that I did to attract such praise, but I had never heard the word before, and at seven years of age I was just very pleased to know that it was a compliment.

When I was ten, I won a scholarship to the 'Medium' school, which was one below a Grammar School, and so in 1932 I moved up. I have no happy memories of my childhood, even though our parents were very good and kind to all of us, simply because we were so poor and life was so hard; it was a struggle just to get through each day. This was the time of the world-wide great depression following the Wall Street crash and in Britain it hit the north-east of England and the Central Lowlands of Scotland particularly badly as these were the areas where the great ships had been built and where the coal mines and steel works were concentrated. There was little other work.

There was no proper welfare state and unemployment benefit only lasted for twenty-six weeks; not much help in a depression which for many people lasted nearly ten years. We were always hungry; there was never enough to eat and what there was, was of very poor nutritional value. We didn't know what new clothes were and the ones we had were threadbare. My boots came from the Mayor's 'Boot Fund' and I didn't own a coat; I was cold from September to May. The north-east coast of Britain may have some lovely beaches but the wind still whips off the North Sea and cuts through you like a knife: a lazy wind we called it, because it went through you not round you.

I was never really interested in politics, but my dad was, as were most men at that time and, because I was the eldest, he would sometimes take me to special occasions in the town. One such occasion was the general election in 1929. Harold Macmillan had been elected as MP for Stockton in 1924, but by the 1929 election, the levels of unemployment, poverty and destitution in the constituency were as bad as anywhere in Britain. It's a good job we didn't know that there was worse to come. The road outside Stockton Town Hall was the widest cobbled street in Britain and Dad, who, unsurprisingly, was out of work, and I went there to hear the election results. I remember the men singing the song, "vote, vote, vote for Mr Riley, kick old Macmillan out upon the field", and they did. Frederick Fox Riley was elected. However, Ramsey MacDonald's second Labour government did not last long, and in 1931, with the depression biting hard, Harold Macmillan was returned and remained MP for Stockton until 1945, when he became the member for Bromley in Kent.

In 1957, and by now Prime Minister, he made a speech about the state of the British economy in which he said, "*Indeed, let us be frank about it… most of our people have never had it so good.*" This is usually paraphrased as "you've never had it so good", and in very many ways he was right; he was certainly right at the time. In 1984, he was elevated to the House of Lords and took the title of 1st Earl of Stockton in fond memory and thanks to the people of the town who had first elected him. A few weeks before his death on 29th December 1986 he reflected that when he had come into Parliament in 1924, the unemployment rate in Stockton had been 29%; sixty-two years later, in November 1986 under Margaret Thatcher's government, it was still at 28%. Despite all the post-war benefits and improvements which the country had achieved after the Second World War, this was a depressing statistic which saddened him greatly.

When Dad was out of work he was given thirty shillings a week (£1.50 today) to feed, clothe and house the six of us; I don't know how my parents managed. When he was working, even as a skilled riveter, he was only paid twice that amount, £3 a week. The shipyard owners, like the mine owners, took advantage of the very high levels of unemployment in these heavily industrialised areas and the fact that families really were starving; men were desperate for work, any work, and so employers paid a pittance, even for skilled labour. During the depression, not just shipbuilding but most of British industry was shut down and the majority of men in towns up and down the country were out of work, so Dad came back to Stockton-on-Tees.

Jarrow, at the mouth of the River Tyne, had been a very prosperous town in the early part of the 20th century, when more than a quarter of the world's shipping tonnage was built on Tyneside. On 5th October 1936, the Jarrow March began and I remember going to Darlington with my dad to see them pass by. There was a woman with them at the front of the march and she had very red hair. I know that their local MP, Ellen Wilkinson, marched with them on several sections of the route. She was known as 'Red Ellen' and I'm sure she must have been the woman with the red hair.

The 207 marchers were very proud and well organised. They carried the petition calling for government aid in Jarrow, signed by 12,000 people, in a wooden box at the front and, whilst this wasn't the only march upon London at this time, for some reason it captured the imagination of the public, which is more than can be said for the politicians at the time. When the marchers arrived in London on 31st October after walking 280 miles, Prime Minister Stanley Baldwin refused to meet them when they got to Downing Street and the House of Commons received the petition with a single sentence of acknowledgement and then went back to its previous business.

We lived in very poor terraced housing in the town and the only running water in the house came through the roof when it rained. There was a cold water tap in the back yard, which would freeze in the bitter winters. When I went to school each day, if I was lucky, Mum would be able to give me a piece of bread and scrape (beef or pork dripping) for my lunch. Sometimes there just wasn't anything to eat at all and I went hungry again, which made concentrating on school work very difficult, because of the gnawing pangs of hunger eating away at me; but then I was no different from most of the children in my school. There was no money to buy anything to eat or drink during the day and although the council could provide free school milk, it didn't, so whenever I was thirsty, I would drink the water out of the nearby lake.

For the most part, we lived on '3d worths'. Mum would send me to the butcher's to ask for 3d worth of 'pieces', the rough scraps which had been trimmed off the better cuts of meat. If they were any good that day, she would send one of the other children to get another 3d worth. She would also buy 3d worth of 'pot stuff'; vegetables that had gone past their best, that only the poorest of families would buy, otherwise they would have to be thrown away. These would be boiled up into a stew or a broth on the kitchen fire. The greengrocer also provided 3d worth of bruised fruit, whilst even the delicatessen could be a source of 3d worth of pieces from the cooked meats counter. It is perhaps then no coincidence that Morrisons supermarket, which was founded by Yorkshireman Sir Kenneth Morrison, to this day sells 'pieces' on its delicatessen counter for roughly the equivalent of 3d. My mother did, though, have one consistent treat for herself, even in the hardest of times. She bought a silk bedspread, which was only ever used on special occasions or if we had to call the doctor in. Mum paid for this bedspread at the rate of 1d per week. The payments went on for years, but eventually she paid for it and it was her pride and joy.

Politicians today like to talk about child poverty in Britain because they think it sounds good to the electors, but they have no idea what real poverty is because they are not old enough to have seen it, never mind experienced it. That's why I say there is no real poverty in Britain today; not like there was before the war. Like Harold Macmillan said, 'you've never had it so good'.

Dad had been a soldier on the Western Front throughout the Great War, rising to the rank of sergeant and he always kept himself very fit. So around 1930, in order to feed us he joined a running club at Ponder Hall because race winners earned prize money and money bought food for the family. He taught me how to run properly, too, and I would go with him when he trained.

My dad was nobody's fool and was a skilled worker; even so, he was out of work for many years during the late 1920s and right up until 1935. I was fourteen at the time and can remember the immense joy in the house when he came home and told Mum that he had got a job again, even though it only paid £3 a week.

The same year that Dad finally got a job, the country celebrated the silver jubilee of King George V. There were street parties, church services and much else, but there was precious little to celebrate in the North East. We barely had enough food to survive on, never mind having a street party. The celebrations were mainly confined to the richer south of the country.

The following year, at fifteen, I left home and went into service with Captain Woolner, DSO, who lived in Stockton. The house had red quarry tiles in the hallway and the kitchen and my first job was to scrub them and keep them clean. I also did a lot of baking whilst I was there, which was a part of my duties that I really enjoyed.

One thing that I did learn whilst with Capt. and Mrs Woolner was the value of education. I had always done well at school and been encouraged to read widely but my time with the Woolners made me realise that education was the key to the doorway out of poverty, and they certainly helped by giving me access to books. Their son, who was about the same age as me, went to a public boarding school and, whilst I knew that I would never have an education like that, it did encourage me to carry on reading as widely as possible so that when I had a chance to leave service, I would be able to make the most of it. Two years later, I saw an advertisement for trainee nurses at St. James' Hospital in Leeds.

St. James', which has always been affectionately known as 'Jimmy's', was originally opened in October 1848 as the Moral and Industrial Training School and run by the Poor Law Guardians for the City of Leeds. At that time it stood in open fields at the top of the hill which is now Beckett Street. In 1858 the workhouse for paupers was added and in 1874 the Leeds Union Infirmary was built nearby. The onset of the Great War transformed Jimmy's when, in 1915, the workhouse was relocated and the whole complex was turned over to a hospital for the endless stream of injured troops coming back from the Western Front. In 1925 it was named St. James' Hospital.

Today, whilst officially called St. James' University Hospital, Leeds, it is still known as Jimmy's and is not only the largest teaching hospital in Europe but has a world reputation for research and education, including a world class Oncology unit. Despite the common misconception, the name Jimmy's has nothing to do with Sir Jimmy Savile, who worked as a volunteer for many years at Leeds General Infirmary. As someone who has always valued the importance of education so much, I am very proud to have trained as a nurse at Jimmy's.

Even though I was still only seventeen, I applied to be taken on at Jimmy's as a trainee and was told that I had to write an essay in which I should say why I wanted to be a nurse. All the skills of composition which my form master at the Norton-on-Tees Board School had taught me and the reading which I had kept up since those days and especially whilst in service came to my aid. I was accepted for training although I was told that I was not allowed to go onto the ward until I was eighteen.

The first thing I had to do was buy a pair of Oxford shoes to go with my uniform, a watch with a second hand and a book on nursing. I couldn't afford to buy a new pair of shoes but I managed to get a nice second-hand pair. They were a little bit small and hurt my feet terribly by the time I had been standing up and walking around all day. We weren't allowed to sit down at all except in the short break we had for our meal. The nursing hierarchy of consultants, matrons, sisters, staff nurses and nurses was very strict in those days and an under-age student nurse was very definitely at the bottom of the ladder.

Although I was supposed to spend all my time in the sluice washing out the bedpans, I did inevitably become involved in what was happening on the ward and it wasn't long before I saw my first dead body and in this case one where rigor mortis had well and truly set in. Nevertheless, I persevered and enjoyed my training, especially after I turned eighteen and was officially allowed onto the ward.

When I was eighteen I had a very small increase in my wages, but I sent all my spare money home to Mum and Dad because I knew that they were still struggling to look after my brother and sisters.

In the days before twenty-four-hour television, people found out about what was happening around the world from the wireless via the BBC National Programme, newspapers or the Pathé newsreels at the cinema. After the Nazis held their Nuremberg Rally in 1935, we knew that the Germans were re-arming and starting to expand in Europe. It all came to a head at the Munich crisis in September 1938, but we couldn't believe that there would be another war; not after the Great War, the war to end all wars, which was still so fresh in people's minds. When Neville Chamberlain returned from Munich with his 'Peace for our time' agreement with Hitler, we all hoped that it was true. It all seemed so remote, all about politics and not real people. However, it very soon became clear that Hitler had no intention of keeping to the agreement and the clouds of war quickly gathered over Europe; it was only a matter of time until another war started. Although I was young, I knew what was happening as the newspapers were full of bad news and then, on 1st September 1939, the Germans invaded Poland. From very early on people came to realise that this war was going to involve everyone and that for the first time in a thousand years the general population would be attacked in their own homes.

Throughout the summer of 1939, I had been having increasing problems with my thyroid gland and in these days before the advent of the National Health Service, I could not afford to see a doctor or even think about an operation. However, training at Jimmy's opened a door for me and I was seen by a very good doctor there, who decided to remove part of my thyroid, which at that time was a pioneering procedure. Whilst the operation was a great success, sadly it put an end to my training and so I returned to my parents' home in Stockton-on-Tees just in time for the start of the Second World War.

Indeed, Neville Chamberlain had made his speech to the nation whilst my operation was taking place, but I don't think the fact was uppermost in his mind. Mum and Dad had moved by now and, although still in Stockton, had a house with a small back garden. Living back at home for my convalescence was not easy as it put an extra burden on the household budget, but at least I was able to help Mum around the house and I gave her my ration card. We put up the blackout curtains, which stayed up for most of the war, at all the windows, although the curtains in one room downstairs were taken down each morning to let some daylight in and then put up again each evening just before dusk.

It wasn't long before our Anderson shelter was delivered and Dad set about installing it in the garden. The idea was to dig a pit over which the curved corrugated iron sheets of the shelter were placed, making the arched roof, and then the soil from the pit was built up at the sides and thrown onto the roof to cover it over. People put various amounts of effort into their shelters, which were designed to help protect against flying debris, shrapnel and bomb blast. They were never designed to withstand a direct hit, which some received.

Because Dad had been in the trenches during the Great War, he knew all about mud and cold and water seepage, so when he dug the deep pit for our shelter he put a sump in it to drain away the water, which helped to keep the shelter dry and warmer than it would otherwise have been. Then he laid duckboards on the floor to keep our feet off the ground and put benches down the sides so that we could sleep in there if necessary. Mum and I put up a metal box which contained candles, matches, tinned milk and bread.

In the event, when the bombing started we all spent many hours in that shelter and were very glad that Dad had made it as comfortable as he had. When the sirens sounded, we each grabbed a blanket from the house and ran out to the shelter. Our house was very close to an ack-ack battery [anti-aircraft], code-named *Kiora* and when the guns started firing, the whole house shook.

The first German bombs of the war to be dropped on Britain fell just north of Edinburgh at South Queensferry, close to the Forth rail bridge. On 16th October 1939, two days after the U-47 had sunk the battleship *Royal Oak* in the Royal Navy anchorage at Scapa Flow, nine Luftwaffe bombers attacked warships anchored in the Firth of Forth. By May 1940, the north-east of England was in the front line of the German bombing offensive against the industrial cities of England. On 25th May, bombs fell across the river on Middlesbrough, and Stockton didn't have long to wait for the same fate.

We had all gone to bed the night the sirens first sounded. I no longer slept very deeply as I was always waiting for that wailing to start so I jumped out of bed, pulled on my jersey and shoes, ripped a blanket from the bed and ran out onto the landing where Dad was getting everyone downstairs.

"Joan, out into the shelter, now. Go, quickly as you can." I could already hear the drone of the bombers and didn't need telling twice.

A few moments later we were all huddled in our blankets in the shelter where Mum already had the candle lit as Dad closed the door. Mum, Dad and I each held one of the other children tightly to give us all comfort and courage. The sirens had stopped now and I could hear the engines of the bombers getting very close: they seemed to fill the little shelter. Then, without warning, the most tremendous thundering started as *Kiora* began firing. The earth around and underneath us shook with each salvo that was sent hurtling skywards in an attempt to shoot down the attackers.

As each shell was fired I could feel my body vibrate; the noise was deafening. I could hear the aeroplane engines even above the tremendous roar of our own ack-ack guns; I knew that the German bombers were right overhead. Then the bombs came with that heart-stopping whistle, the last sound to be heard before death. I was terrified; my teeth were chattering and I couldn't stop my knees knocking against the door of the shelter. I held my breath and squeezed my little sister even tighter. One, two, three; the explosions came in quick succession and although I was expecting them I still flinched and ducked automatically. The crescendo of noise obliterated our crying and the little shelter shook even more violently as *Kiora*'s crew seemed to be firing the gun non-stop. Then the bricks, rafters and roof tiles that had been thrown into the air by the explosion come cascading back to earth, falling around and on top of our precious shelter. I prayed that it wasn't our house which had been destroyed.

I don't know how long it all lasted but eventually I became aware that the guns had stopped and I could no longer hear the sound of aircraft. Dad was talking to us, telling us that things were all right now, the raid had passed and it would not be long before the 'All clear' sounded. With that, he blew out the candle, opened the door and went out into the night. It seemed an age before he returned with the news that the bombs had fallen very close.

I tumbled out of our Anderson shelter, exhausted but relieved to be alive. The greying light of dawn filtered through the gently swirling smoke and dust that hung over the garden like a cloak of death masking its terrible secret. But it couldn't hide the acrid smell of burning houses that overpowered my senses. We had been very lucky and the house was fine but our neighbours were not so; about twenty people lost their lives that night. Looking around at the devastation, dazed and cold, I am glad that I did not know what was waiting for me and that it wouldn't be long before I was destined to miss death again, this time by no more than a few inches in another bombing raid.

Petrol was rationed from the very beginning of the war, but it didn't affect us because we didn't have a car. Transport for us was walking, tram or bus. My brother and sisters were growing up and could earn a little money themselves, giving my parents a bit to spare, so Mum and I would occasionally treat ourselves and catch the bus into Middlesbrough to go to the cinema and watch whatever the latest film was and see the Pathé newsreels.

Not long after the bombing raid, my dad saw an advertisement for a female companion to a lady near Stockton. The lady was Joan Boville-Carr, a well-known optician in the area. In those days it was quite unusual for a woman to be holding a professional position as so many gave up their careers when they got married. However, Joan was single and lived with her mother about seven miles outside Stockton in the small village of Egglescliffe, overlooking the Tees. Her mother was elderly and Joan needed some help to look after her and to be her companion.

Dad was anxious for me to get out of the town, away from the bombing and this job seemed an ideal opportunity. I applied for the post and was interviewed by Joan, who, when she found out that I had some nursing experience, offered me the job. I would receive five shillings a week plus my keep, which suited me very nicely and took the double burdens of finance and worry away from Mum and Dad again. I did have a little difficulty finding Egglescliffe because all the signposts across the length and breadth of Britain had been removed by the authorities to make it difficult for any invading troops to know where they were and get around; unfortunately, it also made it difficult for everyone else to get around, too. Nevertheless, I had left myself plenty of time to walk the seven or eight miles there from my parents' house in Stockton and, after asking for directions, I found the house standing on one side of the village green. It was a beautifully rural setting and one about which I would write a book much later in my life.

Mrs Boville-Carr spent most of her time in bed upstairs, so the first thing I suggested was that we brought her bed downstairs so that she could enjoy the lovely view out of the drawing room bay window across the village green and see the comings and goings. The arrangement we had was that Joan and I would take it in turns to spend three nights in our own bed and then the next three nights sleeping on the camp bed in the drawing room to be with her mother.

I got on very well with Joan and we were all pleased with the way that the arrangement worked out. After the terrifying bombing raids on Stockton and Middlesbrough, it was a pleasant change to feel nice and safe out there at Egglescliffe looking after Mrs Boville-Carr, which is exactly what my dad had wanted for me.

Living in the country had other benefits, too. Although sugar was very scarce, it was always possible to get extra vegetables because people grew what they could in their back gardens. Additional eggs would find their way into the kitchen as well, and the local farmer was happy to fill a jug of cream from the churn for Mrs Boville-Carr at 3d a time. I had to smile to myself when I went to fetch the 3d jug of cream at the thought that even the very affluent Mrs Boville-Carr was also living on a 3d worth. To make the butter go a little further, I would mix some of this cream in with the butter which would give it more bulk.

Vegetable broth became a staple diet for us all and I would make as much stone-ground bread as I could get the flour for. Because offal was not on ration, it was really important to get on well with the butcher. If anyone upset him, they would not get any of the kidneys, liver, hearts, tongue, brawn, chitterlings, trotters and all the other tasty things which he kept under the counter for his best customers, of whom, happily, we were one.

'Under the counter' was a great feature of shopping during the war. Wherever it was that you happened to be living, you had to register with the various local shopkeepers before you could buy anything. The prices for rationed goods were set by the government and when you went to the shops, providing you had enough points in your ration book for the items you wanted, you could buy up to the maximum allowed and everyone paid the same, whether you were rich or poor. However, shopkeepers of foodstuffs generally, but butchers in particular, would keep things under the counter, often the best cuts of meat or some extra delicacy items such as liver, kidneys and so on. This was perfectly legal and had nothing to do with the black market; it was simply the shopkeepers holding back little items for their best or long-standing customers. That was why it was very important to get on well with the local shopkeepers.

As 1940 moved on through the summer and the Battle of Britain raged in the skies above southern England, I would sit with my employer listening intently to the BBC Home Service as Alvar Lidell, John Snagg and Wilfred Pickles read the daily news broadcasts relating the exploits of the RAF, giving us some idea of what was happening. The German invasion fleet was gathering in the Channel ports and we dreaded the news that they were on their way. The bombing raids along the east coast had intensified and most nights we would hear the bombers going over on their way to Manchester, Liverpool or elsewhere. When Stockton or Middlesbrough was the target, we could clearly see the glow of the fires in the night sky. I worried all the time about my family.

Then, from 7th September onwards, the Luftwaffe turned its attention on London and the bombing increased even more. One evening, after I had settled Mrs Boville-Carr for the night, given her a hot drink and her tablets, I said goodnight to Joan, whose turn it was to sleep on the camp bed in the drawing room, and went to my bedroom.

I drew the blackout curtains tightly across the window and changed into my night clothes, pulling my dressing gown over the top to keep me warm whilst I sat on my bed to read the latest letter from my boyfriend. Vincent, who would later become my husband, was in the army and kept me up to date with what was going on as best he could without the censor striking out too much of what he told me. I kept all his letters until a long time after the war.

After reading his letter for the second time, I took off my dressing gown, hung it on the peg on the back of my bedroom door, turned out the light and got into bed. I was just slipping into sleep when I heard the distant drone of aircraft engines. I had heard them so often before, there was no mistaking that sound, I knew that they were German bombers. The muffled crump, crump of explosions crept into my room and I knew that it was Stockton again tonight from the direction of the sounds. As I lay there listening and thinking about my family, I gradually realised that one aircraft sounded different, its engines getting steadily louder. Instinctively I knew that it was coming towards us. I jumped out of my bed and in the dark reached for my dressing gown hanging on the back of the door. To my surprise and a little annoyance, it wasn't there, even though I knew I had hung it up just an hour earlier. I dropped to my knees and started to feel around for it on the floor. The aircraft was very close now; in the quiet stillness of the countryside the roar of its engines was deafening and I knew that it was right above me.

Then I heard that terrible whistle as the bomb hurtled towards me and, unlike when I was in the air-raid shelter at home, I knew that this time it would get me; in that instant I was sure that I was going to die. A moment later my room was filled with utter chaos, the deafening, terrifying noise of splintering timber and shattering brickwork. The wardrobe beside me exploded in a mass of wooden shards as the bomb ripped through, passing so close to my head that I felt the wind in my hair as it went by. Clothes, roof tiles and ceiling plaster fell in on top of me and the door where I had been standing just moments earlier disintegrated in front of me; the landing floor outside my bedroom simply opened up to leave a yawning hole as the bomb continued to plunge earthwards in its final moments. I held my breath, waiting for the explosion to come, for my life to end.

Nothing. Thrown over onto my back, dazed and stunned by the sudden violence of those few moments, I was caught unawares by the stillness that followed. A tile clattered to the ground outside and a piece of plaster fell onto the floor behind me. The old house creaked and groaned in complaint at the assault it had suffered and I felt the cold of the night air wash over me as it tumbled through the gaping hole in the roof; but that was all, no explosion, no blinding flash, no searing pain, no death. I could hear the sound of the aircraft engines receding, growing fainter, and then nothing, just the ticking of my alarm clock, still standing on the shelf. I lay on the bedroom floor listening to my heart pounding in my chest. The peace had folded back over me as suddenly as it had been torn apart, like water folding back over a stone dropped into the river, as if it had never been disturbed, as if nothing had happened.

The cold air continued to waft over me and I shivered. Slowly the realisation that I was very much alive and that the bomb had not gone off began to sink in through my numbed senses. I had to get downstairs. It might explode at any moment, and what of Joan and her mother in the drawing room? Then I heard Joan calling my name and asking if I was all right. I told her that I was fine. Rather shakily, I stood up, gripping the dressing gown that had saved my life. I shook the splinters, plaster and the remnants of my clothes off it and me and gladly wrapped it around my shoulders. I had suddenly gone very cold.

I dared not risk putting a light on, with that gaping hole in the roof, but Joan had a light on downstairs and I could just see enough to carefully make my way down what was left of the staircase. There was so much mess and destruction down here, too.

"What on earth happened?" she asked.

"We've been bombed. I think it's still in the house. It came through my bedroom ceiling."

"Good God, Joan, are you all right, my dear?" she said with eyes as wide as saucers.

Just then a whistle blew outside; it was the local vicar, who was also the ARP warden. We opened the front door to him and told him what had happened.

"I know," he said, "I saw it. You must get out quickly in case it goes off."

"I can't leave Mother, vicar, and it will take too long to get her up. You know how deaf she is; anyway she's still fast asleep."

"Do you know where it is?" he asked, and started following the trail of destruction.

Then from the kitchen he called, "It's all right, I've got it but it's wedged by the gas meter. I think I can get at it."

A few moments later, the vicar emerged, covered in dust carrying a fifty-pound bomb as if it was a sack of potatoes, walked past us and took it across to the village green where he gently unburdened his lethal package, "out of harm's way", as he put it. Thinking back, this was an incredibly courageous thing for the vicar to do because the bomb could have gone off at any moment, but then these sorts of actions were not unusual. People were doing things like this all the time because there was so much danger around us every day that we took a lot of it for granted. It was part of life because death could come at any moment. But I had narrowly missed it twice now; that was enough, I didn't want there to be a third time.

The vicar came back for his bicycle, saying that he would go and arrange for the Home Guard to look after the bomb until the morning when a bomb-disposal team could be contacted to deal with it. And with that, he wished us both goodnight and pedalled off into the dark just as if he had merely stopped to have a chat on a sunny afternoon.

We went back into the house and boiled the kettle for a cup of tea. Joan lit a cigarette and we sat at the kitchen table, which I had earlier set for breakfast. There was shattered glass, plaster, roof tiles, splintered wood, broken furniture all littered about the room. A coating of plaster dust and grit lay over everything. The breakfast table was a shambles. As the smoke curled up from Joan's cigarette and the ash on the end grew longer, I saw her looking around the room, obviously trying to see something.

"What are you looking for, Joan?" I asked.

"Have you seen the ashtray, dear?" she replied, seriously.

I looked at her in astonishment as we sat in the wreckage that had been the kitchen; and then she realised the ridiculousness of what she had said, in the midst of all this chaos. We both roared with laughter until the tears rolled down our cheeks and we felt the release of the emotional tension the last half an hour had brought.

Vincent and I were married in 1942, although I remained in nursing until the end of the war. We had very little time together and two years later he went into Nijmegen on Operation Market-Garden, the plan to capture the bridges through Holland up to the Rhine at Arnhem, the bridge too far.

We were typical of so many couples at that time, when the war was all over, we didn't really know each other. Some had married during or just before the war, others had been separated for years, especially those men who had been prisoners of war. Peace brought a lot of personal problems for many couples, and their children. For some children as young as four or five, they did not know that this man who had come to live with them was their father, and for others, he wasn't.

Vin was demobbed in February 1946; he was given a suit, £81 back pay and that was that. We went to Betws-y-Coed in north Wales for a week's holiday to get to know each other; we stayed for a month. Vin's father had been a farmer, but the farm had been sold and so he had to get a job elsewhere and Ince & Elton at Ellesmere Port provided him with work. He studied whilst he was there and gained his City and Guilds. Like me, Vin valued the benefits of a good education and we made sure that our daughter Pamela did well at school. We were both very proud of her when, much later, she became a head teacher.

Sadly, Vin died when I was 81, so at 83, still focused on education, I decided to get some of the qualifications I hadn't had the chance to take when I was younger. I enrolled at the Telford College of Arts and Technology and obtained my 'A' level in English Literature and then I moved on to a creative writing course. My first book, *Village Green*, a collection of short stories from my own life, followed, and was published in 2007 when I was 86. Now, to celebrate being 91, I have published my second title, *The Storyteller and Other Tales*. I have continued to write and submit articles for the North East papers and to Age Concern, and I have kept my love for literature and what we used to call composition, so I remain very involved with the Wrekin Writers' group, meetings of which I often host at my home.

I have seen life from the bottom up and value and appreciate every day because it could so easily have ended in our Anderson shelter or on the night that I felt the wind ruffle my hair from the bomb as it passed over my head.

Betty in WLA uniform.

Chapter Five
Betty Connor

> *"How it rained when we worked at Flintcombe-Ash,*
> *And could not stand upon the hill trimming swedes for*
> *the slicing mill.*
> *The wet washed through us – plash, plash, plash: how it*
> *rained."*
>
> From 'We Field-Women'. *Thomas Hardy*

There are few places in the world more pleasant than England on a warm, soft, still September day; that special month of peace and bountiful harvest, a time to fill the stores and barns with nature's gifts in the days before the winter storms; the time which John Keats called the season of mists and mellow fruitfulness. It was on such a day in 1923 that I made my appearance into this world at Macclesfield in Cheshire.

And it was on another such September day in 1941 that the postman brought a little brown envelope addressed specially to me by name and marked 'On His Majesty's Service'; I was eighteen and my call-up papers had arrived. It seemed strangely typical of the month of September, a month so often of calm and peaceful weather, that after war had been declared on 3rd September 1939, nothing much happened for the rest of the autumn.

A great deal, however, happened after that. The British Expeditionary Force had been defeated, but over 338,000 men and hundreds of civilian refugees had been rescued from the beaches of Dunkirk and the western French ports of St. Nazaire, Brest, St. Malo, Cherbourg and Le Havre. The Battle of Britain had been fought and won, but now we were losing the Battle of the Atlantic because above all Britain needed food. Although we didn't know it at the time, the U-boats had almost starved us into submission; there was just two weeks' supply of food in the country. By late 1941, the government's slogan *Dig for Victory* would have been more accurate if it had read *Dig for Survival*.

The choice that my call-up gave to me was to work in a munitions factory or join the Women's Land Army, the WLA. The work in the munitions factory consisted of three eight-hour shifts, 6am to 2pm, 2pm to 10pm and 10pm to 6am, although many shifts were longer. The pay was much better than it was in the WLA and although munitions work was amongst the best paid of all the factory work which women did, it was still not as much as the men were paid for doing the same job – but then that applied everywhere, even in the Services.

Working in a factory would have entailed a train journey each way, which would add to the length of the working day, and the trains were often delayed and disrupted by enemy air raids and by the movement of troops and other essential supplies. I would also have spent much of my time travelling to and from work in the blackout and as a young single girl of eighteen, it was not a prospect that endeared itself to me. I had always lived in Macclesfield, which was a much smaller town before the war than it is now and was surrounded by the open Cheshire countryside. The WLA recruitment posters and propaganda painted a picture of working on the land as being a job of health, fun and vitality in the company of lots of other freckled-faced girls all enjoying the country life; the Women's Land Army seemed a much better option than the munitions factory. Of course, the posters didn't say anything about the long hours, the winter ice and snow, the summer heat, the rain, the wind, the back-breaking work, the cracked hands or the lower wages; but even so, I would still have joined because I really did not want to work in a factory.

The WLA was first formed in 1917, when during the Great War Britain's food reserves were down to just three weeks' supply. The then Minister of Agriculture, Mr Prothero (later Lord Ernle), created a completely new branch of the Ministry, the Women's Land Army, run and staffed entirely by women. Britain had almost been starved into submission by the

German U-boats but the increased food production generated by those women had prevented that happening. Although it had been quickly disbanded in 1919, Neville Chamberlain's government remembered the lessons and in July 1939, before the war with Germany started again, the WLA was re-formed.

In October 1940, the Rt. Hon. RS Hudson, PC, MP the then Minister of Agriculture and Fisheries sent this message to the WLA:

> "*The events of the past six months have made increased food production at home even more urgent. Total war is a war of endurance, and to ensure winning it we must make the most use of all our resources, especially the land. Milking the cows, feeding the pigs and the poultry or driving a tractor, day after day, is unspectacular and at times may seem to you very dull.*
>
> *"But without the food you help to produce the bravery of the fighting services would be of no avail and the machinery in our munitions factories would be silent and still. Famine could achieve what no bomb or blitzkrieg or invading force will ever bring about. It is your vital task to see that such a thing could in no conceivable circumstance arise, and is driven even further from the realms of possibilities."*
>
> [from *Land Girl: the Manual of the Women's Land Army 1941*;
> WE Shewell-Cooper [1941] Amberley Publishing Plc 2011]

So, having made up my mind to join the Land Army, a few days later, as instructed, I presented myself for a medical examination and then went on to Derby Street in Macclesfield to be measured for my uniform, which was very basic. The uniform consisted of a pair each of overalls and dungarees, two shirts, a tie, a pullover, a mackintosh, a great coat, a hat, a pair of lace-up shoes, which we always kept for walking out, woollen stockings, a pair of gum boots for working in, a badge and an armlet. Anything else we had to buy for ourselves, such as underwear, skirts or a jacket for walking out in. About four weeks later, my uniform was sent to me at home where I lived with my parents and I was given my start date of 31st October.

The rates of pay for Land Army girls, including those who were in the Women's Timber Corps, often known as the 'Lumberjills', were set by the government and applied throughout the WLA authorities although the actual money which we received was paid to us by the farmers. Starting pay was generally one pound and twelve shillings a week in 1941, of which around sixteen shillings went towards the cost of lodgings, although this did vary depending upon the lodgings and whether they were on the farm, in the village or in the Land Army Hostel. The wages could be a little higher, up to one pound and eighteen shillings a week, if the general wages in the county were high, but this really only applied around London.

Some farmers were very good and kind to the Land Army girls; others didn't make us feel particularly welcome but just accepted us on their farms for the duration, whilst a few others took advantage of the girls sent to them by making them work longer hours or not paying them the proper rate, or in some cases, at all. However, we were not simply abandoned on these farms; the WLA supervisors came around every month to make sure that everything was all right and that we were being properly treated. Those farmers who did not abide by the rules very quickly lost the help the scheme provided to them – but they still had to meet their production quotas, so abuses of our labour were fairly rare and short lived. The supervisors also checked up on our general health and organised the replacement of any items of kit which had worn out.

At 2.15pm on the afternoon of Thursday 30th October 1941, standing outside our front door, I said goodbye to my mother, gave her a hug and a kiss and set off to walk to the bus station in Macclesfield. From there I caught the single-deck bus for the five or six mile journey to Mottram St. Andrews and the start of my Land Army service.

The welcome which I received could not be described as warm, but the farmer's wife was kind to me. Margaret, the other WLA girl on the farm, had already been working there for some time, but since her parents' house was very close she lived at home, whereas I lived with the family in the farmhouse. I had my own room on the top floor of the main farmhouse, up a winding stone staircase. There was a bed, a small chest of drawers and a wash stand with a jug of cold water and a bowl for me to wash in. There was no carpet on the floor, just the oak floor boards. Nobody had carpets in their bedrooms unless they were very rich in those days. Whilst the wages were always low for Land Army girls, at least we ate well, and things like eggs, bread, milk and wild rabbit were always in plentiful supply; after all, the production of food was what we did.

After tea, I went to look around the small farm before going up to my room to unpack and put my few possessions into the chest of drawers. By that time it was dark and, not having been invited back downstairs, I set my alarm for 06.30 the next morning and tried to get an early night. The bed, however, was very uncomfortable and I did not sleep well at all and was already wide awake when the alarm sounded. After washing in the bowl with the bitterly cold water from the jug, I dressed and went downstairs to the kitchen for a quick cup of tea. It was still dark when Margaret arrived a few minutes later and greeted me with,

"Morning, Betty. Have you ever milked a cow?"

"No, never."

"Well, now it's time to learn. Follow me."

Milking by hand is definitely an acquired skill and cows know straight away whether they are being milked by an experienced hand or not. There is more to it than simply pulling on the cow's teats; that won't produce anything except a good kick. In addition to learning how to milk properly, I also had to learn the trick of keeping the pail between my knees at the same time and not letting the cow put her foot in it or kick it over. The farm had about thirty milking cows and they all had to be milked before breakfast, a task which took about two hours, even with the four of us at it, and of course they had to be fed, too, since at this time of year they were inside and would stay there until the grass started to grow again the next spring.

Breakfast at last, followed by mucking out the byre, and then out into the fields to harvest the root crops, turnips and especially the last of the potatoes before the frost got to them. This was hard, back-breaking work, but in time I got used to it, and of course, as each day passed I got fitter, quicker and more efficient in the work. The only motive power on the farm was horse power, and I had to learn how to look after the horses, tack them up and harness them to the plough or scarifier or cart or whatever they were to pull and also how to work them.

It was a long hard winter but the spring of 1942 came round and the routine of work started to change slightly. We still started at 6.30 each morning by milking the cows before breakfast, but as the warmer days came, so the cows were turned out into the fields for the day time. It would be a few weeks yet before they stayed out all night. After mucking out it would be time to start sowing the fields with barley and oats and wheat. This was all done by hand, by broadcast sowing, that is by walking up and down the fields scattering the seed as evenly as possible over the ground. It then had to be covered up, again by hand using a rake, to stop the birds eating all the seed.

The spring also brought a change of farm for me. The WLA increased our wages a little, but the farmer at Mottram St. Andrews refused to pay the higher wages. So it was that in May 1942 I left and went to Mr Warburton's farm at Daresbury, near Warrington. I don't know what Margaret did, as we lost contact, but she probably stayed at Mottram St. Andrews despite not being paid the higher wages, because she could live at home whilst working there.

I was now to live in the Land Army Hostel, which was home to about forty girls and was run by a matron. There was a very good atmosphere in the hostel and we had a lot of fun. On my first day, I arrived in the evening and the matron showed me round and introduced me to some of the other girls who were in from the various farms. She showed me where the bathroom was and when she opened the door there were two girls having a bath together in the great big tub.

"Good evening, girls. This is Betty. She has come to join us and will be working at Warburton's farm."

"Hello, Betty," they rejoined and waved through the splashes, "see you at tea."

The matron explained the house rule that if you wanted a bath, you just jumped in with whoever else was in there at the time. The sooner you got in, the cleaner the water would be for you to wash in; fuel for heating bath water was in short supply. An hour later, I went through to the dining room as everyone was sitting down to a well-earned tea and took my place at the table next to a very bubbly girl.

"Hello again, Betty. Has matron finished showing you round? Are you settling in all right? Which room are you in?" the words tumbling out of her faster than I could take them in.

I didn't say anything but just looked at her, desperately trying to think where I had met her before and how she knew my name. Then the penny dropped. "Oh, yes, fine thank you. I'm so sorry; I didn't recognise you with your clothes on."

A great burst of giggling and laughter followed and I realised what I had said. I was made to feel very welcome in the hostel and went to bed much happier than on my first night at Mottram St. Andrews. At the hostel, we slept six to a room and the company made a nice change after being on my own, especially in the evenings. I soon got along very well with the other five girls in my room and we had a lot of fun.

On average, we had a twelve-hour day, although in the winter we worked fewer hours and in the summer, especially at harvest time, more. As was typical at that time, the working week was six days with alternate Saturday and Sundays off. Sunday was always the most popular day off because it gave a lie-in after a Saturday night out dancing. When we could, we would catch the bus and go into Warrington to the cinema or to a dance, but the curfew on the hostel was 10pm, so it was always a rush to get back. At other times, an ENSA group would come to the hostel to entertain us. ENSA was the Entertainments National Services Association and during the war just about everyone who was in entertainment but not in one of the Services, ended up in ENSA. They entertained British and Allied troops all over the world as well as the WLA. Over those years they gave more than 2.5 million performances to more than 500 million troops; a staggering achievement. Inevitably, some of the acts were better than others and some definitely left a lot to be desired. Consequently, ENSA also became known as 'Every Night Something Awful'!

One lovely summer evening in August 1942, three of us were waiting at the bus stop to go to a dance in Warrington, dressed in our best walking-out uniforms, when a couple of American GIs pulled up in their open-top Jeep. The passenger spoke to one of my friends in typical GI style,

"Hey, honey, would you and your friends like a lift into town?"

"Oh, yes please," she quickly replied, thinking the same as me, that it would save the bus fare and would look really good in front of the other girls when we got there.

"Great, jump in then."

We were very impressed with their beautiful uniforms and the novelty of having the Americans over here. The local lads were, of course, less impressed to see the Americans. Thanking them for their offer, we jumped into the back of the Jeep as the driver crashed the gears and sped off. A few moments later, there was a crack and jolt underneath us and as I looked to the side, I saw a tyre rolling past us and down the road.

The back of the Jeep dropped with a thump onto the tarmac as we careered, bounced and swerved along the road on three wheels until coming to an abrupt halt in the bottom of a hedge. Dazed but otherwise unhurt, the five of us slowly clambered out and stared at the marooned Jeep. The Americans looked glum. We looked disappointed. The three of us inspected each others' clothes to make sure they were not damaged, checked our make-up and, much to the embarrassment of the GIs, thanked them for the lift and walked to the next bus stop.

Supplying the dairies in Warrington, Warburton's was a big dairy farm of about forty milking cows, some of whom even had names, and I had joined three other Land Girls who were already working there. Once again, all these cows had to be hand milked twice a day, but with four of us at it, the job was soon done, and then after the morning milking, it was out into the fields. Breakfast was served at the hostel before we left in the morning and each girl had a packed lunch to take with her. The farm was not very far from the hostel and I would walk there and back each day.

The daily routine was much as at Mottram St. Andrews, and although the farm was quite a bit larger, because there were more of us to do the work, it didn't seem as hard. One of the things that Mrs Warburton insisted upon, though, was total cleanliness in the dairy and we had to scrub it daily with donkey stone.

Today, with more food than we can eat and with so much waste, it must be difficult for people to realise just how short of everything we were during the war. Nothing was ever wasted. Even at the hay harvest, we would collect the wild grass growing on the verges of the lanes and throw it up onto the cart as the horse slowly plodded along towards the farm. It would soon dry and just become more hay. We didn't have to worry about any chemicals or traffic fumes on that grass; there weren't any, it was just more good wholesome grass.

I stayed at Warburton's for nearly a year and then in early 1943 I moved to Gawsworth on the Leek to Congleton road and the farm of Arthur Trueman. I stayed here for about eighteen months, living on the farm and, although I was the only Land Girl, there was another farm worker who also stayed on the farm occasionally. I was very happy and only left after being injured in an accident. As usual, the money was not very good and my meagre wages were paid to me in cash each week, but there was plenty of food and I wanted for nothing to eat, which during the war was really something to be thankful for. There were not many people who could say that because everyone was rationed equally, rich and poor alike. Although there was the black market, it was mainly in the towns and cities, but was very limited anyway in what it could supply; quite simply there wasn't the food to be had. Inevitably, things were better in the country and a few 'arrangements' were arrived at to make sure that the local villagers were fed as well as could be managed; and there were always rabbits, pigeons and, if you were lucky, pheasant, duck or wild goose to be shot, although officially only rabbits and pigeons were to be shot as these were classed as crop pests.

Arthur Trueman's milking herd was about twenty cows with a lot of land under the plough, but although there were horses on the farm, he had what very few of the others farmers had: a tractor. Arthur worked alongside me, whatever the weather, and we always got through the tasks of the day. His brother had the next farm and they shared the labour force between them at harvest time, which was very efficient.

I worked the smaller horses as well as driving the American-made John Deere tractor, although I did stay away from the farm's Shire horse. They were beautiful animals but gentle as they were, they were just too big and powerful for me to handle, weighing as they did about a ton each. It is sad to think, though, that the days when these gentle creatures were the main source of power on a farm are now all gone, part of an altogether more innocent and genuine bygone age, despite the two world wars which ripped so many families apart and brought so much devastation.

An example of how a horse would have been much better than a tractor was an occasion when I was towing a scarifier, a kind of harrow, with the tractor and I got too close to the river before I turned to go back up the field. I stopped just short of the bank and as I tried to turn, the tractor began to tilt over. Had I gone any further it would have toppled into the river and taken me with it. I went back to the next field to get Jack, who was Arthur Trueman's brother, and told him what had happened. He came and took one look at the precious tractor, precariously perched on the lip of the river bank. With a very worried expression on his face, he sent me to a neighbouring farm to get another tractor, as all the horses were already working in the other fields. Having carefully uncoupled the scarifier and pulled it out of the way, we were able to chain the two tractors together and pull the first one away from the river bank. Much to my relief, and Jack's, the John Deere inched back onto an even keel and no harm was done. If I had had a horse pulling the scarifier, I wouldn't have had that trouble as the horse would have been able to turn. Tractors have their limitations.

Although the milking of the cows happened twice a day irrespective of the season or the day of the week, the field work did vary and was determined according to the season. Springtime was for sowing seed and planting potatoes, but unlike my first farm, Mr Trueman had a seed drill which was towed behind either the horses or the tractor. It made sowing much quicker, easier and less wasteful, and because it drilled the seed into the ground, there was no need to follow behind covering up the grain.

When the summer came, everyone helped to get the various harvests in. Firstly there was the hay, which was done with a grass cutter attached to the tractor. The cut grass was left in the field to dry, although we had to turn it by hand using a pykle, a long-handled twin-pronged fork, so that the sunshine would help it to dry all through. Then when it was ready to bring in, using a pykle again, we would throw the hay up onto the carts which the horses pulled back to the farm. There the hay was stored in the barn and whatever was left over was made into hayricks in the yard.

The next harvest was grain; oats and wheat. Sharing the labour and equipment between the two farms, the two reaper machines would be pulled by the horses and tractors. They would cut the stalks of grain and automatically tie about an armful of stalks into a sheaf using a coarse string called binder twine. The sheaves were then dropped onto the field as the reaper moved along and we followed behind to stand them up in stooks of ten across the field. Once these had dried, they were loaded onto the carts and taken back to the farm where the threshing machine would separate the grain from the straw stalks. As always, the whole farming year was a race against time and a battle with the weather.

Autumn was a time for ploughing and for harvesting the root crops, and there were many lovely warm days in late September and early October when it felt really good to be out in the fresh air. But the days were growing short and nights were getting cold; another winter was not far away now. Sometimes, if the weather really was too bad to be able to get out into the fields, then there would be a list of inside jobs to be done. Snow and ice, though, unless very severe, were not reasons to stay in; the cattle still had to be fed, and if that meant cutting kale by hand for several hours on an icy morning in the biting wind, then there was nothing for it but to try to wrap up in my greatcoat and get to it. Through my boots and woollen socks, my feet were soon too cold to feel, standing for hours on the snow and frozen ground and even though I wore gloves, it was so cold that my fingers became numb and red raw from handling the icy kale. When the job was done, and inside once more, my hands and feet would begin to thaw out, but the pain was so great that sometimes it would make me cry as the feeling slowly seeped back into fingers and toes. Many girls suffered from frostbite and I was very lucky not to have been one of them.

Friday nights during the winter, when the dark had put an end to the outside work, were something to look forward to, for it was then that the village dances were held in the various communities and provided an opportunity for me to meet my friends from the other farms and for us to let our hair down. Not living in the hostel now, there was no curfew to observe, which was just as well since the dances didn't start until 10 o'clock. The first part of the evening's entertainment was always a whist drive and since none of the village halls and schools were big enough to hold a dance and a whist drive at the same time, the dance, which was really for us younger ones, had to wait. They never finished before 1 o'clock in the morning, then it was perhaps a three-mile cycle home to bed and up again at 06.30 to milk the cows before breakfast and another hard day on the farm. You had to be young and fit to do that each week.

Fate is a strange companion to compass each one of us through life. After I had been at Arthur Trueman's farm for around eighteen months, I had an accident one day which changed the course of my war service. In the summer of 1944, we had almost finished getting the grain harvest in. As usual, I was riding on top of the cart, which was stacked up high with sheaves of grain and being pulled along by our great gentle Shire horse. It was a beautiful late August day, the hedgerows along the lanes were laden with ripening blackberries, sloes and damsons. Overhead those aerobatic Olympians of the sky, the swifts, swallows and martins swooped and wheeled and soared as they hungrily scooped up copious quantities of the protein-rich insects that filled the air around the harvest fields. In truth, I was not so much riding on top of the cart, but lying on my back, gazing up into the cornflower blue of the sky, watching the birds and, high above them, the silhouettes of Lancaster bombers with their escorting fighters flying south on another operation, the distant drone of their engines disturbing the tranquillity of the unfolding ageless performance far below them in which we were the principal actors.

The courage of those airmen up there, and thousands of other people, had brought us to the point that we now believed that we would eventually win this war: that the Germans really could be beaten. The sight and sound of enemy bombers over Britain was now a rarity rather than the norm, the threat of starvation from the U-boat blockade had been lifted, D-Day had happened and we were pushing the Germans out of France, back towards their own borders. We couldn't yet see the end, but surely it must come soon. Perhaps by Christmas?

It had been a long day already, with an early start, and it would be a late finish to get the harvest in before the weather broke. The afternoon heat of the August sun beat down upon me as I wallowed in the sheaves of wheat, soft and giving like a huge feather bed, the gentle bounce and sway of the hay cart keeping time to the benign rhythmic plodding of the great horse. I closed my eyes and relaxed, letting the relief from work wash over me and the arms of sleep embrace me.

I hit the ground hard and the searing pain that shot through my arm was certainly not a dream. Whilst I had been dozing, one of the wheels of the hay cart had run over a large cobble stone in the lane, the load of sheaves had rocked violently and the heavy, loose part of the load on the top, me, had come tumbling down to earth in every sense. In that moment, my Land Army days were ended. Although I had not broken my arm, I had ripped the ligaments and tendons. According to the doctor, milking and heavy farm work were both out of the question if I was to regain the full use of my arm and I was duly signed off. However, the work of the farm did not stop because I was injured and so the WLA supervisor arranged a replacement for me whilst I was sent home to recover. It soon became clear that my injury was going to take some time to heal and so I left the Land Army altogether.

My father was the owner of a small factory business making ladies' clothing, and as soon as I was able, I started to work in his factory. I did not receive any sort of preferential treatment and was paid piece-work rates – no work, no money.

Christmas came and went, and like so many wars before it, this one had not ended by Christmas. The winter of 1944 turned into the early spring of 1945 and then at last it came, the news that Hitler was dead. Surely now the war must end, and on 8th May 1945 it did: at least the war in Europe did.

A year earlier, I had taken an afternoon off to enable me to go to visit the dentist; not really what I would have chosen to do on my afternoon off, but it had to be done. Whilst I was in Macclesfield, quite by chance, I met a young soldier called Arthur Connor, who was on leave from the Royal Tank Corps. I had always liked Arthur and I was pleased to see him. I had known him for many years as we had lived close to one another and had both worshipped at St. George's Church. On that warm pleasant afternoon we had stood in the sunshine and chatted about what each of us was doing and had caught up on the news around the town. All too soon, though, it had been time for me to say goodbye and cycle back to the farm in time for the afternoon milking, but before we parted we had exchanged addresses. Arthur had been due to rejoin his regiment the following day and had gone into Normandy on D+1, 7th June 1944 and had been in heavy fighting during the battle for Caen.

After our chance meeting that afternoon, we had written to each other for the rest of the war, although it had been much easier for me in the peaceful surroundings of the farm and then home, than it had been for Arthur as he had fought his way across France and then into Germany.

The war officially ended at midnight 7th/8th May and VE Day was one long celebration for many people, Arthur and me included. I was lucky, Arthur had survived the war and he was home on leave again for VE Day. We went down into

Macclesfield to the Town Hall. In those days, the Town Hall was the place where people would congregate to hear news of national importance, be it good or bad. Now, of course, we all get it direct from our televisions. After the civic speeches everyone there had a wonderful time. The whole town came to a standstill. The only people working seemed to be the pub landlords and, occasionally, the police.

By and by, Arthur and I left the town centre and went to the park. Fortunately, the weather was lovely that day and the park was full of couples and families and people just enjoying themselves as the relief of Hitler's defeat sunk in. We spent the rest of that wonderful day in and around the park, eventually arriving back home at 1 o'clock in the morning. I kissed Arthur goodnight and crept quietly into the house, which was all in darkness, and up to my bedroom. I thought that my dad would throw me out for coming home at such an hour, which was, of course, ridiculous since I was now twenty-two and had very often come in at 1 o'clock in the morning from a dance; the difference was that on those occasions, my dad had not been on the other side of the door. Next morning when I came down to breakfast, all he said was, "You were late in last night, Betty." I needn't have worried.

With the war in Europe over at long last, the newspapers were looking to the Far East and the prospect of a protracted battle across the Pacific against the Japanese. Arthur, like so many servicemen and women, returned to their duties after VE Day and started to focus on the battle that was to be fought on the other side of the world. The RAF and Royal Navy in particular were preparing for this: then the atomic bombs were dropped on Hiroshima and Nagasaki and it really was all over.

On 20th March 1946, Arthur and I married in St. George's Church, Macclesfield, and started our life together. However, the army had not quite finished with him yet and after a short leave he returned to Germany until he was demobbed in January 1947, when at last we could have a happy settled life together, although the post-war years, with continued rationing and shortages were sometimes just as hard as during the war, only without the bombs; but we got through. Sadly, Arthur died in 1990, but we had a wonderful life together and, with nine grandchildren and seven great-grandchildren, I have a lot to be thankful for.

Betty – back-breaking work.   *Betty on her way to bring the cows in.*

Helping hands at hay making time.

Betty on the farm in winter.

Betty on a visit home.

The Women's Timber Corps Memorial

Chapter Six
Monica Oxenham

> *"I remember, I remember, the fir trees dark and high;*
> *I used to think their slender tops were close against the*
> *sky;..."*
>
> From 'I remember, I remember'. *Thomas Hood*

The Women's Timber Corps, which came into being in April 1942, was part of the Women's Land Army, except that we were trained for the specific work in the forests rather than on farms and we became known as 'Lumberjills' or 'Polecats'.

I was quite grown-up for my age as I was older than my two sisters and had always helped Mum look after them so that she could work in the factory. Jobs were scarce during the 1920s and things only got worse as we moved into the great depression of the 1930s, especially in the north of England where I was born. Mum was really lucky to have a job, as Dad was often out of work and she needed to keep hers at all costs, and so even though I was still quite young, I looked after and cared for my two sisters when Mum was out. I wasn't unusual in this; it was just the way life was then. Neighbours would help each other out whenever they could as communities were much closer then than they are today. Everybody knew everyone else and that was really important when times were hard, as they were then for most of the time. It is strange to think that the war actually gave poorer families a better standard of living because war meant jobs and that meant wages.

My first experience of what war was really like was when I was fourteen, just before I left school. One day in the early summer of 1940, we were in our classroom having a lesson, although I don't remember what it was about. I do remember that it was a beautiful day and that I wasn't really paying much attention to what my teacher, Miss Ettingshaw, was saying. I knew that I was going to leave school in a few weeks at the end of the summer term and I was thinking about all the things I was going to do when I left and that I would much rather be outside in the sunshine than in this stuffy classroom.

Gazing up at the clear blue sky from my seat by the window, I could see dozens of little black dots coming towards us, dots that I thought were birds flying very high. As I looked more intently at them, I realised that they were aeroplanes and that I had, unwittingly, stood up to get a better look. As I did so, Miss Ettingshaw said, "Monica, what are you doing? What are you looking at?"

"Aeroplanes, Miss. Hundreds of them," I replied urgently, pointing up at the approaching dots.

The other children rushed to the window to look at them too and at that moment we heard the air-raid sirens wailing out their warning to take cover. We had practised this so many times since the war had started but we had never had to leave the school for a real air raid before; at first, it was all very exciting. Doing as we had been told, we left the classroom very quickly and in orderly fashion, on our way each of us picking up the books that we had been studying when the sirens had sounded. For many schoolchildren in Britain, a daytime air raid simply meant that lessons would continue as best they could in the shelter.

The young teacher guided us out of the classroom and into the playground where the younger children from the other class were running towards us. We set off towards the gate and everything was going well until we heard the sounds of exploding bombs coming towards us from across the town. Suddenly it wasn't exciting any more, but terrifying. We ran as fast as we could towards the air-raid shelter, which was the basement of a building on the other side of the street just opposite the school gate. As the oldest girl in the school, I helped our two teachers with the younger children, trying to get them safely across the road and into the shelter. I held on to one with each hand saying, "quickly now, run as fast as you can. Quick as your legs will go."

We just got there in time. One teacher went down with the first group of the youngest children whilst I stayed to help Miss Ettingshaw usher the others down the steps. Everything seemed to be so loud now; the bombs were falling very close, their explosions shaking the ground; the air was full of noise, full of the sounds of terror. The sirens were still wailing, louder than ever it seemed; people who had been just passing or working in nearby buildings were running past us to get to safety, some shouting to each other as they plunged down the basement steps. A few stopped momentarily to snatch one of the smaller children as they went down into the shelter; one man even carried a child under each arm as he disappeared down the steps. Then, taking hold of my hand tightly and pulling me close to her away from the doorway, my teacher said, "That's everyone, Monica, hurry now, down the stairs."

It must have happened so quickly and yet when I replay it in my mind it seems as if it all took place in slow motion. As she was speaking to me, I turned round to look back across the street just in time to see a stick of three bombs fall in quick succession on our school. At the same moment Miss Ettingshaw shouted, "Get down, Monica," and took hold of my shoulders, pulling me down with her onto the concrete floor at the top of the shelter steps, her body sprawled across mine and her arms holding my head.

There was a series of shattering explosions in quick succession and our little school was ripped apart. Even though my teacher was lying across me, my ears hurt, the ground beneath us shook and the power of the blast pushed me over the edge of the steps. A moment later the blast carrying a wall of debris crashed in through the open doorway, lethal shards of glass, roof tiles, pieces of wood, bricks and masonry smashed against the wall above us, tumbling down and covering us; death in a cloud. I tried to get up but she held me down,

"Keep still, Monica. It's all right. Oh God, no," I heard her whisper.

We lay there for what seemed an age, Miss Ettingshaw holding me close, as the dust and debris settled over us and, though my ears were still hurting, I could hear more explosions which seemed very close. After what was probably only a few moments, I tried again to get up but couldn't move.

"Miss Ettingshaw, are you all right? Can we get up, I can't move."

She didn't answer me and I realised that a large wooden beam was lying on top of her, pinning us both down.

"Miss Ettingshaw," I called softly again to her, but still there was no answer.

Then two men were lifting the beam from us and the other teacher was bending over me, wiping the dust from my face and asking, "Monica, are you hurt, my dear?"

"It's Miss Ettingshaw, she won't answer me," was all I could say, and felt the tears well up in my eyes.

One of the men picked me up and carried me down the steps into the basement, laid me on a camp bed and someone started to clean up the scratches on my face, arms and legs. Then they brought Miss Ettingshaw down, her hair all out of place and full of dust, her clothes ripped. Everyone else from the school was safe, but when I tried to stand up, the room started to spin and I fainted. When I woke up, I was lying on the camp bed again and being given a cup of tea, but I couldn't see Miss Ettingshaw. I fell asleep then until I was awoken by the other teacher gently shaking me and telling me that it was all clear now and that we could go home.

I was a bit unsteady on my feet at first, but gradually got my balance and looked around the underground room. Nearly everyone had gone; there were just a few people clearing up. I asked the teacher, whose name I can't remember, where Miss Ettingshaw was and she told me that she had been taken to hospital because she had one or two cuts.

After the raid, the news that the school had been hit went quickly round the streets and those mothers not at work came to find their children. The ARPs had directed the mothers down to the shelter to collect their children and the WVS organised getting the rest home. I was left until last because I was asleep and had been hurt and the other teacher wanted to take me home as she knew that my mum would be at work.

I was undoubtedly saved from serious injury by having been blown over the edge of the steps by the force of the blast and the protection given to me by my teacher's body. Even so, I was badly shaken and had dozens of cuts and bruises from the brick ends and glass that we had been showered with. I later learned that Miss Ettingshaw had been very badly injured and that was why she had been taken to hospital. She had used her own body to protect mine and had taken the full impact of the blast. I didn't see her again, but I have never forgotten that it was her courage that saved me.

That was the end of my school days and the start of my war, but much sooner and more violently than I had ever thought it would be. I spent the next eighteen months until just before my sixteenth birthday doing whatever I could to earn a little money for the family. My dad was away in the army by now and my mother had the three children to take care of alone. Much of what I did involved looking after my younger sisters so that Mum could work longer hours in the factory.

However, by early 1942 they were old enough to look after themselves and so, even before I was sixteen, together with two friends from my school days who were also survivors of that bombing raid, I lied about my age by claiming to be nearly eighteen and joined the Women's Land Army. Nobody asked too many questions about my real age; the war made us all grow up so quickly and look older than we were anyway, even as children, and so with my appointment time written on a piece of paper in my pocket, I presented myself for a medical examination. After having satisfied the doctor that I was as fit and healthy as anyone who had lived on war rations for the past two and a half years could reasonably be, I set off to be measured for my uniform. My official date of entry into the WLA was 16th February 1942. Three weeks later, with my new uniform in a suitcase, I set off with my two friends for the Land Army Hostel. However, we were not destined to work on farms but with the Forestry Commission.

Officially, the full uniform kit issue consisted of two green jerseys, two pairs of riding breeches, two overall coats, two pairs of dungarees, six pairs of woollen knee-length socks, three beige shirts, one green tie, one pair of boots, one pair of brown shoes, one pair of gumboots or boots with leggings, one green belt, one green beret, one greatcoat, one oilskin or mackintosh, two towels, one green armlet with a metal badge and a Bakelite cap badge. We were actually issued with about half of that kit and were promised that the rest would be sent on to us: it never was, of course, and we had to try to top it up as best we could by whatever means.

After hanging around at the hostel for a couple of days, we were on the move again, this time to start our training with the Forestry Commission. Since the Great War, the forests had been managed by the Commission, but in April 1942 the responsibility for timber was passed to the Home Timber Production Department of the Ministry of Supply. WLA women like me who were already working for the Forestry Commission transferred to the new Women's Timber Corps, which, although part of the WLA, kept a separate identity. We received six weeks' training on the work we would undertake in the forests including felling, two-handed cross-cut sawing, snedding, powered circular saw work, stacking, feeding logs into the saw cut, working the horses, tractor driving and such other delights. At the end of our training we were posted to our places of work. Unfortunately, I was split up from my two school friends and lost contact with them.

The first forest I was sent to was in Wales. I had digs arranged for me, which I shared with two other girls who arrived at the same time. One of them, Betty, and I shared a bedroom and we became very close friends indeed and managed to stay in touch with each other after the war. We gave our ration books to the owner of the house where we stayed, and she treated the three of us very well. She was widowed and I think she looked upon us as her daughters.

We had breakfast in the morning and our dinner at night in our digs, but because we were out in the woods all day with no access to a canteen, every day our landlady gave us a packed lunch to eat during the day. The girls of the WLA worked incredibly hard, but even by those standards our work was demanding and physically hard, simply because of the weight of the timber that we were handling. Physical fitness and energy were essential, so I think our landlady must have had extra rations of certain foods for us. She certainly fed us very well even if the choice was limited to cheese, onion or fish paste for lunch.

We were collected by truck each morning from our digs and went out every day, whatever the weather; hot or cold, wet or dry, clear or foggy, sunshine or deep snow, we went into the forests to work. The trees which were to be felled were chosen by another team, known as selectors, and marked with a whitewash cross or a code, depending on what the tree was to be used for when we had felled it. We would then come along and cut down all the trees that were marked. The felling was mostly done by hand with an axe or a two-handed cross-saw. That is, one girl on each side of the tree, working together with a push-pull motion on the saw until the tree came crashing down, the most dangerous part of the whole operation. We also used the cross-saw to cut the trees up into logs ready for shipping out of the forest.

The logs were put to a myriad of uses, including telegraph poles, pit props, railway sleepers, gun-mats, ladders, newsprint, ships' masts and planks for accommodation huts on RAF bases and army camps. They were even used to make wooden crosses to mark the graves of fallen service men and women.

In all, there were about 6,000 women in the WTC and it was a very mobile work force in that we could be sent to work anywhere in Britain. Even though we were told that our work was vital to the war effort, we were treated very badly by the authorities, both during and after the war, probably because we worked in such isolated locations and were out of the way. The pay was very poor to start with and then the cost of our board and lodgings were taken out of it too, so we didn't have much money in our pay packets at the end of each month. Also, once in the WTC, there was no escape because a transfer to the other services was not allowed, as those who tried it found out. Nor was there any interchange within the WLA to farm work because that would have required a different training.

The work was desperately hard and dangerous too. There were always several trees being cut down at the same time, tractors and horses dragging the felled trees out to the cut-up points, logs being stacked high and always at risk of rolling, and together with swinging axes and razor-sharp saws of various types in operation, the forest was a dangerous place to work in. Inevitably, there were many accidents, most fairly minor but others more serious, including a few fatalities.

Officially, we were allowed half a day a week off and seven days holiday a year, which was not long enough to really go anywhere to get a proper rest from the long, hard days of work. However, in practice, we didn't even get that little bit of leave. Like many others, I managed the occasional forty-eight-hour pass for a weekend away when things were quieter in the woods, usually in the winter when the days were shorter. Betty and I would always take our time off together and try to get to one or other's home when we could go out dancing or to the pictures, but then it was back to the camp. I just don't remember ever getting away for a week or more. In general we made our own entertainment or went to the dances in the local villages, though these were often several miles away.

Sometimes we would get a lift in one of the trucks, but otherwise we just walked; there was no alternative, other than to miss the dance altogether, which no-one ever did unless they were ill.

But for all that, we had a lot of fun and I remember my time in the Corps with fondness. We all had blisters for the first few days and in winter it was bitterly cold, but in summer it was good to be out in the clean fresh air. I was never fitter nor stronger than I was when with the WTC. It was very important to understand and get on with the person you worked with. Betty and I worked very well together and had a lot of fun. We pooled our resources and shared everything, our clothes, our food, and even the same bed on the bitterly cold winter nights. We also made sure that we stuck together when being sent to different forests to work so that we didn't get split up into different digs.

The end of the war though did not bring the end of our time in the WTC. Some of the girls were sent to Germany to see what could be retrieved from the sawmills over there to save us having to send timber from Britain. However, Betty and I remained working in the British forests until just before the Christmas of 1946 when the WTC was being disbanded. After almost five years of working long hours in all weathers, pretty much miles from anywhere, sawing, cutting and lugging timber out of the woods, I felt that I had done my bit and that it was time for a change.

My official release date from the WTC came on 21st December 1946 and when I handed in my uniform, in return I received my certificate of service from Her Royal Highness Queen Elizabeth, who later became the Queen Mother, and was the patron of the WLA.

> "*By this personal message I wish to express to you Miss M Oxenham WLA 68157 my appreciation of your loyal and devoted service as a member of the Women's Land Army from 16th February 1942 to 21st December 1946. Your unsparing*

efforts at a time when the victory of our cause depended upon the utmost use of the resources of our land have earned for you the Country's gratitude.

Elizabeth R"

Betty's release date from the WTC was also 21st December and we left our last forest, which was in Northumberland, together and travelled by train to our demob centre. I went and stayed with Betty for a few days before returning home and starting a new life in post-war Britain. In time we both married and raised our families, but we kept in touch with each other for very many years and would see each other whenever we could. We had a wonderful friendship forged from the war and the hardship of working for the WTC in the isolation of the forests of Britain; I will always remember her with great affection.

A long time later, when Gordon Brown was Prime Minister, an official medal was issued to the WLA/WTC and with it came another certificate.

"Monica Jones, the Government wishes to express to you its profound gratitude for your unsparing efforts as a loyal and devoted member of the WLA/WTC at a time when our country depended upon you for its survival.

Gordon Brown"

Today, at long last there is a permanent memorial in the form of a Lumberjill statue in the Queen Elizabeth Forest at Aberfoyle in Scotland. It is a great pity that that same grateful country didn't do a bit more for us at the time because there is no doubt that we were exploited by the authorities. Nevertheless, we got through, many girls made lasting friendships and I wouldn't have missed it for the world.

Women's Timber Corps
1942 – 1946

This statue is dedicated to the members of the Women's Timber Corps or "LUMBERJILLS" as they were affectionately known, who worked in woodlands throughout the country during World War II. It recognises their dedication, hard work and effort which was immeasurable.

"THANK YOU"

WTC inscription

Frank Parker.

Chapter Seven
Frank Parker [4854008]

> "*This story shall the man teach his son; and Crispin Crispian shall ne-er go by, from this day to the end of the world, but we in it shall be remembered – we few, we happy few, we band of brothers; for he today that sheds his blood with me shall be my brother...*"
>
> From 'King Henry V' [Act 4, scene 3]. *William Shakespeare*

D rawing heavily upon the Woodbine cigarette, I gazed down at the scattered jumble of assorted passengers who, in the stifling heat of the afternoon sun, had slowly made their way on board the HMT *Laconia*, moored at the quayside in the port of Suez on that late July day in 1942.

Built in 1922 at the Swan Hunter & Wigham Richardson yard in Wallsend-on-Tyne, the 19,695-ton *Laconia* was a pre-war passenger liner of the Cunard White Star Line, a later sister ship of *Titanic*. As I stood on her deck that day in 1942 I had no idea that not only would she would suffer a similar fate but that she would also become almost as famous. She had been requisitioned by the government in 1941 and was now a troopship. Her wartime crew of 136 men would be joined on this voyage by some 1,800 Italian prisoners of war together with their 160 Polish guards, 80 civilians, mainly women and children, and 286 British servicemen, including 20 RAF airmen and Royal Navy sailors, but mostly they were my fellow soldiers of the Royal Leicestershire Regiment, some of whom were wounded. We had been serving in Palestine and were on our way home for some well-earned and overdue leave.

The battle of El Alamein was still three months away and the route to Britain through the Mediterranean Sea was too dangerous, with attacks from German and Italian aircraft and submarines a certainty, particularly for an unescorted troopship travelling alone; information which made me shudder. The *Laconia* was to return to her home port of Liverpool from Suez via Aden, Mombasa, Durban, Cape Town and Freetown.

We had come aboard the *Laconia* on Tuesday 28th July, just in time for an attack by German aircraft upon the docks as she was moored at the quay in Suez. Embarkation had been delayed for as long as possible because, whilst conditions on shore were not particularly pleasant, they were much worse on a crowded troopship in the searing temperatures which we all experienced below decks. As a sergeant, it was my responsibility to get my men on board without losing any into the fleshpots of the port and then report to the officer that we were all present and correct. The Italian prisoners of war with some of their guards had boarded first, followed by us. The civilian families, together with the RAF and RN officers, were last to embark.

The ship had escaped any damage during the raid and in the lingering heat of the following afternoon, the last of the *Laconia*'s mooring ropes lazily dropped into the murky water of the dock as the tug strained on the hawsers to pull us clear of the quayside and out into the Gulf of Suez. Making plenty of smoke from her coal-fired boilers, we entered the Red Sea and steamed all night towards our first port of call, Aden at the southern tip of what is now South Yemen.

The next morning, about a quarter of the way to Aden, we passed the island of Jazirat Zabarjad on our starboard side and half an hour later, the *Laconia*'s Master, Rudolph Sharp, OBE, announced that we were crossing the Tropic of Cancer. It was hot and getting hotter by the hour. There was little or no wind and the steel on the ship burned to the touch. Time slipped by painfully slowly, but I had the chance to chart something of our progress by the many islands along the way and the Dahlak Archipelago. In time, I felt the *Laconia* start to turn, the land became clearer and we entered the port of Aden, where we replenished our stocks of fresh water and supplies.

A few hours later we were on the move again, out into the Indian Ocean, round the Horn of Africa and heading for Mombasa, the principal sea port of Kenya. The tropical heat during the daytime on the ship was only eased by the gentle sea breeze, but it wasn't until nightfall that we experienced anything approaching cool air. The closer to the equator we got, the hotter it became and the less benefit we had from the breeze. It was baking hot in the shade of the deck, what it must have been like for the Italian prisoners locked in the hold, God only knows.

Most of us had crossed the equator on the way out to Palestine and, in any event, no-one was in any mood for 'crossing the line' rituals. We were tired and, conscious of the long and dangerous journey we had to make, just yearned to see the twin towers of the Liver Building as we steamed up the River Mersey into Liverpool. However, for the time being we would have to be satisfied with Mombasa harbour and the knowledge that two of the six stages of our voyage were behind us. Again, fresh water, coal and supplies were taken on in the blistering heat.

I suppose that the temperatures must have dropped a little as we moved from the equator towards the Tropic of Capricorn, but it really didn't seem like it. I carried out daily inspections of the men in my company, but I knew that they were tired and needed some rest. A few of them played cards during the day, but most just dozed in the shade of the decks or their bunks, and in the evening the officers tried to ensure that there was some sort of activity to keep the men occupied.

Two days out of Mombasa, we saw Zanzibar slip by to starboard as we plodded our way down the eastern coast of Africa in the unrelenting, dazzling, stifling heat. Mealtimes came and went as the only relief from the whooshing sound of the bow wave and the rhythmic throbbing of the old engines deep below the water line of the ship. Far in the distance, out to the east, I was just able to make out the clouds that hung over the mountains of Madagascar: we were making progress.

The Tropic of Capricorn was crossed with only two more days' sailing until we made it to Durban. The heat was being turned down a little, the breeze got slightly cooler, the voyage more comfortable, home a little nearer.

We made Durban for fresh supplies and then, towards the end of August, passed Port Elizabeth, rounded the southern end of Africa and with some considerable relief sighted Table Mountain, the Cape of Good Hope and at last sailed into Cape Town harbour. It was early spring down here in the southern hemisphere and the weather was very pleasant, although it had been less settled recently and we had come through a couple of stormy days not long before passing Port Elizabeth.

Cape Town meant a chance to go ashore and leave the ship for twenty-four hours. The bars around the port area of Cape Town were a microcosm of the world's maritime nations. During the war, however, they teemed with not only sailors but also thousands of soldiers and a fair number of RAF lads, too, on their way around the Cape to various destinations. The bar owners and the girls who worked in and around them had a bounteous time in every respect. However, for Service personnel enjoying the company of some of these girls, there was the ever present and almost inevitable risk of contracting some form of venereal disease. Classed as SIW, a self-inflicted wound, a dose of VD would almost always also lead to being placed on a charge, just to add insult to injury. As usual, advice was given about where was safe to visit and where was not; not everyone heeded the warnings and I had to deal with a number of mishaps, but in the end all my men were present and correct when we left.

In the early-morning light of 1st September 1942 the HMT *Laconia* slipped her moorings for the very last time and steamed out of Cape Town harbour and into the annals of 20th-century naval wartime history.

The pleasant spring weather of the Cape soon turned once more into the sweltering heat of the tropics as we plied north, this time through the Atlantic Ocean along the western seaboard of Africa. We were about halfway through our journey home, another five weeks aboard the *Laconia* stretched out in front of us, but at least now we were sailing north and towards home instead of further away from it. However, I knew that that comfort was over-shadowed by three very sobering factors which I did not dare share with my men.

Firstly, we remained unescorted and on our own; a twenty-year-old coal-fired converted liner, making about ten to twelve knots. Secondly, those twenty-year-old coal-fired boilers were pumping out a veritable cloud of sooty smoke high up into the still air of the tropics every minute of every hour and that cloud could be seen a hundred miles away. Thirdly, and most worrying of all, we were entering some of the most dangerous waters in the world, for German U-boats patrolled all of the Atlantic Ocean. If we were found, we were lost.

For two weeks we made steady, monotonous progress, with nothing to see except the sea. The heat grew again as the ship approached the equator, but somehow did not seem as intense as it had been in the Indian Ocean; either that or I had just got more used to it. Despite this, I kept my men much more on their toes than I had done on the way from Suez to Cape Town. They had had a good rest by now and needed to be occupied. Drill each day, PT and an occasional kit inspection all helped to keep them alert.

The 12th September found the *Laconia* still a little way south of the equator and approaching Ascension Island, though about a hundred miles to the east. The day had been still, the sea almost flat with a long, barely discernible swell, undetected by the ship. Almost desperate to see another ship for company, to break the solitude of our voyage, I had looked out from the deck rails time and again; there was nothing but the vast ocean. With the approach of Ascension Island, my thoughts of making Freetown safely and another few hours in port before setting off on the final leg of the trip to Liverpool, possibly as part of a convoy or with an escort, began to turn to hope.

The twelve hours of equatorial daylight had passed without incident and the ship, now shrouded in the darkness of blackout order, was settling down for the corresponding twelve-hour night. I had finished my tour of D deck where my men were billeted and had, as so often over the last few weeks, been up to stand at the rails on the port side, thinking of home and the comfort of sleeping in my own bed. I had looked down and idly watched the flashes of phosphorous sparkling over the darkened water as the ship resolutely ploughed its way through the peaceful ocean. The thick palls of smoke from the funnel had still been gushing out into the night air, but at least with the dark I hoped they couldn't be seen by an enemy lying in wait beneath the glassy surface of that peaceful ocean.

It seemed that we had got through another day. Dressed in just shorts and singlet, I had flicked the last dregs from my mug of tea over the side and gone below once more to set about my very popular task of issuing the day's beer ration in the Sergeants' Mess on D deck, and business was understandably brisk in the sweltering heat of the equatorial evening.

The torpedo ripped into *Laconia*'s starboard side just below the main dining saloon. Like a fleeing deer pierced by the hunter's arrow, the old ship stumbled, trembled and finally faltered in her stride as if knowing that she had been mortally wounded, that her time had come. It was 20.07 hours.

For an instant there seemed to be nothing; silence, then my ears were filled with a crescendo of noise, the shouts of the men around me on D deck, the ship's alarm siren, and people running past me. Horror and disbelief gripped my body as I joined the desperate scramble for the staircase to the deck above and escape. In a few seconds the stairs were a heaving mass of frightened men, fighting to reach the top. Then, I was thrown forward by the force of another rending blast which tore the side out of Number Two hold. We had been hit by a second torpedo. The staircase could not stand the strain and gave way, torn from its supports by the weight of bodies and the force of the explosion. There was already a noticeable list to starboard and the engines were quiet; the *Laconia*'s heartbeat had stopped. I found myself at the right end of the collapsed stairs and continued up and out into the chaos on the main deck. Already crewmen were at the few remaining starboard lifeboats preparing them to be swung out and people were gathering around them. The ship listed further to starboard; she was lost and the port side lifeboats were out of reach. The *Laconia* was already preparing to go.

At 20.12 the ship's First Radio Officer sent the following message in plain English on the international 600 meters frequency to notify any vessel in the area that the *Laconia* had been torpedoed:

"*SOS SOS 0434 south/1125 west* Laconia *torpedoed.*"

The order to abandon ship came almost immediately and there was an almighty rush to the remaining lifeboats as nearly two thousand people, mostly the remaining Italian prisoners released from below, sought refuge in them. The first torpedo had hit one of the holds containing 450 prisoners, most of whom died instantly, and the Polish guards who had brought the remaining fourteen hundred up on deck now acted quickly and restored some calm. The order from Captain Sharp was women, children and the wounded into the boats first. After that it was every man for himself.

The *Laconia* was settling fast; time was against us and the darkness of the sea beyond the glare of the fires on the ship made everything seem even more frightening than it already was. There were pitifully few boats to launch now. Those on the port side could not be used and the two explosions had destroyed several of the starboard boats. Standing by the rail trying to get my eyes accustomed to the darkness and deciding upon my best chance, I could see that there were already hundreds of people thrashing around in the water at the side of the ship. Urgency had turned to panic and the lifeboats were being lowered far too quickly and unevenly. People were being thrown out of them, even before they hit the water; women and children were screaming, men were shouting and crying out.

Then I heard terrified screams from the sea as one of the lifeboats went careering down the side of the ship, the gantry pulleys squealing like a stuck pig. A rope had snapped and sent the overloaded boat crashing down into the sea on top of the struggling people in the water, crushing them and ending their torment. The sound of splintering wood as the lifeboat hit the water and the agonised cries of the shattered bodies of men, women and children in the sea reached up to me, even above the pandemonium on the deck. Even as a battle-hardened soldier, it made me feel sick.

The noise around me was shattering, deafening in its intensity and disturbing in its relentless constancy. Below decks, the ship was burning, roaring and crackling as the flames, fighting a losing battle with the incoming sea, engulfed everything combustible in their path, making the deck plates hot, whilst steam whooshed and hissed each time the *Laconia* settled a little further and the water doused the fires. There were muffled explosions beneath me and the steel plates of the stricken vessel cried out in the twisted agony of her death throes. Dozens at a time, people were jumping off the deck and into the water to join those already there screaming, some in panic, some in fear, others in pain, with bleeding, broken limbs, needing help that wasn't going to come; some with their last drowning breath as they slipped beneath the water. Men were running across the decks shouting orders, others simply shouting, terrified of what awaited them in the water.

I knew what awaited us in there; I had seen them earlier in the day and I shuddered, trying not to think about them. But it was too late. "Sharks, sharks!" The hysterical screams rang out above everything else that night from dozens of terrified, thrashing souls far below me in the sea.

By now, the stern was coming up out of the water and those who could not swim or who dared not risk the water were retreating past me up the deck from the sinking bow. In the faint glow of the remaining fires, I could see an empty life raft drifting by not far from the ship. It meant a jump of a hundred feet and I would have to risk the growing number of sharks to get to it but it was my only hope. I made up my mind, took a deep breath, focused on where the raft was and jumped. I hit the water hard, which was surprisingly cold after the heat of the fires on board, and it knocked some of my breath out of me, but I was full of adrenalin and desperate to get to the raft. I swam across to it as quickly as I could without making too much splashing, keeping my legs together, and pulled myself onto it. I lay there for a few minutes gasping for breath, trying to take in that I no longer had the solid feel of the deck plates beneath my feet but that I was at least out of the water and away from the sharks.

As I recovered, I realised that I had to get the raft away from there or I would be sucked into the vortex and pulled down by the power of 20,000 tons of ship heading to the seabed; a force from which there could be no escape. I looked across the few yards of water to where the *Laconia* had settled even lower in the short time since I had jumped. Her forward decks were awash now, the fires burned less fiercely and the light cast across the water from them was little more than a dim glow; the sea would have her soon, the old ship was about to go.

Then, out of the gloom I saw someone splashing around near to my raft, almost exhausted, eyes wide with fear. He said something to me which I didn't understand but I realised that he was one of the Italian prisoners. Kneeling up, I shouted and beckoned to him, holding out my hand. He struggled across the last few feet of open water, grasped the edge of the raft and held his other hand up to me for help. I seized his wrist and forearm with both hands and, though he slipped back into the sea a couple of times, I managed to pull his oil-covered body up out of the water and onto the comparative safety of the little raft.

"Grazie. Grazie," he gasped between spluttered coughs of foul, fuel-oil-tainted sea water. We may have been enemies whose countries were at war with each other, but out here in the Atlantic Ocean, we were the same; we were shipwrecked survivors and I had done for him what I hope he would have done for me.

There was a lifeboat not too far away and, using the raft's little paddle, I put all my strength into making for it in case they had room for two more. Trying to close my mind to the terrified and agonised screams that followed each shark attack on some poor soul, I was concentrating so hard upon getting us away from the pull of the vortex that I knew would soon come, I didn't hear the sound of the diesel engines.

The black sinister shape of the conning tower broke the surface some little way off and the rest of the U-boat followed in a great gushing cascade of sea water. After everything we had been through in the last hour, were we now to be machine gunned and left for shark food after all? The dim orange glow cast across the water by the remaining fires on the *Laconia* was split by the intense beam of the high-powered deck light and the clear sound of voices, German voices.

At once the Italians in the water and the boats started to shout and wave at the sailors on the U-boat, their Axis allies. They at least would be rescued. Slowly the U-156 edged towards the mass of struggling bodies and the crew began the slow and laborious task of pulling as many survivors as they could, of whatever nationality, from the sea and the grasp of the encircling, gorging sharks. We weren't to be machine gunned, but rescued by our attacker.

"She's going," came the agonised cry from one of the seamen of the lifeboat I had been paddling towards. I stopped paddling and watched, transfixed. Most of the bow section was well under the water and in the dim light of the remaining fires I could see hundreds of people, mainly Italian prisoners, still on her decks, crowding to the uplifted stern, destined to go down with her. The once lovely White Star passenger liner gave a lurch, tipped up more steeply and with screaming, terrified men falling off her into the sea, the HMT *Laconia* slipped gracefully beneath the surface amidst a boiling ferment of sea water. In a few dramatic moments she was gone. It was 21.16, barely an hour since the first torpedo had struck.

I took in my good fortune to be alive balanced by the desperation of the predicament; we were 350 miles from Ascension Island, the nearest land, some 750 miles from Freetown, and had an enemy U-boat in our midst. There had been more than 2,700 people on the *Laconia* and even though many had already been lost, the submarine could not rescue everyone who was left, even if the captain was prepared to try. What was to be our fate? Now that the *Laconia* had gone, it suddenly seemed very dark, even with the moonlight. In the time that I had stopped paddling to watch the *Laconia*'s final moments, I had lost contact with the lifeboat and the sweep of the U-boat's searchlight told me that we were too far away to be picked up any time soon.

The backwash from the vortex hit us hard and slopped up over the raft. My Italian companion and I had to hold on tightly not to be swept off our refuge, but in that moment, without him realising it, his left leg slipped into the water. Many survivors were still in the sea, clinging to whatever they could find to keep them afloat during the night, whilst in the bright moonlight of a tropical night, I could make out the unmistakable ghostly forms of bodies drifting past the raft, face down, as if searching for the lost ship.

We were wet and cold; even though this was almost the equator, the water had chilled us to the bone. Exhaustion, fear, adrenalin fatigue, whatever, we just lay on the raft, drifting in the vastness of the ocean awaiting the dawn that would come in about six hours, at around 06.00. Determined not to fall asleep, into what the Scandinavians call 'the long sleep' from which there is no awakening, I tried to occupy my mind with everything I could remember about the journey since we had left Suez.

I lay on my back gazing up at the millions of stars above me, thankful to be alive, the raft now gently rising and falling in the long lazy swell which rolled endlessly across the ocean. My travelling companion lay next to me, asleep or deep in his own thoughts, his left leg still trailing in the water like bait on a line. I saw it but was too cold and tired to recognise the significance of what I was seeing. Voices drifted across the water to me from the activity around the U-boat and others from the sea closer to me; a jumble of languages and emotions. Some calling for help, others quietly crying, someone nearby praying, others just slipping away from life and into the vastness of the sea.

I didn't see the shark, only a flash of white water followed by a scream that rose in a crescendo of unimaginable pain. My companion seemed to be catapulted almost on top of me, sobbing with shock as he clutched his footless leg. Trailing in the water, it had at last attracted unwanted attention. I pulled my singlet over my head, wrapped it around the poor man's foot and tied it tightly with the shoulder straps to stem the flow of blood as best I could. It was all that I had on the raft. Before I finished my makeshift first aid, the Italian had passed out.

Whilst I lay there in the dark wondering how all this would end, unbeknown to me, a chain of events had started to unfold which would draw a direct line between the sinking of the *Laconia*, Hitler and the German High Command, the Nuremberg war crimes trials and ultimately my wife and I having dinner with Großadmiral [Grand Admiral] Karl Dönitz and Korvettenkapitän Adalbert Schnee in Hamburg.

The Italian survivors rescued from the water very quickly told the captain of U-156, Kapitänleutnant Werner Hartenstein KC, that the *Laconia* was a troopship carrying mainly Italian prisoners of war en route from North Africa to Britain.

The thirty-two-year-old Hartenstein was faced with a dreadful dilemma. At this stage of the war, Germany and Italy were still allies and a German U-boat had just sunk a ship that was full of Italian soldiers. It was not particularly unusual for U-boats to stop and pick up survivors from their victims where there were no escorts around, so no-one really knows whether Hartenstein acted out of genuine humanitarian concern or the realisation of the political implications between Germany and Italy when the news of what had happened got out: probably both.

Whatever the motivation, and faced with well over a thousand survivors, including some women and children, Hartenstein needed help if he was not to condemn them all to death. At 01.25 hours on 13th September he radioed news of the *Laconia*'s fate to Befehlshaber der Unterseeboote [BdU] headquarters:

> "*Versenkt von Hartenstein Brite* Laconia. *Marinequadrat FF 7721 310 Grad. Leider mit 1,500 Italienischen Kriegsgefangenen. Bisher 90 gefischt. 157 cbm. 19 Aale, Passat 3, erbitte Befehle.*"

Translation:

> "*Sunk by Hartenstein British* Laconia. *Grid FF 7721 310 degrees. Unfortunately with 1,500 Italian POWs. Till now 90 fished. 157 cbm* [cubic meters of oil]. *19 eels 3 torpedoes, trade wind, ask for orders.*"

All night long I watched as the crew of U-156 worked to pick up as many survivors as they could. The lights showed people standing, sitting and lying on the deck as the crew went about their mission of mercy. Whilst all this activity was going on some distance from me, I was having my own dreadful dilemma to resolve. I did not want to be captured and become a prisoner of war. However, my still-unconscious companion was in need of medical attention. I had stopped the bleeding from the ragged wound left by the shark's teeth, but he would probably not survive floating on a raft for several hundred miles. I didn't know whether I would survive such an ordeal, but a prison camp was not an attractive choice. For the time being, I did nothing to draw attention to ourselves and resolved to see what daybreak brought in another few hours.

Dawn found the crew of U-156 still doing all they could. They had pulled 193 people from the water, including five women, and had taken four lifeboats in tow, each containing over a hundred survivors. At 06.00 on 13th September, things took a dramatic turn when Hartenstein took the unprecedented step of sending out a message in English on the international communication wavelength:

> *"If any ship will assist the ship wrecked* Laconia *crew I will not attack provided I am not being attacked by ship or air forces. I have picked up 193 men. 4° 53' S 11° 26' W. German submarine."*

This message, which confirmed the position of the sinking of the *Laconia* at about 350 miles north-east of Ascension Island, was intercepted by the British in Freetown, but, thinking that it might be a trap, they failed to act upon it or to pass it on to the Americans. Out at sea, there was no answer to Hartenstein's plea for help but the Allies now had an exact fix on U-156. What none of us knew at the time was that there was a secret American air base on Ascension Island, Wideawake Airfield, which was part of the lend-lease arrangement and was critical to the American support for the Allies' war effort in North Africa, India and Russia. The British did not want to compromise this secrecy and so did not pass on Hartenstein's English message to the Americans, a decision which was to prove pivotal to the fate of so many survivors and to have far-reaching consequences in the *Laconia* incident.

Meanwhile in Berlin, even Hitler was involved in the discussions with Admiral Dönitz and others of the German High Command about what to do over the sinking of the *Laconia* and how to pacify Mussolini at a critical time for the war in North Africa in the run-up to the decisive battle at El

Alamein. Hartenstein had asked for a 'cease fire' order, a truce, to allow all the survivors to be picked up and also for help in the form of German ships or submarines to come to the area.

The Germans did not trust the Allies any more than the Allies trusted the Germans; both sides were wary of a trap and of treachery. In a compromise, the German High Command requested that the French Vichy government send warships from Dakar and the Ivory Coast to effect a rescue, but it refused Hartenstein's request for a truce. In his rage over the whole affair, Hitler ordered that the Allies should not be informed of the efforts being made by the Axis powers to rescue the Italians and as a consequence, the British survivors.

Moreover, at that time, the Nazis had their own secret, which was Operation Eisbär, the gathering of U-boats in the southern Atlantic to attack Allied shipping around the Cape of Good Hope, the very waters we had just sailed through a few days earlier. Hitler did not want this operation to be compromised in any way, but even so, Admiral Dönitz, who was not a Nazi, defied Hitler and, being well aware of the public relations disaster looming with the Italians, ordered two of his U-boats to the area to help us. The U-506 commanded by Kapitänleutnant Erich Würdemann and U-507 commanded by Korvettenkapitän Harro Schacht had both been positioned in the waters off Sierra Leone, watching for ships in and out of Freetown; waiting for us if Hartenstein had missed.

The Italians sent the submarine *Cappellini* under the command of Marco Revedin and, following the request from Berlin, the Vichy government sent the cruiser *Gloire* and two sloops, the *Dumont d'Urville* and the *Annamite*. The British reportedly diverted two freighters just in case it was true, but otherwise sat on their hands.

Out on the ocean, the sky began to lighten and then the sun slipped silently into view on the distant eastern horizon like a burning discus, reminding me of just how far it was to the nearest land. My companion was stirring now from his pain-induced stupor and I knew that I had to get him to a lifeboat where he could be made more comfortable with the possibility of medical attention. At least my mind was made up, my dilemma settled. Slowly and laboriously I paddled the little raft towards the nearest lifeboat. There was no point in rushing; no-one was going anywhere. The crew of the submarine had seen me and from time to time casually watched my progress across the open stretch of glassy water from the conning tower.

All the while I was paddling, I kept talking to the Italian telling him that help was on its way. I have no idea whether he understood anything that I said, but I think he got the gist of the fact that I was trying to help him. After about an hour I got close enough to the lifeboat for someone to throw me a rope and pull me in until I felt the comforting bump of the raft against the side planking of the boat.

There was a merchant navy officer in charge and I explained to him what had happened and that the Italian needed help and to get into the boat. Even in their state of desperation, willing hands reached out to steady the raft and lift my floating companion aboard as I lifted his injured leg. Once he was safely transferred, it was with no little relief that I heard the officer say that there was room in the boat for me as well. With grateful thanks, I clambered in, leaving the raft that had been my saviour for the last eight hours for someone else to find and use. The lifeboat was equipped and designed to hold sixty people; the Italian and I made a hundred and twenty-seven. Once in the boat, the Italian was given proper first aid and I was glad to retrieve my singlet which, blood-stained though it was, would save me from sunburn.

Kapitänleutnant Hartenstein had ordered his crew to give whatever help they could to those on board and in the lifeboats, and hot soup, water and even some coffee was handed out wherever possible. Throughout that first day, U-156 took on board the wounded together with the women and children from the lifeboats. My Italian companion, now conscious, was one of those who were transferred. As he was about to be lifted onto the deck of the submarine, I was shaken from my thoughts by a cry and a shout. I looked to the bow of the lifeboat where he was sitting on the side, about to be lifted off.

"Per favore, venite," he called and beckoned to me. I carefully stepped between the others to reach my erstwhile raft companion. In true Italian style, he flung his arms around me and hugged me.

"Vi ringrazio, amico mio, vi ringrazio." He turned to another Italian, pointed to his missing foot and seemingly explained what had happened. His friend, who could speak English, helped me out.

"He says thank you for saving his life. He will never forget you."

We were not the only survivors. There were several lifeboats being towed by the submarine as well as others in the area, and many people were still in the water, clinging to whatever wreckage floated by. The crew of the submarine did what they could to shoot those sharks which came within range and undoubtedly saved many more lives this way.

For the next two and a half days, U-156 remained on the surface, a strange spectacle with nearly two hundred survivors crammed on and below her decks and hundreds more in four lifeboats strung out astern, like ducklings behind their mother. For a submarine crew at war this was an outstanding commitment to their humanitarian efforts, and without the life support given by U-156, many would not have lived at all.

After the first day, we drifted away from U-156, and together with three other boats, decided to set sail for Africa, six or seven hundred miles to the east, despite the poor strength of the wind. The choice was stark; do nothing but sit in the sun and wait for who knew what or try to make our own way to land. Rescue was what everyone wanted, but rescue by whom and would it come at all? For me, it almost certainly meant a prison camp, but that was infinitely preferable to a slow death in the unbearable heat which beat down upon us, hour after hour, with no shade and little wind to cool us. The sailing was debilitating and exhausting because the heat sapped our energy. The cool of the night air brought a welcome relief from the sun and, on the first night, a chance to attend to the necessities of nature in the dark over the back of the boat. From then on there was no call. We slept sitting up or slumped against each other, or against the side of the boat. Sleep now was the best way of surviving because it made the hours pass unnoticed.

Early-morning conversations quickly dwindled; it took too much energy to talk, tongues were thick from the heat, mouths dry from dehydration; words were only used as a necessity. The daytime brought more unabated, blistering heat and the meagre, life-preserving ration of an ounce of water and a Horlicks tablet handed out by the officer in charge. Silence returned, broken only by the rhythmic creaking of the oars on the rowlocks and the timbers of the boat as it rose and fell with the long gentle swell of the ocean, followed by the slap of the sail against the mast as it searched for the wind to fill its fabric and push us on towards the elusive goal of land. It became hypnotic in its monotony.

Once or twice, from one of the other boats we would see some movement, and then a body would be slipped over the side to join the hundreds we had already left behind. There was no shock in it, we had endured too much since the first torpedo for that; it was just another body, someone else who hadn't made it. If we didn't make land soon we would all end up like that. On the third day, the sun seemed hotter than ever. By mid-morning the air was lifeless, even the sea had given up any pretence of movement, its surface flat and dazzling, reflecting the sun like a mirror. Nothing moved except for the slow steady rhythm of the oars. We were in the Doldrums.

However, for those in the lifeboats that had stayed with the U-156, there was about to be a development. Gradually they became aware that they could feel something moving in that inert expanse of ocean. The planks of the lifeboats began to reverberate then they heard the unmistakeable throb of a diesel engine. On the U-156, sitting two hundred yards in front of them, there was definite activity amongst the crew.

At 11.30, with a great resounding crash of cascading water, U-506 broke the surface and gently eased her way alongside her sister U-boat. By 15.00 hours they had been joined by U-507 and the Italian submarine *Cappellini*. The three newcomers set about picking up the remaining survivors in the water and rounding up the other lifeboats. The four submarines were well spread out in a staggered formation around the lifeboats and from time to time would dive out of sight for a while, resurfacing to hand out hot soup and water to the survivors. Whenever on the surface, all the submarines had large Red Cross flags draped over their gun decks in an effort to minimise the risk of attack from the air.

Wednesday 16th September once more dawned clear and bright, just as every day had done for the last week. In the lifeboat, we stretched and yawned as the daylight crept over the horizon and quickly spread across the still, flat calm surface of the sea. We had not yet been picked up by any of the Axis U-boats and were still making some progress towards the African coast. Once again there was no wind, so rigging the sails was pointless. However, the merchant navy officer in the boat kept us rowing in the direction we had been heading. Although Ascension Island was the nearest land, it was a fairly small target to aim for and if we missed it, the whole of the south Atlantic would be spread out before us.

Meanwhile, the four U-boats and the lifeboats they were towing were making good progress towards the rendezvous point with the Vichy French ships. At 11.25 that morning, there was a sudden flurry of activity on the U-156 and Kapitänleutnant Hartenstein, standing in the conning tower, gazed up into the sky through his binoculars. He strained to see the source of his concern in the cloudless azure that hung above him, until at last he had it. Coming from the south-west, he saw the tiny black speck slowly grow in size and shape until he could hear the unmistakeable drone of an aircraft.

The USAAF Liberator bomber circled as the American pilot, Lieutenant James D. Harden looked down, trying to take in the meaning of the unlikely scene he could see below him, an enemy submarine openly sailing on the surface towing four lifeboats. His job was to seek out and destroy such craft, and yet, not only were they not trying to avoid him, they were signalling to him. The signaller on U-156 sent a message to the Liberator, in English, that these were Allied survivors from the *Laconia* and help was needed. When no reply was received from the circling Liberator, an RAF officer on the deck of the U-156 took the lamp and signalled who he was and that they needed help, having been rescued by the submarine and that they really were survivors of the *Laconia*.

Still without answering the submarine, Lt. Harden decided to hedge his bets and contacted his base for orders; and so the tragedy started to unfold. In the meantime, he turned the Liberator away to the north-east. At Wideawake Airfield on Ascension Island, the senior duty officer who received Lt. Harden's reported findings and request for orders that morning was Captain Robert Richardson III, who was now faced with the most dreadful dilemma of his life. He was not aware of the open language messages which Hartenstein had sent and which had been received by the British in Freetown, because the British had not passed them on to the base at Ascension. The intention and purpose of the humanitarian convoy was clear, but Richardson's great worry, unaware of the planned rendezvous with the Vichy French ships, was that it would turn to Ascension Island, which was the nearest land. If it did so, the Germans would learn of the highly secret air base there and its purpose to give logistical support the North Africa campaign.

Faced with a clear operational decision, Captain Richardson answered Lieutenant Harden's message with an unequivocal order: "*Sink the sub*". At 12.32 the Liberator returned with the clear intention to attack. Hartenstein ordered his gun crew not to retaliate. The Liberator dropped two bombs which straddled U-156, sending tons of sea water crashing down upon the terrified survivors huddled upon her decks. So much water fell down upon the submarine that it simply washed several hapless souls straight into the sea. In all the lifeboats, survivors were standing, waving and shouting to the crew of the Liberator, but of course they couldn't hear them, and anyway, they now had their orders.

With disbelief, they saw the Liberator coming back round again for another attack. Again, Hartenstein ordered no retaliatory fire from his gun crew. This time, the American bomb aimer released a single depth charge which landed amongst the lifeboats, destroying the one closest to U-156 and killing many of those in it. The water from the exploding depth charge cascaded down over the remaining three boats in the line and almost swamped them.

Hartenstein now had to look to the safety of his own men and craft. The men, women and children crowded onto the decks were ordered into the water, the tow ropes were cut and the submarines dived before the Liberator could come round again. All those who had reached the safety of the U-boat decks were once more at the mercy of the sharks.

One of those who lost their lives that day was the master of the *Laconia*, Captain Sharp. This was his second sinking in as many years; his previous ship had been the HMT *Lancastria*, which was sunk by a Junkers Ju88 bomber off Saint-Nazaire on 17th June 1940 whilst rescuing troops and civilians.

The submarine commanders had been given no choice; they had to dive to save their own crews and indeed could have done so without clearing the decks first and giving people the chance to swim away. Even as the Liberator droned away back to Ascension Island, people were starting to drown. They were tired, thirsty, and hungry and weakened by the days and nights out in the open since the *Laconia* had sunk. Few had the stamina to survive long in the water once again. All afternoon, struggling swimmers clung to the sides of the remaining lifeboats, desperately trying to summon the last of their strength to hang on. Some succeeded, but others lost their battle with exhaustion and slipped quietly away into the ocean, their place at the side of the boat being gratefully filled.

For us, like everyone else, the day brought more hours of blistering heat as the sun continued to accost us. However, we felt that we were making good progress, although in fact we had not gone as far as we thought. In the late afternoon, one of the submarines, the U-507, I think, surfaced close by and an understandably irate officer berated us with the news that an American aircraft had attacked them. Of course, we knew nothing about the attack at that stage, but even so, they were still trying to help us, and towed us back to where the *Laconia* had sunk, taking the view that we would have a better chance of rescue there than trying to make land or meet the ships on our own. It was very disappointing but proved to be the right decision.

Rescue was now our only hope of survival and since we had been told that Vichy French ships were on the way, we could do nothing now but sit and wait in the blistering equatorial heat of the south Atlantic. For the next four days and nights we sat out in those open boats, watching the lifeless bodies that slowly performed their macabre dance in the water around our boats, condemned to drift on the current until they became a part of the sea itself.

In the late afternoon of 19th September, the eighth day after the *Laconia* had been torpedoed, I heard a shout from the stern of the boat, "Smoke, dead ahead, sir." Painfully and stiffly, I turned and strained my eyes towards the distant horizon, but I couldn't see anything; it all looked the same as it had done for days.

"Are you sure, Mac?"

"Yes sir, positive."

"All right, keep your eyes on it, then. If Mac says he's seen smoke, then he has and that means a ship." For the first time in days, our spirits were lifted; we might survive after all if this was the promised French ship.

Five minutes later, the sighting was confirmed. Sure enough, a ship was approaching. The French cruiser *Gloire* took shape until at last we were alongside and being helped aboard. At around 17.30 hours and just before the sun set, ushering in an end to that fateful ordeal, having survived on an ounce of water and a Horlicks tablet each day, I no longer had the strength to struggle up the scrambling nets or rope ladders draped over the side of the *Gloire* and had to be hoisted up, as did most people in our boat. We were all exhausted and in a terrible state, but now I was a prisoner of war, and I wondered how I would be treated. In the event, I was treated very well; we all were. The Italians amongst us were of course the happiest, because they were now free again, although this news was received with mixed emotions, many having lost good friends, whilst others would have preferred the prospect of a POW camp in Britain to that of going back into the front line, which was almost certainly what now awaited them. However, the immediate need for everyone was to be given a hot drink, hot food, and where necessary, medical attention and dry clothes.

The steady flow of bedraggled, weary survivors continued to struggle onto the deck of the warship, either up the scrambling nets or by being lifted in a hoist or a stretcher. Once on deck, before being segregated, we were given a steaming mug of tea and a blanket. Very shakily, I stood at the rail drinking my tea, happy to be able to stand properly after so many days sitting in the lifeboat. I looked out to the west, watching the sun dip lower to the horizon; the last time I had watched that with a mug of tea in my hand was exactly a week ago, just before the first torpedo struck.

Together with other British NCO survivors, I was taken to one of the lower decks and given a hot meal and the use of a hammock. During the meal I had felt the *Gloire* get under way and knew that we were leaving the area. We had been rescued again, importantly before nightfall. In all, 1,084 of the original 2,741 men, women and children on board the *Laconia* had endured attacks by both sides in this war as well as by nature; torpedoes, bombs, depth charges, sharks, thirst, heat and the ocean had all tried to kill us, but we had survived. Now, lying in the hammock, I realised just how exhausted I was; emotionally and physically drained from the ordeal, I closed my eyes and let the welcome sleep wash over me.

Two days later, along with the sloops *Dumont d'Urville* and *Annamite*, the *Gloire* put in to Dakar where the business of sorting everybody out began. The Italians were taken off to begin their journey of repatriation, whilst the rest of us, military and civilians alike, were collected together from the three ships and brought onto the *Gloire*. In all, there were 668 people: one Royal Navy officer with 178 NCOs and ratings, seventeen army officers with eighty-seven NCOs and other ranks, nine RAF officers with seventy NCOs and airmen, eight officers of the Merchant Navy with 178 men, one officer and sixty-nine NCOs and other ranks of the Free Polish Army and fifty civilian women and children.

After another two days, we set sail again, this time for Casablanca in Morocco where we arrived on Saturday 26th September. However, an evening's entertainment enjoying the pleasures of Rick's Bar with Ingrid Bergman and the strains of 'As time goes by' was not what our captors had planned for us. Instead we were put into waiting trucks and transferred to a prisoner of war camp. Once more we were treated very well by the Italians, who by and large, like us, would much rather have been at home with their families than fighting this bloody war which their dictator Mussolini had got them into. We were fairly well fed as far as POWs went, and from time to time received a Red Cross food parcel from home.

At the beginning of November the Allies launched Operation Torch, the seaborne invasion of North Africa, which cut off Rommel's retreating Afrika Corps and pushed east to link up with Montgomery's Eighth Army, the Desert Rats. Most of the German troops of the Afrika Corps withdrew across the Mediterranean leaving the Italians to fight the rear-guard action and ultimately get captured. Within a few days of the invasion, our prison camp was relieved by US troops of the American 1st Army, and I was on my way again, this time to the States in a Liberty ship and then from New York back across the Atlantic in the freezing cold of a winter storm, arriving in Glasgow on 29th December 1942, just in time for the New Year.

Whilst I was being rescued by the *Gloire*, the German High Command, and Admiral Dönitz in particular, grappled with the implications of the sinking of the *Laconia* and the events which had followed. We were at war with Germany and Kapitänleutnant Hartenstein had done what he and his crew were trained to do and what their country expected them to do; he had sunk an enemy ship. What he did afterwards was not an act of war, but one of genuine humanitarian concern for those of us left in the sea.

In those first few days after the sinking, two opportunities had presented themselves to the Allies to prevent the attack by the American Liberator and to have produced an altogether different outcome; both were missed. Had the British Intelligence officer in Freetown shared Hartenstein's humanitarian message for help with the Americans on Ascension Island, Captain Richardson would have had a wider understanding of what was happening 350 miles away when his Liberator crew asked for orders. Regardless of the paucity of intelligence at Richardson's disposal, the second opportunity fell to him alone. Since his primary concern was to maintain the secrecy surrounding Wideawake, he could have ordered the Liberator crew to keep a watch over U-156 and the other submarines and only attack if any of them turned towards Ascension Island. Had he chosen that option, not only would he have saved many lives from the *Laconia* but also from many other ships during the course of the war.

Although conscious of the political and military damage which the sinking was likely to cause with their Italian allies, the German High Command, and Hitler in particular, was at best ambivalent in its response to Hartenstein's request for help. The dispatch of U-506 and U-507 to the area was at the sole initiative and responsibility of Admiral Dönitz. It also emphasised the great rapport which he had with his crews. He knew that Hartenstein would have weighed the risks carefully and that if he was asking for help, then it should be sent.

Dönitz had put at risk three of his U-boats and their crews, together with the Italians in the *Cappellini* to try to save his enemies and must have felt betrayed by the actions, and inaction, of the British and Americans; he was not going to put his men in that position again. As it was, the U-156 had been damaged by the Liberator's bombs and had to return to port for repairs. A few days after the attack, Dönitz issued a new order to his submarine commanders, an order which became universally known as the '*Laconia* Order', the translation of which is as follows:

> "*All efforts to save survivors of sunken ships, such as the fishing out of swimming men and putting them on board lifeboats, the righting of overturned lifeboats, or the handing over of food and water, must stop. Rescue contradicts the most basic demands of war: the destruction of hostile ships and their crews. The orders concerning the bringing in of skippers and chief engineers stay in effect. Survivors are to be saved only if their statements are important for the boat. Stay firm. Remember that the enemy has no regard for women and children when bombing German cities.*"

The sinking of the *Laconia* shows how a single tactical decision can have strategic impact across the expanse of history and can resonate with unforeseen consequences for years to come. As a result of this order, all future attempts by U-boat commanders to save survivors from the ships they had sunk ceased and there can be little doubt that this led to the needless deaths of many merchant seamen, creating the impression of a generally more ruthless attitude of U-boat crews to their victims.

On 23rd May 1945, Großadmiral Karl Dönitz, who since the death of Adolf Hitler had become the head of the German people, was arrested and imprisoned on indictment of war crimes. Along with Rudolph Hess, Herman Göring, William Joyce, better known as 'Lord Haw-Haw', and many others, he was put on trial at Nuremberg the following year, charged with having issued the *Laconia* Order, together with the earlier War Order No.154 of 1939.

Karl Dönitz was not a Nazi; he was a life-long German navy career sailor having worked his way through the ranks of the Kaiserliche Marine and the Kriegsmarine since joining as a *seekadett* on 1st April 1910. He was drawn into the German High Command because by 1935 he had attained the senior rank of Kapitän ze See and was ordered by Generaladmiral Raeder to build up the German U-boat fleet.

During his trial, in answer to a question put to him, Dönitz answered, "*My life was devoted to my profession and, therefore, to the service to the German people. As last Commander-in-Chief of the German Navy and as last head of state I felt responsible to the German people for everything I did and did not do.*"

The trial of Großadmiral Karl Dönitz was a farce, in that he was charged with purported offences which could have equally been brought against any naval officer from the Royal Navy or United States Navy at that time. In addition to issuing the *Laconia* Order, he was also charged with conducting an offensive war and preparing and training his men for battle; which is exactly what every officer in every armed service across the world is supposed to do.

Dönitz's defence advocate was the very able Flottenrichter Otto Kranzbühler, who, to the great consternation of the prosecution, called the Commander-in-Chief of the American Pacific Fleet, Admiral of the Fleet Chester Nimitz to give evidence in support of his client. Nimitz's sworn evidence was that, from the very outset of war with Japan, the US Fleet had conducted unrestricted submarine warfare against its enemy. As the Commander-in-Chief of the American Pacific Fleet that was what his job was and he would have failed in his duty had he not done so, in exactly the same way that Dönitz, as commander of the Befehlshaber der Unterseeboote, had done. Admiral Nimitz saw no distinction between his own duty and actions and those of Großadmiral Dönitz. In the face of such compelling evidence by one of the Allies' own most senior commanders, the judges could not convict Dönitz on a charge arising from the very same strategy just because he was German. The *Laconia* Order charge was dismissed.

Nevertheless, there was a political imperative to see Dönitz, as head of the German State, convicted, and he was found guilty on the ludicrous charge, which has never again been brought against anyone else since that day, of preparing his men for war. He was sentenced to ten years imprisonment in solitary confinement, which even by the standards of 1946 was seen as a particularly harsh punishment. He had been a prisoner of war at Redmires in England at the end of the Great War, having been captured in 1918; but this was different.

When the sentence was handed down, Otto Kranzbühler addressed the Court with heavy sarcasm, saying that the sentence reflected the minimum penalty to be expected in a case of proven innocence. Even the Allied judges were uncomfortable with it.

Sometime afterwards, Otto Kranzbühler said, "*This conviction was born out of the dilemma to take the Großadmiral into prison for political reasons. As I learned later on, the American law advisor made the proposal to the Allied control office to nullify the verdict.*"

As a man, Karl Dönitz enjoyed the greatest admiration and respect from his Allied contemporaries, who knew that he was a professional seaman, not a politician or a Nazi. The verdict was generally regarded as an outrageous injustice, and officers from around the world, including more than one hundred and twenty admirals of the United States Navy, condemned the sentence as an attack upon one of their brother officers. Within a short space of time following his imprisonment, Karl Dönitz received over four hundred letters of support, sympathy and deep regret from admirals, generals, politicians, historians and journalists world wide. I was to come to understand why.

I had been born on 24ᵗʰ June 1910 at Shipston-on-Stour and at sixteen, had joined the Royal Leicestershire Regiment as a drummer boy. In 1946, after twenty years' service and a world war, I was demobbed.

I was thirty-six, married and needed a job in Civvy Street to support my family, but in 1946, jobs were not that easy to find. Britain was just about bankrupt and had to borrow money from America under the 'Marshall Plan'. At first I worked on the buses for Birmingham Corporation and then I became the landlord of the Queen's pub in Aston. Four years later I moved to the Phantom Coach in what was left of Coventry, where I stayed until 1958 when I took over the Bradford Arms at Wheaton Aston near Stafford on the A5, the old Watling Street Roman road. After the Bradford Arms, in 1965, the family moved back to Coventry to the Brickmakers, from where in 1969 I finally retired.

In early 1963, whilst at Wheaton Aston, I became aware that a book called *U-boats to the Rescue* by the French writer Leonce Peillard, which told the story of the *Laconia*, was about to be published. After twenty years, all the images of that night came flooding back to me; the gripping panic below decks to get out, the collapsing staircase, the horrors of the people crushed by the falling lifeboat, the sharks and the days in the open boat, but most of all of the efforts made by the U-boat commanders to save as many of us as they could.

I became driven by a desire to say thank you to those who had helped my survival. I wrote to the author of the book, told him of my own experiences and that I wanted to thank Admiral Dönitz for sending his U-boats to pick us up.

On 17th July that year I received a reply to my letter written by Monsieur Peillard, from the offices of the Conseiller du Commerce Exterieur at 22, Rue Henri Rochefort, Paris:

> *"Dear Mr Parker, I thank you for your long et very interesting letter about the sinking of the LACONIA.*
>
> *I know, of course, what you said about the lifeboat lowered and crashed down and your lifeboat, the story of the rope broken. You will find this in the SUNDAY EXPRESS and further in my book.*
>
> *Regretting not to know you - and your personal story before, when I was enquiring for survivors, I hope that you will find a true-to-life story of the LACONIA.*
>
> *I can say that all the survivors agreed that Captain Hartenstein was a gentleman and I am glad to tell this.*
>
> *I thank again, dear M. Parker, and I remain,*
>
> *Yours very truly,*
>
> *L Peillard"*

Encouraged by this reply, I eventually managed to get an address for Admiral Dönitz, who had been released from Berlin-Spandau prison in 1956 after nearly eleven years. In his retirement, together with his wife Ingeborg, he lived an almost reclusive life in the small town of Aumühle, Holstein, near Hamburg. There he spent most of his time writing his memoirs, helping journalists and historians from many nations with answers to their questions about German naval warfare and giving occasional lectures.

I must say that as I dropped my letter, which was written in English, into our village Victorian post box on 29th December 1963, I really did not expect a reply from such a distinguished and revered wartime officer, who had been both the Commander-in-Chief of his country's navy and its head of state. Why would he be bothered to reply to me, a man completely unknown to him and linked only by one incident of war in a six-year-long struggle which had occurred over twenty years earlier? A man who at fifty-five years of age had been condemned to spend more than ten years in solitary confinement on a trumped-up charge; a man entitled to be bitter and resentful towards the British.

Nothing could have been further from the truth. During the first week of 1964 I had a delightful reply to say that he would indeed like to meet me, but he modestly declined to take any credit for the rescue operation, saying that the decision was Kapitänleutnant Hartenstein's alone. However, I was very sad to learn from him that Werner Hartenstein had not survived the war. Indeed, tragically none of the U-boat commanders who had done so much to save the *Laconia*'s passengers and crew had survived the war.

I quickly made some arrangements and suggested that my wife Dorothy and I visited him on 20th January. Within a few days I received a reply written in German, which translated reads:

"Very Dear Mr Parker,

Thank you very much for your letter from 29th December and I am looking forward to your visit, but I am very sorry to say that 20th January is not suitable. So I want to ask you if it is possible on Sunday 19th January. I want to suggest the following things for your visit: I will be very pleased if you and your wife will meet me at my house [Aumühle] on Sunday 19th at 11.00. I am sorry that I cannot invite you for lunch at my house, but that is because I am alone. My wife died in May 1962.

I will accept your very kind invitation for a meal. I suggest we have a meal at 19.00 on Sunday evening in the Four Seasons Hotel, Hamburg, Neuer, Jungfernstieg 9. I want to invite, of course as my guests, Korvettenkapitän AD Adalbert Schnee and his very charming wife. In the last war, Schnee was a U-boat commander and now he is President of the German U-boat Association.

I hope that these arrangements suit you and I am waiting for your answer. I suggest you also stay in the Four Seasons Hotel.

With best regards, also to your wife,

Yours,

Dönitz."

I was overwhelmed, captivated by the charm and warmth of his letter to me. This was a man of immense stature during the war and after, not just in Germany but throughout the world, and he was still revered in Germany. For him to embrace Dorothy and me, to be so welcoming and helpful to his former enemies whom he had never met, was something that impressed and humbled me. I replied by return thanking him for making the arrangements and confirming that they suited us very well. I had obtained a copy of *U-boats to the Rescue* from Leonce Peillard to present to my host when I met him and, together with Dorothy, set off on a bitterly cold and foggy January day for Heathrow to fly to Hamburg.

By the time we reached the airport, the fog had cleared and we were able to take off on time in a Vickers Viscount. In the fading light of the late afternoon, the Viscount began to lose height and speed as it circled Hamburg on its approach to the main runway. Looking out of the window, I could see vast open spaces covered in fresh snow like an endless starched white cloth spread across a dinner table. At the far end of this cloth was a great forest which seemed to stretch for miles, the trees stripped of their summer decoration standing bare and gaunt, a vast maze of inter-twined snow-laden braches, like some heathen army waiting to advance upon the city. Lower yet the Viscount slipped, now over the city, showing me the remaining evidence of the heavy bombing which it had suffered during the war. RAF Bomber Command had visited the heavily defended city on many occasions, although bad weather over Hamburg had saved it from receiving the very first one-thousand-bomber raid in history on the night of 29th May 1942; the force went to Cologne instead.

Then the runway was flashing past the window; a solid bump and we were down, racing towards the far end, the propeller blades becoming less of a blur as the brakes slowed the aircraft and the engines sounded more relaxed. A few more moments and we turned onto one of the taxiways, finally coming to a stop on the concrete apron. I couldn't help thinking of the irony of this moment. A British four-engine aircraft landing at this airfield twenty years earlier would have heralded capture and imprisonment for its occupants; tonight, I was going to sleep in a comfortable hotel and on Sunday would be the guest of one of Germany's most prominent wartime leaders. Strange the way things turn out.

Despite the scattered bomb sites, by 1964 Hamburg was once more a bustling modern metropolis with much of its pre-war charm restored. Part of that charm was the imposing Hotel 4 Jahreszeiten, the Four Seasons Hotel. Built in 1897, it had substantially survived the bombing and still stood at the edge of the lake in all its grandeur. The hotel entrance was very impressive, with a beige marble floor and matching marble columns supporting the high ceiling. When we presented ourselves at the reception desk, we found that not only were the staff expecting us, they knew who we had come to see and why. They could not do enough for us. After our long journey, we were shown to a most comfortable room and were very grateful to the Admiral for his recommendation. He had kindly made the reservation for us and also for the dinner on Sunday evening, so the staff knew that he was coming to their hotel. The German people worshipped Dönitz, and anyone who was his guest was to be given the warmest of welcomes. If the roles had been reversed, I only hope that any hotel in Britain would have made an ordinary German soldier and his wife just as welcome as these people made Dorothy and me.

Karl Dönitz had been one of the most powerful men in Germany during the war. In 1943 he succeeded Admiral Raeder and became Großadmiral, the Commander-in-Chief of the entire German navy, not just the BdU. And yet when I met him, I found not an arrogant man full of his own importance and undoubted place in history, but a genteel seventy-two-year-old of great charm, courtesy, intelligence and interest. It was impossible to identify him with the Nazis, probably because he had never been one. He was not at all as I had imagined him, and yet in a way he was, because, having met him, I came to understand the compassion in the man which had led him to support Hartenstein and to order U-506 and U-507 to come to our assistance and save us from certain death in those shark-infested tropical waters of the Atlantic.

On Sunday morning, Dorothy and I got into the pre-booked taxi outside the grand entrance of the hotel and made our way through the streets of Hamburg towards Aumühle. At 11.00 precisely we arrived at the very comfortable home of Großadmiral Karl Dönitz, who met us at the front door and ushered us inside away from the bitter wind. The house was set in its own grounds of open laid-out gardens and mature trees, and at the height of summer this would be a most beautiful garden to walk in. However, in the biting cold of January in northern Germany, we were happy just to look out at this snow-covered winter wonderland from the warmth and cosiness of the drawing room.

We were entertained to a splendid reception of sherry and cocktails. Dönitz had taken the trouble to invite a number of other people along, including Adalbert and Frau Schnee, who were joining us for dinner that evening and who kindly acted as interpreters for us. From the beginning, I was impressed that these were men who were genuinely interested in my experiences on the *Laconia*. Those present were mostly former senior German navy officers and particularly from the BdU. I was probably one of the very few survivors, perhaps the only survivor, of their actions whom they had met in peacetime and, particularly as a survivor of the *Laconia* with all that resonated from her sinking, they wanted to know what I felt about my experience and what had actually happened to me. They were also interested to know about the part that Werner Hartenstein had played in the incident and what I thought of the man who had put me into the sea in the first place. After all, Dönitz's *Laconia* Order had affected these men as much as anyone during the war since it had fallen to them to carry it out.

I was very conscious not only that Hartenstein wasn't there with us to speak for himself, but also that he had been a well-respected comrade who had not been as fortunate as the rest of us and had not survived the war. In the event, I felt nothing but admiration for the commander of U-156. Sinking the *Laconia* had been as much a part of his duty as pulling the trigger on my rifle had been a part of mine and it was neither his fault nor mine that we had been enemies. What earned Hartenstein such acclaim and affection from the survivors was what he had done after he had fired the torpedoes. He had been motivated by a genuine concern for his fellow human beings and had demonstrated that concern by doing all in his power to save us.

We discussed the incident along these lines for some time, including the parts played by the British Intelligence officer in Freetown and by the Americans. It was at the end of this discussion that I presented Dönitz with the copy of *U-boats to the Rescue* which I had brought with me, and in doing so, I thanked him for saving my life. He still refused to accept any praise or thanks for his actions, maintaining that it was Hartenstein who should be thanked if he was still alive. I did not disagree with that, but I also knew that the other submarines and ships had come to us upon Dönitz's orders. He could have ordered Hartenstein to leave us floating in the ocean and go about his business of sinking ships; but he didn't and, having met him, I understood why he didn't. He was a most gracious host and we spent a very easy and pleasant couple of hours with him and his other guests before leaving to return to the Hotel 4 Jahreszeiten.

That evening, it was my turn to play host. Having met Dönitz together with Herr Schnee and his wife, Dorothy and I were looking forward to the evening and the opportunity to talk again with these remarkable people. I was still overwhelmed by the whole thing, finding it hard to believe that I was going to have a private dinner with not only one of the greatest German wartime commanders of all time and the man who had been the head of the German State at the end of the war, but also the man who had been instrumental in saving my life twenty-two years earlier.

At exactly 19.00 a large black Mercedes drew up outside the front door and the hotel staff escorted the man who is about as close to German hearts as it is possible to get, into the entrance foyer where we were waiting. Many of today's so-called 'A' list celebrities could not even stand in the shadow of this man; Dönitz was a true celebrity, quiet, gracious and dignified amidst the genuine adoration of the people around him. Once more I realised what an immense privilege it was for us that he had entertained us at his home and had now accepted our invitation to dinner. As we had hoped, he was accompanied by Adalbert and Frau Schnee.

The hotel provided a sumptuous meal for us in one of its ornate marble and classically decorated restaurants, during which we talked about many subjects in a wide-ranging and light-hearted conversation. By 1942, Adalbert Schnee had been awarded the Knights Cross with Oak Leaves, Germany's highest gallantry award in war time, and finished the war with the rank of Korvettenkapitän, equivalent to Lieutenant Commander in the Royal Navy. He told us all about his very interesting work as President of the U-boat Association and that led us to very briefly touch upon some of the wider issues of the war. Having shared my own wartime experiences, I was anxious to hear about theirs. It appeared that they had first met each other in 1934 when Dönitz, then a Fregattenkapitän, was the commander of the cruiser *Emden*, where German naval officer cadets got their basic training on a year-long cruise around the world. The future U-boat ace Adalbert Schnee, was one of those young cadets aboard the *Emden*, and thirty years and a lifetime of experiences later, they had become close friends in retirement.

We talked a little about Hitler and his relationship with his senior commanders. Dönitz told me that Hitler, whilst sometimes a most charming man, was, like all dictators, unbalanced and therefore unpredictable. He could fly into great rages, as he did over the *Laconia* for no rational reason. From the High Command's point of view, this proved disastrous on a number of occasions because poor or wrong decisions were made against the advice of his trained military commanders. He just shrugged his shoulders saying, "Hitler war nie ein Offizer" (Hitler was never an officer) and observed that after the assassination attempt in July 1944, his paranoia became even greater, unfortunately matched by his ruthlessness. It was a great pity that the attempt failed, because the war might well have ended within days or weeks had it been successful, and tens of thousands of lives would have been saved.

The Nuremberg trials came up in the conversation and I asked Dönitz about his time in Berlin-Spandau prison, in solitary confinement and how he felt about it. Remarkably, he felt no bitterness towards the British but accepted it philosophically as the price that had to be paid by the head of the German State. Since Hitler had committed suicide, someone had to be held to account, and he bore that burden, however unjustified. To him, it was more important that he had been acquitted on the ridiculous charge arising from the *Laconia* Order; but I could tell that he didn't want to dwell upon these things.

Although we didn't talk about it, I knew, too, that Karl Dönitz had suffered great personal tragedy during the war; both his sons had been killed on active service. His younger son, Peter, was killed whilst serving as Watch Officer aboard U-954 when the boat was depth charged and sunk with the loss of all hands by the Frigate HMS *Jed* and the sloop HMS *Sennen* in the North Atlantic on 19th May 1943. His elder son, Klaus, had been killed on his twenty-fourth birthday whilst aboard the fast boat S-141 when it attacked Selsey on the south coast of England near Bognor Regis on 13th May 1944, almost a year to the day after Peter's death.

All too soon, however, the evening was over and it was time for our guests to leave, but before doing so, Herr Dönitz handed me a portrait photograph of himself taken during the war when he was Großadmiral Karl Dönitz. He had signed it and written the following message to me in German, "*To Mr Frank Parker with best wishes. I was very pleased to meet Mrs Parker and you. Yours, Dönitz*". We bade them farewell and as I watched this most respected of wartime leaders get back into Herr Schnee's car and be driven away, I knew that Dorothy and I had been privileged to relax and enjoy the company of a truly great man. I have treasured that signed photograph and my memories of that day ever since.

HMT Laconia.

U-156.

U-506 and U-507 rescuing survivors.

Korvettenkapitän Adalbert
Schnee, Knights Cross
with oak Leaves.

Großadmiral Karl Dönitz,
Knights Cross with Oak
Leaves.

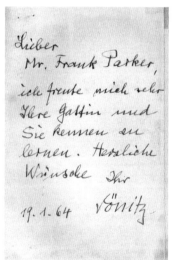

Lieber
Mr. Frank Parker,
ich freute mich sehr
Ihre Gattin und
Sie kennen zu
lernen. Herzliche
Wünsche Ihr

19. 1. 64   Dönitz

A hand-written greeting from Dönitz to Frank.

Top centre: Frank at the time of the Hamburg meeting.
Bottom left: Dönitz at the time of the Hamburg meeting.
Bottom right: Adalbert Schnee at the time of the Hamburg meeting.

Anne with another Wren.

Chapter Eight

Anne Gray

> *"At Viscount Nelson's lavish funeral, While the mob
> milled and yelled about St. Paul's, A General chatted
> with an Admiral:
> 'And, Sir, the secret of his victories?' 'By his
> unServicelike, familiar ways, Sir, he made the whole
> Fleet love him, damn his eyes!'"*
>
> *From '1805'. Robert Graves*

The WRNS, the Women's Royal Naval Service was first formed during the Great War in 1918, when at long last the Admiralty recognised the valuable role that women could perform in many shore-based jobs within the navy, thereby releasing men for active fighting duty.

However, the following year, the WRNS was promptly disbanded along with great swathes of all the armed forces. It was re-formed twenty years later in 1939 when war with Germany was once more an inescapable inevitability and the lessons of the value of a female workforce, both in and out of uniform, learned from the Great War were recognised by Neville Chamberlain's government.

My father was an army officer, a career soldier, and my secondary education was obtained in the magnificent surroundings of Drumlanrig Castle girls' boarding school which was, and still is, owned by the Duke of Buccleuch. The castle stands back from the A76 Dumfries to Kilmarnock road in Dumfriesshire, and whilst I was there in the late 1930s and early 1940s, I met several members of the royal family. My own family originate from Manchester and I am a direct descendent of Oliver Cromwell.

Summer 1939 was filled with the long, warm sunny days of childhood, when the problems of the world seemed so distant and irrelevant. Although my parents, and most other adults, knew that war with Germany was imminent, at fourteen I didn't really understand the full implications of it all. School had broken up in mid-July and the summer holidays beckoned. However, I knew that things must be getting serious when my parents arranged for Mother, my seven-year-old sister Joan and I to stay at Kippford, near Castle Douglas on the southern coast of Scotland because they felt that Manchester would not be very safe when the war came. We filled our days dressed in little more than shorts and shirts playing on the sea shore, running on the golden sands, catching crabs in the rock pools, exploring the sand dunes and swimming in the warm waters of the Solway Firth looking across to the hills of Cumberland and the Lake District which lay to the south.

Father had left home to return to active service and as August ran its course, I could tell that Mother and all the adults around us were becoming increasingly anxious. Although we weren't officially classed as evacuees, that is in essence exactly what we were and the news was full of reports of other children being moved out of the big cities to the safety of the countryside. September dawned and on that Friday morning we awoke to the news that the Germans had invaded Poland. The British government had issued Hitler with an ultimatum to withdraw his troops from Poland by 11 o'clock on Sunday morning or Britain would declare war. Of course, Hitler ignored the threat and the Prime Minister solemnly addressed the nation.

Not everyone owned a wireless set in those days and because the whole country was holding its breath, hoping against the odds that the Germans would step back from the brink, people gathered wherever they could to hear the broadcast. In Kippford, one of the main gatherings was in the local pub, and because this was such a momentous occasion, even I, at fourteen, was allowed to go in and listen. At 11.15 on that Sunday morning, 3rd September 1939, Neville Chamberlain announced to an expectant nation that we were henceforth at war with Germany. On that day the world changed forever.

It was a very strange feeling and nobody really knew what to do. Gradually, people drifted away from the pub back to their own homes or else they huddled together in small groups, talking in hushed voices and shaking their heads in a gesture of resigned disbelief. Were we really at war with Germany once again and so soon after the 'war to end all wars' was supposed to prevent such a thing? I was ushered from the premises and went back to the cottage with my mother. Alvar Lidell reading the BBC News during the next few days did not report immediate and massive bombing attacks on Britain's cities, as had been expected, and so a sense of normality returned. I saw out the last of my summer holidays at Kippford much as they had begun and helped Mother pack my school trunk and arrange for its collection and delivery to Thornhill station, PLA, Passenger Luggage in Advance.

I went back to school at Drumlanrig later that month and my education continued uninterrupted. The autumn that year turned into an Indian summer and was wonderfully pleasant, adding to the sense of normality which lasted through much of the winter as the phoney war dragged on with something of a standoff in France, whilst the majority of German forces rested and Hitler focused upon Denmark and particularly the capture and occupation of Norway.

However, for the people of Scotland, 'phoney war' was something of a misnomer because on the night of 14th October 1939, the German submarine U-47, commanded by Kapitänleutnant Günther Prien, crept past the defences of the Royal Navy's supposedly impregnable main anchorage at Scapa Flow on Orkney and sank the World War I battleship HMS *Royal Oak* with great loss of life. Fortunately, most of our more modern capital ships were out at sea, but nevertheless the sinking of *Royal Oak* inside Scapa Flow was a tremendous propaganda coup for the Germans and was equally embarrassing to the Royal Navy.

Two days later, at lunch time on 16th October, out of a clear blue sky, nine enemy bombers flew up the Firth of Forth to attack our warships at anchor off South Queensferry, which is just north of Edinburgh. These were the first bombs of the Second World War to fall on Britain and three of our ships were struck, but no serious damage was caused, although there were casualties, including fifteen sailors being killed. Two Spitfire squadrons, 602 and 603 were scrambled to intercept the intruders and a few minutes later Squadron Leader Ernest H. Stevens of 603 claimed the first RAF 'kill' of the war when he shot down one of the bombers.

Not to be outdone, within moments, George Pinkerton of No602 Squadron secured a second bomber, whilst a third was shot down by anti-aircraft fire. There were two survivors from the bomber downed by George Pinkerton and he later went to visit them in hospital after they had been rescued from the cold waters of the Firth by the crew of a local trawler. In November 1939, Archie McKellar, also of No602 Squadron, shot down a Heinkel He111 bomber near Edinburgh, which became the first German aircraft to hit British soil, since all three shot down on 16th October had landed in the waters of the Firth of Forth.

The winter of 1939/40 was one of the most severe on record and in the rolling hills of the Scottish Southern Uplands it was particularly harsh. In due course the snow and ice gave way to some early warmth in the sun and the green shoots of spring started to burst forth in the woods and across the moorland grasses surrounding Thornhill.

Most of the girls at the school had fathers or older brothers in the Forces and so any development in the war was very keenly followed. On Friday 10th May 1940, Winston Churchill replaced Neville Chamberlain as Prime Minister and the Germans unleashed their *Blitzkrieg* attack upon Holland and then Belgium, pushing around the Maginot Line and into France.

At home we believed that France, which had more than five million men in its armed services, the largest standing army in the world at that time, together with the 350,000-strong British

Expeditionary Force supporting it, would easily repel the German advance. We were in for a very big shock. Within a month, that optimism had vanished and we were facing total defeat. June saw the rescue of some 338,000 men of the BEF from the beaches of Dunkirk and the French Atlantic ports such as St. Nazaire, but France was on the verge of surrender and Britain now stood alone to face the expected and imminent German invasion. What General Weygand called the 'Battle for France' was over; the Battle of Britain was about to begin.

My most lasting memory of the early weeks of the summer of 1940 and the days around the Dunkirk evacuation was that my father was somewhere over there and that Mother had had no news from him for some time. We didn't know where he was or what had happened to him, but on my birthday a telegram arrived at school from my father wishing me a very happy day. It was; he had certainly made it so. Amidst all the chaos of those perilous hours, amidst everything else that my father must have had to think about and do, he had remembered me and been able to send me a birthday telegram. I was amazed and so grateful to him.

Once more the long summer term drew to a close and after prayers were said by the school Chaplin for the deliverance of our nation and its troops, for our families and ourselves, we said goodbye to friends with a mixture of excitement and sadness. Because of petrol rationing, there was no school transport to take us the two miles to Thornhill railway station and so, along with everyone else leaving by train, I walked along the narrow lane to the station to await the local passenger trains that would take us north, south, east and west for the holidays. The great express trains of the London Midland & Scottish Railway Company did not stop at Thornhill, which was a fairly small mining community in the Southern Uplands; however, the local trains did.

I am sure that the railway staff must have dreaded the end of term at the school and the invasion of so many girls into their beautifully kept station. For twenty minutes, the two platforms were crowded with dozens of girls who all seemed to be chattering at the same time, disturbing the rural tranquillity of the setting. Presently, however, the stopping train from Kilmarnock arrived and, together with the others who were travelling south, I scrambled into a compartment in one of the four carriages behind the engine painted in wartime black. A little under an hour later, we pulled into Dumfries station where I changed platforms for the Kirkcudbright local, which sported only two carriages, neither of which had a corridor and which was waiting and ready to leave. I settled into my seat and then, with a short toot on its whistle, the little tank engine cheerfully chuffed out of the station; I was in high spirits at the start of another summer holiday and would soon be running along the sea shore at Kippford again.

The engine clattered noisily along the track, its plume of smoke swirling past the windows, the carriages swaying to the clickity-clack rhythm of the rails. Presently I felt the train slow as we approached Castle Douglas; excited and anxious to see my mother and little sister, I jumped up and pulled down the window slide so that I could lean out and wave to them as we came into the station. Sure enough, there they were waiting on the platform to take me to Kippford; the summer holidays had truly begun.

The Battle of Britain dominated the news and we eagerly awaited the reports from the BBC Home Service of the exploits of Fighter Command pilots over the south coast of England. However, the threat of invasion and a complete end to the way of life that we knew was very real and I was old enough to understand it now. During August the reality of war came to me in a very stark way. One beautiful day in that long, lovely summer, Joan and I were walking along the fresh golden sands of the bay with no visible signs of a war that seemed so far away and almost unreal. The tide was slowly slipping out, having once more washed the beach clean leaving only a thin string of seaweed to show its furthest advance up the shore. The water shimmered and sparkled in the bright sunlight, the retreating wavelets barely touched the sand as they ran across it, frightened to disturb the peace by making more than the merest sound. It was a perfect day.

Some way off along the shore I saw a dark shape gently lolling and bumping back and forth, trapped in the shallow water, unable to reach dry land, unable to return to the sea with the ebbing tide. It was difficult to make out what it was at first, but as we got closer I realised exactly what the sea had brought us on that perfect day, but by then I was too late to prevent Joan from seeing too; it was the body of an airman, still in his flying clothes and Mae West life jacket, but I could tell that he was dead. This was the first body I had seen but I was to see many more such sights before the war finished.

My stomach tightened as if I was being squeezed and I took my sister's hand as we ran up the beach to find our mother to tell her what we had discovered. The look on our faces and our drained complexions told her that something was very wrong and she soon realised that we had had quite a shock as our story tumbled out of me faster than I could think about it.

Mother made a telephone call to the police, who recovered the airman's body. However, it put an end to our walks along the sea shore because the word was spreading that German bombers were flying over in daylight and shooting at anybody and anything that they could. Too many people had already been killed that way.

Despite our gruesome discovery, the holiday was wonderful, August flew by and the long summer days once more began to shorten, the nights started to draw in and become cooler, and I returned to school once more. But with the passing of September, so too did the immediate threat of invasion, to be replaced by intense aerial bombardment. Britain's cities other than London had been bombed since May, but now the Luftwaffe turned its attention on the capital with a vengeance. Nevertheless, despite the very heavy bombing of Manchester on the nights of $22^{nd}/23^{rd}$ and $23^{rd}/24^{th}$ December, I did spend Christmas 1940 in our house there.

By 1942 I was seventeen and had left school; it was time to join up. Probably because my father was in the army, he didn't want me to join the ATS; he thought that the WRNS would be ideal after my time at Drumlanrig and, as he put it, would be the best finishing school I could possibly have.

So, later that year I started my training at Millhill in London. The very first night that I was there, the bombers came over to attack that part of London. I really had no idea what to do, not having experienced an air raid at such close quarters, even in Manchester at Christmas 1940. All the other girls were under their beds in double quick time, so I just followed their example.

As always with initial training, drill and marching were top of the list to be taught, but we must have driven our drill instructor frantic with despair because we were hopeless. There were girls who could not keep in step no matter how hard they tried and others who couldn't help putting their left arm forward at the same time as they put their left foot forward. We certainly had a lot of laughs learning to march.

At the end of my training, I wanted to go to the secret code-breaking centre at Bletchley Park, but instead I became an ambulance driver for the navy. My first posting was to Leeds, just in time for Christmas. On my first day I was put into a 3-ton truck and told to drive it. That was fine except that I couldn't really drive properly and in the back of this truck were a number of sailors, all of whom were standing up and swaying about as I swung the truck this way and that on the journey. Each time the truck swerved, the men swayed, which made the truck swerve even more, which made the men sway even more; I thought that we were going to turn over. Eventually we got to our destination and I think that the sailors were even more relieved that the journey was over than I was.

At Leeds I learned how to drive and how engines worked. We were taught the theory first and then shown the practical evidence, which included being instructed how to take an engine apart and then put it back together again. This was something we each had to learn and until you could do it, you just had to keep trying until all the bits had gone back together again.

Leeds was definitely an education for a girl with a sheltered upbringing; I had never seen so much drinking. Most of it seemed to take place in the Officers' Mess, where, as women, irrespective of not being officers, we were generally welcome, on invitation only, of course. Christmas arrived and the inevitable parties were in full swing. I lay on my bunk in the dormitory one night, quietly reading when the door burst open and two WRNS came in carrying one of the Mess stewards between them. They threw the steward down on her bed and turned to leave.

Full of innocent concern, I asked, "Is she not well?"

"Of course she's all right. She's just bloody pissed," was the response and they disappeared through the door, leaving me alone with this girl who was definitely in need of some help.

For a few minutes I sat and looked at my companion sprawled across her bed and decided that I could not just leave her there in that state; she needed to get into bed and keep warm. Her uniform skirt was rucked up, her tunic was undone and her tie was already fairly loose, so I started to undress her; tunic, tie, white shirt, skirt. I struggled to get her out of her clothes as she was so drunk that she could hardly help me. However, when I at last managed to get her clothes off, I stood back in wonderment and shock; I had never seen a woman wearing underwear like this before. She had on matching black knickers, bra and suspenders. This was quite a revelation to me and I was completely taken aback, astounded. This wasn't the regulation school underwear that I wore and that I thought everyone else wore; I really didn't know what to make of it. From that night on, I grew up very fast in the navy.

After Leeds, it was a posting to Arbroath, on the east coast of Scotland, north of Edinburgh, and the start of my war service in earnest. One of my first jobs at Arbroath was to take a group of navy officers, who were all in their best uniforms, to a party which was being hosted by the commanding officer of the nearby RAF station. In early 1943, the blackout was rigorously enforced because, although the intensive blitz bombardments of our cities were over, there were still plenty of German bomber attacks. The need for the blackout was particularly important around operational airfields, where, if they could, Luftwaffe fighters would infiltrate the returning bomber stream and attack our aircraft as they were coming in to land when they were especially vulnerable.

With little idea of the roads leading to the airfield, I jumped into my little Tilley pick-up truck, a 5cwt general-purpose run around or utility vehicle, which is the origin of its affectionate nickname, and drove it over to the Officers' Mess, pulled up outside and waited. After a few minutes a group of three or four officers wandered out of the doorway and clambered into the Tilley, having quite clearly been in the Mess for more than one gin and tonic. The headlamps were shielded for the blackout and once off the base, I had some real difficulty seeing the road in the pitch black of the night.

Anxious to get to the party, one of the officers told me to get a move on as they wanted to get there that night. My eyes were becoming accustomed to the dark but I was now driving faster than I could see and we had a couple of close shaves on the bends in the road. A little way from the gates of the airfield, the officer in the front seat next to me lit a cigarette; in the glare of the flame from her lighter my night vision was gone, the Tilley hit the verge, swerved across the road, hit the verge on the other side and careered into the ditch amid a torrent of screeches from my female passengers.

One by one, the officers struggled out of the lop-sided Tilley, gathered on the road, straightened their uniforms and with a "Don't bother, we'll walk the rest of the way," set off for the airfield gate house, no doubt to call for safer transport to the Mess. Uninjured, other than for a few bruises and a dent to my pride, there was nothing for it but to set off after them, report the accident at the guardroom and await the inevitable consequences.

Driving the rum ration, however, was always a pleasure. The rum was stored in a large copper cylinder which was set up in the back of the Tilley and I would drive it around the base, whereupon the CPO, the Chief Petty Officer, would draw off each person's ration for the day. Some days I think that I was completely intoxicated without any having passed my lips, just from the fumes coming through to me from the back of the Tilley.

Arbroath was a Fleet Air Arm training 'ship' which involved ground-based work, followed by training on an anchored aircraft carrier and then putting to sea on the carrier. The WRNS officers didn't care too much for the drivers because we were able to go on board the ships in the harbour and go into all sorts of places that some of them were not able to access.

One dull and miserable day, I was sent over to the airfield to pick up some documents. As I drove around the perimeter, the traffic lights at the point where the road crossed the end of the main runway were showing red, indicating that aircraft were landing or taking off. I slowed my Tilley pick-up, gently came to a stop by the lights and turned off the engine. I could see the ambulance and the fire tender standing by on the far side of the runway, waiting for the aircraft to come; all usual routine and nothing to suggest the tragedy that the next few minutes would bring.

I sat leaning on the steering wheel, idling thinking about the party I had been to the night before. My thoughts were interrupted by the growing sound of an engine. I looked to my right to see a single-engine fighter, its undercarriage down, making its final approach to the runway. I watched the aircraft gradually lose height as it sank inexorably towards the earth, side-slipping slightly in the wind that gusted across the airfield. A few moments later, the roar of the engine filled the cab of my

Tilley and the fighter passed a few yards in front on me. With little more than detached interest, I watched the wheels touch the concrete runway and then, almost in slow motion, part of the undercarriage collapsed. The nose of the aircraft hit the runway with a grinding, rending pain as the propeller buckled and one of the wings dug into the surface. The little fighter, engulfed in a cascading eruption of sparks and fire, turned and twisted to an abrupt halt not far from where I was now standing beside my vehicle, unable to believe what I was witnessing.

I could plainly see the terror on the face of the pilot, trapped in his cockpit and struggling to get the canopy open, fighting with all his might to slide it back, to work the release handle, to escape. I could see that he was screaming as the fire took hold; I held my breath, praying for him to get out. There was nothing else I could do, I felt so helpless. I watched, transfixed by the horror unfolding before me, as the flames spread up through the cockpit. In those few moments on the face of that young airman I saw naked terror turn to excruciating pain, and then to nothing, a blankness as life slipped out of him, engulfed by the furnace that his aircraft had become. The ambulance and fire engine raced across the grass to the stricken aircraft and its hapless pilot, but they were too late, he had gone long before they doused the flames and lifted his charred body from what remained of the cockpit. Vivid images that have stayed with me ever since. As I said, I grew up very quickly in the navy.

Not long afterwards, I was on detachment to Edinburgh where I was driver for the King's Messenger. First created in 1497 by Richard III, the King's Messenger carried diplomatic secrets by 'safe hand' on behalf of the monarch. Even today the Foreign and Commonwealth Office employ a number of Queen's Messengers to carry highly sensitive state documents that can only be delivered in person. During the war, the King's Messengers undertook many highly dangerous journeys.

One such mission involved a Norwegian-speaking messenger on a journey back to his own occupied country with secrets for the Norwegian government. I was detailed to take a senior officer to meet him from the London train at Waverley Station in central Edinburgh and then drive them both to the RAF base at North Berwick, which was situated immediately opposite the Bass Rock. The conversation in the back of my car was conducted entirely in Norwegian and although I couldn't understand a word of what was being said, it was quite obvious from their serious and subdued tones that the whole matter was of the utmost importance.

After Edinburgh, by way of complete contrast, I was given a posting to Newcastle-upon-Tyne where I was detailed to be an ambulance driver. Newcastle was one of the major ports of the North Sea with a hospital and was where the injured and shipwrecked sailors from the Russian convoys to Murmansk and Archangel were brought.

The first convoys had started in August 1941 and ran fairly continuously throughout the rest of the war. The most disastrous convoy of all was PQ17, which left Reykjavik in Iceland on 27th June 1942 with thirty-six ships. Following the Admiralty order for the escorts to be withdrawn and the convoy to scatter, the German U-boats and Luftwaffe dive bombers sank twenty vessels. The responsibility for that order and the terrible loss of men and ships which followed was Admiral Pound's. Sitting at his desk in London, he believed that the German battleship *Tirpitz*, the pocket battleship *Admiral Scheer* and the heavy cruiser *Admiral Hipper* had left the Norwegian fjords to attack the convoy. He refused to accept the intelligence coming out of Bletchley Park, where the Enigma messages had been decoded, that the enemy capital ships had aborted their mission and returned to the fjords.

As an ambulance driver, I would be on duty for eight or nine hours at a time, and once we knew that there was a vessel with wounded and shipwrecked sailors on board we would just wait at the quayside until it berthed. I had two hospital orderlies with me who would give whatever immediate medical attention was needed before we got to the hospital. I had a bell fitted to the front of the ambulance and there were many times that I had to put it to good use in order to get through to the hospital as quickly as possible.

The walking wounded would make their own way down the gangplanks, but the more seriously injured lads would be hoisted off the ship in a Bosun's chair or simply in the stretcher on which they lay. Some of these men had terrible injuries. Many were burned, others had fuel-oil poisoning from swallowing mouthfuls of sea water when they were swimming away from the sinking ship through the oil that had spilled into the sea around them. Others still had blast and shrapnel injuries caused by the exploding bombs dropped from attacking aircraft. On most occasions, I was confronted by some terrible and pitiful sights, but it was something that I was used to by now, but no less compassionate for the familiarity of it all.

I stayed at Newcastle until we received news that the base was being closed down and that we would be posted. The war was nearly over at this time, and although the convoys to Russia continued, there were far fewer. The last convoy of the war sailed on 29th April 1945. There was one more to come back from Russia, but not until after the hostilities were ended. The CPO in charge of us was a good sort and she told me to take the ambulance home at the weekend and to take whatever I wanted from the base with me as it was closing and most of the equipment would be thrown away. I took a good supply of blankets. So much valuable equipment was destroyed, broken up or just left to rot after the war, it was as if everyone wanted to put it all behind them as soon as possible.

After leaving Newcastle I was posted to Helensburgh, which is outside Glasgow on the shores of Loch Long. However, when VE Day arrived, 8th May 1945, as fate would have it, I was sitting in the very same pub in Kippford that I had sat in on that Sunday morning six years earlier as a young fourteen-year-old schoolgirl, listening to the voice of Neville Chamberlain on the wireless set in the bar announcing that we were at war with Germany. Now as I sat in that same bar listening to that same wireless set, dressed in my WRNS uniform, much wiser and older than my twenty years, it was Winston Churchill who was telling us that we were no longer at war with Germany because Grand Admiral Dönitz, the head of the German State since the death of Adolf Hitler, had agreed to his country's unconditional surrender.

The response to the two Prime Minister's messages couldn't have been more different. In 1939, everyone had sat in stunned silence for some time, even though the declaration of war had been of no surprise. Now, a great cheer went up, glasses were filled and much merriment followed. What else could be expected! Moreover, this time I stayed in the bar and joined in the fun.

It should, though, never be forgotten that victory, after six years of bloody and ruthless war, both in Europe and in the Far East, was only won though the courage of hundreds of thousands of ordinary men and women and through the lives of far too many. On VE Day and then VJ Day, 15th August 1945, there were many people in Britain and across the world who did not feel like celebrating. Pleased and relieved though they were that the killing had stopped, they had lost someone close and dear to them. For some the loss was of more than one family member and the pain was multiplied. To celebrate the end of the war was good and it was necessary, but let us not forget those who didn't see it and those that they left behind.

After Helensburgh, I was on the move again. I was offered a commission but I was enjoying my work too much. It got me out and about and I did not want to be tied to an office desk, which would have been the inevitable consequence of taking a commission, so I declined the Admiralty's kind offer. However, it wasn't long before I had cause to reflect upon my decision. We were often invited by officers to parties in their Mess, but once more, some of the WRNS officers disliked this intensely.

On this occasion, along with a few other girls, I had been invited by some of the officers to a dinner party in their Mess and, as requested, my friend and I went in our civilian clothes. However, the WRNS officers who disliked us being invited in the first place asked for us to be removed for coming to the Mess in civvies, much to the embarrassment of our host. However, the Chief Petty Officer took pity and the four of us had dinner with him instead.

Nevertheless, we were put on a charge and next morning were on the Captain's Parade, which was a little awkward for him because my friend was his driver; we were given twenty-seven days confined to barracks.

In addition to not being allowed out, confined to barracks, or CB as it was referred to, meant that we had to report to the CPO every three hours in full dress uniform, but I'm afraid that I did not take this very seriously and would very often report with my curlers in; definitely improperly dressed. I think that the CPO thought that we had had rather a raw deal. This was the winter of 1945 and it was freezing cold in the barracks; we would light the fire in the room and huddle around it to try to keep warm. Then, in the midst of all this, my demob papers came through and I was posted to Chatham Barracks, one of our largest naval headquarters.

The WRNS was the one service that one could walk away from without being arrested for desertion. They didn't make it easy, but it was possible. If that winter had got any colder in those perishing barracks, I might just have thought about it. In time, though, the cold winter passed, the spring brought the sunshine and warmer weather, and then the late summer of 1946 saw the end of my military service in the WRNS.

Despite some of the sights which I witnessed, I would not have wanted to miss my time in the Royal Navy. I had certainly grown up and my father was right; it had been the best finishing school I could have had. But the world had also changed and, although I had undoubtedly found much satisfaction in my years of navy service, I was glad to be going home.

Anne and friends.

Mary & Ken Bryant, 24 April 1943

Chapter Nine
Mary Bryant

> " *The butterfly, a cabbage-white, (his honest idiocy of flight) will never now, it is too late, master the art of flying straight, yet has, - who knows so well as I? – a just sense of how not to fly: he lurches here and here by guess and God and hope and hopelessness. Even the aerobatic swift has not his flying crooked gift.* "
>
> 'Flying Crooked'. *Robert Graves*

Britain in the autumn of 1940 was a dangerous place to be living and the Aston area of Birmingham was particularly so, since the frequency of the German air raids had increased as the nights started to draw in. Like most people, we had an Anderson shelter in our garden and each evening when my dad came home from work he would go straight down into the shelter where my mother would take his dinner to him. He remained there all night until time to get ready to go to work again the next morning.

A few weeks earlier, on a clear bright August morning during that beautiful summer of 1940, I was called to see Olive, my section leader at the Lucas factory where I worked as a secretary and with whom I got on very well. Briskly walking along the corridor to her office, I wondered what this meeting could be about; I hoped that nothing was going to put the dampers on the sunshine that was streaming in through the windows. I knocked on the glass panel of the door and went in. Olive got up from behind her desk and came to meet me, looking worried and a little upset.

"Mary, thank you for coming to see me, my dear; please do sit down." She beckoned to the chair beside her desk, whilst returning to her own seat. "I have asked to see you on a very important matter which will probably change your life, and I'm so sorry, but there is nothing that I can do about it."

"Oh dear, what is it, Olive?" I replied with matching concern, having no idea of what was coming.

"I have been told that I must lose a member of my clerical staff to go into military service. I was going to take the opportunity to send Maisie, of course; but she has told me that she is about to go off and marry a Canadian so will be leaving anyway. But that hasn't helped me with finding someone for military service, so I have no alternative than to let you go instead. I'm so sorry, Mary. You will have to finish at the end of the week and of course I'll make sure that you are paid a further week's wages in lieu of notice. I feel so bad about this."

"Oh, Olive, that's wonderful. Thank you," I replied, hardly able to contain myself. "I know I shall miss it here, but I can't wait to join the WAAF."

"Thank you, Mary, I'm really pleased that you are happy about it. I was so worried that you would be upset."

I turned and left her office walking on air. I couldn't believe my luck; I had a terrible job not to shout for joy as I walked back down the long corridor. I had wanted to leave home for a long time and now I was going to do so. It wasn't that I was unhappy at home, because I was actually very happy there; I simply wanted my independence. That's what the war gave to me and thousands of other women my age who would otherwise have gone from home to marriage to raising a family and known nothing else.

In early 1940, I had a boyfriend who was in the army and had been sent overseas. Not long after his embarkation, he had been reported MBK, Missing Believed Killed. He had been on his way to Crete when his ship had been torpedoed and he was drowned when the ship sank. Not long afterwards, I went to a dance at Springfield in Birmingham, and, I later found out, met Ken Bryant on the toss of a coin between him and his friend. Ken had also worked at Lucas and had been given reserved occupation status by the company, but in early 1939 the government passed a law requiring all young men of twenty and twenty-one to register for six months' military training in the Militia, a forerunner to conscription and later, National Service. It just so happened that Ken was doing his six months with the Militia when the war broke out, and so instead of returning to Lucas he happily remained in the RAF for the next six years.

A few days after my chat with Olive, I presented myself for recruitment at the Albert Hall at Six Ways in Aston and was interviewed by a rather genial army lieutenant who, I could tell by his medals, had served in the Great War. He was about the same age as my father and, sitting behind the decidedly wobbly table, asked me if I would like to join the Auxiliary Territorial Service, the ATS. I thanked him, but declined his offer, saying that I didn't want to join the army because I didn't like the colour of the uniform and that Royal Air Force blue suited my complexion and hair much better and that therefore I would like to volunteer for the WAAF instead.

He cleared his throat, took off his glasses and began to polish them whilst blinking at me rather like a startled owl. After slowly replacing his spectacles, he told me that he was sure that my talents would be much more in tune with the RAF and that he would do everything he could to ensure that my preference for the Junior Service was met. However, I had the distinct impression that having listened, with increasing disbelief, to my reason for wanting to join the WAAF, he was rather pleased that he was in a position to ensure that I would definitely not be heading for the ATS. So, with an excited feeling that I was at last on my way, I went home to eagerly await the outcome of the interview.

Several days later I was notified that the recruiting officer had indeed made sure that the ATS were not to be graced by my presence and that I had been accepted for the WAAF. I was told to report to Gloucester in three weeks' time where I would be given a medical examination, sworn in and kitted out. When the day came for me to leave, my mother sobbed and no amount of reassurances could stop the tears rolling down her cheeks; her little girl was leaving home. I said goodbye to my parents and younger brother and set off for Birmingham New Street railway station. And so, in the autumn of 1940, at the age of nineteen, my war service began.

We stayed at Gloucester for five days, just long enough to fill in all the forms, receive our kit and be issued with travel warrants to our Initial Training Wing [ITW] destination, which in my case was Morecambe in the north-west of England.

All the former boarding houses in Morecambe had been requisitioned by the government as billets and each bedroom had been kitted out with two, three or four beds, depending upon the size of the room. There were six of us allocated to our billet and to say that we were made to feel unwelcome was an understatement. We arrived at the house and rang the bell.

The landlady opened the front door, took one disdainful look at us and said, "Oh, WAAFs. I'd rather have the men."

The whole house stank of onions and she gave us dripping to light the fire in the bedroom with. The next day I met one of the other WAAFs, also called Mary, and we became very good friends, helping each other through our initial training. We would often go to Mary's billet together where her landlady would give us tea. This was a proper boarding house and so different from my own billet. Nevertheless, in spite of the onions, the dripping and the cold bedroom, the six weeks soon went by, which was probably just as well since by now the weather was becoming decidedly wintry as the northwest wind blew in off the sea and cut through us, especially when we were learning to march, salute and do all sorts of fitness exercises along the sea front promenade.

At the end of our course, one of the local cinemas was temporarily commandeered and everyone gathered in the auditorium to be told of their various postings. Mary and I had become really good friends and were very anxious to be posted to the same station, so we went to the Adjutant and asked that if it was at all possible, could we please be posted together. We were, and even more luckily, we were being sent to RAF Oakington in Cambridgeshire, part of No5 Group Bomber Command. We were thrilled as this was an operational bomber station, the home of No7 Squadron, which would later be equipped with Lancasters and become one of the Command's finest pathfinder squadrons. At the end of 1940, however, the squadron was already leading the way as it became the first squadron to fly the new four-engine Short Stirling bomber, the first of the three main four-engine heavy bombers operated by the Command during the war; the other two being the Handley Page Halifax and of course the Avro Lancaster, the most famous bomber of World War Two.

Mary and I were duly issued with our travel warrants and early the next morning with no regrets at all, I bade farewell to my landlady along with her onion-smelling house, told her that I hoped she had airmen not WAAFs next time and, complete with my kitbag over my shoulder, excitedly set off to meet Mary at the corner of Skipton Street. In the grey light of that winter dawn as I happily walked along the promenade road looking out across the bay, I saw several warships steaming up the Irish Sea. I slowed to watch them for a few minutes, a reminder that this was war and that I was now on my way to help in that war. However, I was now late and Mary was waiting for me,

"Come on, Mary, where have you been? We'll miss the train if we're not quick."

"Sorry, I was watching the ships go by."

"You'll be watching the train go by if we don't step on it, then we'll be for it."

We couldn't run because of the weight in our kitbags but we walked as quickly as we could and, a little breathless, got to the station just in time. Most of the carriage doors were still open but all the compartments seemed full; there were WAAFs and airmen everywhere. A whistle blew from somewhere near the back of the train, so we jumped in through the nearest door and squeezed along the corridor. Another whistle blew and the carriage doors started to slam shut.

"I told you we were cutting it fine," laughed Mary as she saw an empty seat in a compartment, slid the door back and almost fell into it as the train gave a jerk and started to move off. A very kind and chivalrous young airmen sitting opposite to Mary offered me his seat, saying that he had to get off at Lancaster to change trains anyway.

We chatted for a while but it was a very long and tedious journey through Lancaster, Preston, Wigan, Warrington, Crewe, Birmingham and finally London Euston. We had been given two packs of sandwiches each for the journey, and mine would definitely have tasted better if my landlady had put something in it besides margarine. I was so very hungry when we arrived in London late that evening, but fortunately the WVS trolley was still on the platform and both of us bought an extremely welcome mug of hot tea and a decent sandwich. Our train for Oakington left from King's Cross station, so with kitbags once more slung on our shoulders, we walked the half mile along Euston Road, passed the beautiful St. Pancras Station and into King's Cross.

There were far fewer people waiting for the Cambridgeshire train and the compartments were much quieter. We were tired out after our long trip from Morecambe and managed to sleep most of the way to Oakington despite the lack of heating. Eventually, the train pulled into the station and we tumbled out of our cold but comfortable compartment. We were met by the driver of a 15cwt truck who had been sent to pick us up and take us to the aerodrome, which was just as well, since that late at night and in the blackout, we would have never found it ourselves.

Once through the main gate, we were taken to the WAAF area where two very glamorous WAAF sergeants greeted us with "Hut number five", and that was all that was said to us. Our driver gave us directions and, carrying our kitbags again, which by now seemed much heavier than they had that morning, we made our way past the other huts until we stood in front of number five. Rather timidly, I opened the door of the hut to be greeted by the sight, not of an orderly, regimented billet as we had been used to at ITW, but by washed underwear hanging up on lines across the room, WAAFs playing cards and everyone in various stages of undress and hair styling. This was life on an operational station.

By now, Ken had completed his training as an air gunner and had been posted to No115 Squadron at RAF Marham just outside King's Lynn, flying Vickers Wellingtons. A posting to nearby RAF Oakington suited me very nicely as it would make seeing each other much easier than had our postings been further apart. It was all a matter of luck; it worked out well for us but many others were not so lucky.

The next day we were shown around the base but since the Waafery was not yet completed, Mary and I were moved out to the Shrubbery, a large house outside the station where we had no beds to sleep in, just a mattress on the floor. I hadn't been at the Shrubbery for more than an hour or so when I started chatting to another WAAF and asked her if she had been at the aerodrome long.

"No, I only got here yesterday," she replied.

"Me too. Where did you come from?" I asked.

"King's Lynn."

"Oh, my boyfriend is stationed at Marham."

"Is he. I know some of the chaps there. What's his name?" she asked, smiling.

"Ken Bryant," I replied cheerfully.

Her smile faded as she answered slowly, "Oh dear! I went to the cinema with him last night."

When I was at Morecambe, I had applied to be a Motor Transport driver so that I could drive the aircrews out to their aircraft. Unfortunately, I was an inch too short and so Mary suggested that I should do as she had done and apply to work in the station post office, because all the young airmen went in there to collect their letters and parcels. That seemed like a good idea and as a result we both worked in the post office at RAF Oakington.

On the very first morning that I was in the post room, the senior WAAF in there was sorting through the parcels that had arrived. After stacking five or six on the counter, she picked up another one, looked hard at the name on it, grunted and threw it in a corner. I picked it up and looked at the parcel which had been so neatly wrapped with crisp brown paper, tied with good-quality string, the knots covered with red sealing wax to ensure they wouldn't come undone and the label beautifully written in a woman's handwriting. Someone had taken a great deal of care, time and no doubt love to wrap that parcel. I asked the WAAF why she had thrown it into the corner.

"Oh well, he won't be coming for that," she said, not even bothering to look up from her work, "he's gone for a Burton."

I was stunned, caught unawares by the starkness of the reality that along with the glamour, the relaxed discipline and easy atmosphere on an operational station, there was death and destruction on an almost daily basis. A mother, sister or girlfriend had sent the young airman that parcel with their love, but he had been killed before it had arrived and now he would never receive it. I felt my throat tighten and the tears start to sting my eyes as I turned away so the others would not see me. The harsh lesson of war and the finality of death cast a cloud over me for the rest of the day. I also vowed never to become hardened to it in the way that other WAAF had become, but I suppose that was just her defence mechanism. One way or another, we saw a great deal of sadness pass through that post room and we all dealt with it differently.

At last the Waafery was finished and we all moved in. There were five or six huts to the Waafery and about twenty girls to each hut. It wasn't long before I met Joan, who was the base hairdresser and who was very sweet on an airman named Bob. Because we handled all the post that came onto the station, she asked Mary and me to check all letters that came for Bob by holding them up to the light to see if they were from a girl.

I needed a bicycle. It was long way to walk from the Waafery to the post room every day, and then back again at night, so I bought a bike, obtained the necessary ID papers for it and, in between the two of them falling around laughing at my early attempts to stay on the saddle, pedal and steer all at the same time, Mary and Joan taught me to ride it. They were very patient as I fell off it more than I was on it at first, but then I got the hang of it and I was away; however, I still couldn't take my hands off the handlebars otherwise I would have fallen off. This was a bit of a problem for me since I needed to ring the bell when approaching the main gate to let the Service Police there know that I was arriving. In the end, I just used to shout, "Excuse me," and they would wave me through. I don't think that they viewed me as a security threat and I even managed to make them smile.

Now that I had my bicycle I could really get around and because the post room was not open at night, I had most evenings off duty. Bomber Command flew operations on most nights of the entire war, although as a general rule, if it was a full-moon period, the crews were stood down. No7 Squadron was by now flying the four-engine Stirling heavy bomber and was called on more and more. Whenever the squadron was on operations and the crews were going out to their aircraft, I would cycle around to all the dispersal pans to wish the boys good luck and a safe return. I made a point of doing this as often as I could because I knew that it was really important for them to know that whilst they were away, taking the war to the enemy, those of us left behind were thinking about them and waiting for them to come back home.

So often, though, next morning as the dawn brought a new day there would be one or two, sometimes more, overdue crews, their seats at the breakfast table left unfilled, their beds left unslept in, their return time on the watchtower blackboard left blank; out on the aerodrome the expectant ground crews waited on the empty dispersal pans anxiously listening for the distant drone of engines, fighting the realisation that their aircraft and crew was not going to return, that it was gone forever. Another aircraft lost, more young men killed, like the one whose parcel had lain in the post room corner. The crushing emptiness of those vacant concrete circles, which only a few hours before had held a proud aircraft and a group of vibrant young men full of life, now lying forlorn and bare in the dull morning light, never lessened, never eased its intensity, never ceased to be painful, no matter how many times it was repeated.

The whole station felt each loss, whether we knew the crew or not: but then we moved on, there would be new crews to fly new aircraft on new operations, to have more successes, to suffer more losses. The war still had a long way to go. Despite the sadness of these crews failing to return, I continued to ride around on my bicycle before each raid to let them know that we were all thinking of them. At this stage of the war, it was only the RAF that was able to take the fight all the way to the German heartland, all the way to the homes of the German people, to remind them of what the Nazis had started, to return what had been meted out to Coventry, Hull, Clydeside, London and cities all over Britain.

Soon enough, Joan got her airman and started seeing Bob on a regular basis. Whenever he was not on operations, they would join the rest of us in one or other of the local pubs. We lived every day to the full and the evenings in the pubs were an important part of that. One of Joan's party tricks was to pour beer over Bob's head and then set his hair, much to the amusement and entertainment of everyone else.

Throughout the war, the average age of Bomber Command aircrew, who were all volunteers, was just twenty-two; they were very young men. No matter how skilled they were, ultimately luck played the greater part in determining the survival or loss of a crew. However, one way that they helped their luck was to ensure that they all got along very well. There are, of course, a handful of exceptions, but for the great majority of crews, there was no room for big egos, nor depressing introverts for that matter. Any such personalities tended to be dropped out very quickly. Each bomber crew forged a very tight, close-knit bond which held them together during the most unimaginable of combat circumstances, where for many hours at a time they were likely to be attacked and blown out of the sky by fighters or anti-aircraft fire, to say nothing of accidents during training, on take-off and landing or of being hit by bombs dropped from another aircraft flying above them.

Ken's crew was one such tightly knit group and he worshipped the ground Bill Berry, his American pilot, walked upon. Just before Ken and I were married I suggested that he should marry Bill instead and I would be the bridesmaid. Although it was said in jest, we both knew how important to Ken's survival was this absolute faith which the members of his crew had in each other's ability because the lives of them all depended upon each of them.

With Ken being stationed so close at Marham, when the crew were on flight tests or daylight bombing practice exercises, Bill would often land their Wellington at Oakington so that Ken could call in to see me. He would clamber out of the aircraft and walk over to where I was working in the post room. I was very impressed and the envy of many of the WAAFs there. Ken did this fairly often in order to see me and so did a lot of other crews; that's how so many managed to keep their relationships going when every day might have been their last.

We had decided to get married and one day just before I left RAF Oakington, I was in the post room telling one of the other girls that I had seen a lovely pair of pyjamas in Dorothy Perkins that I wanted to buy but that I didn't yet have enough clothing coupons. Whilst I was bemoaning my plight, an officer came in to collect his post and listened to what I was saying. Before he left the room, the officer took out his wallet and handed me the clothing coupons that he had, saying that they were a wedding present from him. They were enough for me to get the pyjamas. It was very kind of him and I do hope that he survived the war.

There are two parts to Royal Air Force Station Cranwell in Lincolnshire; there is the Royal Air Force College which was opened on 5th February 1920 under the command of Air Commodore CAH Longcroft, and was the first military air academy in the world, and there is the aerodrome part from where the flying takes place.

In late 1942, Mary and I were posted to the aerodrome part of RAF Cranwell on a teleprinter course. Whilst there, along with the other WAAFs on the course, we were billeted in the married quarters attached to the College. At the end of the short course, just as we had done at Morecambe and again when we knew that we were leaving Oakington, we went to the Adjutant to ask if we could be posted somewhere together, and on 4th December 1942 we were sent to RAF Stafford.

Before we left Cranwell, we had a few days' leave and I met up with Ken, who had by now been commissioned, completed his first tour of operations and was an instructor at Abingdon. To save us carrying our kitbags on the journey across the country from Lincoln to Stafford, he told us to put them on the train, which was actually an offence, since they should always stay with the person. Mary's kit went to Grantham and mine was labelled for Birmingham New Street, but it didn't arrive. In fact, it never arrived and all I had was the uniform that I stood up in, which caused me all sorts of difficulties.

I stayed with Mary during my leave and at the end of it we caught the train to take us to Birmingham and then on to Stafford. As the crowded train pulled slowly into the railway station, we found out that the Americans had just arrived on another train. We jumped down from the compartment and were accompanied by wolf whistles and cat calls from the GIs leaning out of the train windows. I thought that the officers had very smart uniforms, and within a few minutes one of them, who told me that his name was Curly, asked me where he could get the bus to Stone.

He walked up to the bus station with me and on the way he asked me out for a date. I agreed to see him that night and we arranged that Mary would come with me on a blind date with one of Curly's fellow officers.

Later, when I was getting ready, because these were the first Americans that I had been out with, I put on my best stockings making sure that they were inside out, and carefully smoothing them up my legs to the suspender belt so keeping them nice and flat with no wrinkles or creases; the trick being that by turning them inside out the seams were darker and showed up better, like the actresses in the Hollywood films. You learn these things when you grow up in a city.

We met Curly and his friend on the steps of the Swan Hotel in Stafford. Mary took an instant liking to her blind date and we all went into the Swan for a drink. Eventually, Curly told me how he got his nickname; he took off his cap and was completely bald. He was a lovely man, very polite and showed me pictures of his wife and children back in America and I told him all about Ken and that we were soon to be married. Like so many Americans here at that time, he was a long way from home, lonely, in a foreign country and fighting a war that seemed very far away from America.

At RAF Stafford, the teleprinters were staffed twenty-four hours every day and we worked them in eight-hour shifts, although if it was very quiet, the officer in charge would usually let us off early, especially during the night shift so that we could catch up on some sleep. Whenever we could, we would try to get a forty-eight-hour leave pass. Not having access to a car, and with the passenger trains always very crowded and often delayed by enemy action or priority traffic, getting anywhere more than a few miles away was difficult, so Mary and I would hide in the back of the post van just before it was about to leave the station and that way get a lift into Nottingham or Sutton Coalfield. It was great fun and very effective.

I had my twenty-second birthday on 28th February 1943 and eight weeks later, on 24th April, Ken and I were married during our first proper leave together at Erdington Parish Church. But it wasn't long before he was back at OTU getting ready to go on operations again for his second tour. I seemed to worry about him even more now that we were married.

In January 1944, he was posted to No214 Squadron at RAF Sculthorpe, near Fakenham in Norfolk, part of No100 (Bomber Support) Group. The squadron was equipped with the American Boeing B17 Flying Fortress and their job was to interfere with and disrupt the German radio and radar signals during Bomber Command missions. The wireless operator in Ken's crew was a fluent German speaker and would tune in to the German controller's wavelength and then give false and misleading instructions to the Luftwaffe night fighters, so that they flew out in the wrong direction and away from the bomber stream. Of course, it wasn't too long before the Germans realised what was happening, but the fighter pilots were never altogether sure after that whether they were getting the right messages or not.

If the hoax messages didn't work, the radio equipment on Ken's B17 allowed the wireless operator to jam the German signals or to track the night fighters so that they lost the element of surprise over the bomber stream. It was rather like cat and mouse, with both sides trying to outwit the other.

These missions were top secret and even the rest of Bomber Command did not know about the work that Ken and the crew were carrying out. The radio transmitter in their B17 was sufficiently powerful that from around 18,000 feet, it could transmit over an area the size of Wales as it moved across the darkened expanse of Western Europe. The Luftwaffe night fighter force had become the greatest threat to the survival of RAF bomber crews. The pilots of the night fighters were directed to the bomber stream by ground controllers, and the RAF thinking was that if they could be led to the stream, they could equally be led away from it.

When the German controllers realised what was happening, they prefixed their instructions with a coded message and changed wavelengths. Even the skills of the Bletchley Park code breakers couldn't decipher these coded messages that quickly and so some other device had to be contrived. The solution was found far away from the sophistication of technology; through the powerful airborne transmitter in Ken's Flying Fortress, they belted out a mish-mash of hurdy-gurdy music, which drowned out the messages of the German controllers. Sometimes the simplest of solutions is the most effective.

Superstitions, omens and gremlins were a very important, and to some almost a religious, part of life in Bomber Command. Different crew members would each have their own particular idiosyncrasies and talismans; Ken's rear gunner Paddy More had invented 'the Man in the Bowler Hat'. Gazing down from his exposed position in the rear turret, Paddy was convinced that he saw the image of this man on many occasions, such as at a crossroads in the target area or guiding them out of searchlight beams by pointing in the direction of safety with his umbrella. Far from ridiculing this apparition, the rest of the crew embraced it for it was part of survival. When the crew, who were all officers, were together in the Mess, or when they went to the pub, they would always keep a seat free for 'the Man in the Bowler Hat'.

Finally, and thankfully for me, Ken's second tour came to an end. However, the skipper wanted a photograph of the ten-man B17 crew and hurriedly gathered them all together before they split up and went their separate ways. The photograph was quickly taken and the film slipped over to the photographic unit for developing and a copy was made for each crew member. They were sitting having tea when one of the boys brought the picture in for them to see, and Ken told me that when he looked at the photograph he could feel the hairs on the back of his neck start to rise. Paddy More was standing on the extreme right of the picture and Ken was next to him; between the two of them could clearly be seen the image of 'the Man in the Bowler Hat'.

Bomber Command aircrew were given a week's leave every six weeks that they were on operations, so when Ken had his leave after we were married, he would come up to Stafford and fix a sleeping-out pass for me. It was so much easier for him to arrange that now that he was an officer and we stayed with two elderly ladies who had a big old house opposite the base. They treated us so well and made us very comfortable whenever Ken could get to see me. I don't know whether they looked upon Ken as an adopted son or me as an adopted daughter, but they did like to spoil us.

Later in 1944 and after completing fifty-nine operations, Ken, now a Flight Lieutenant was tour expired for a second time and given a ground job as CO at RAF Kingswear, a radar surveillance station in south Devon, near to Brixham, with forty-four men and WAAFs under his command. As the CO, he was billeted with Mr and Mrs Thomas at Coleton Farm, adjacent to the radar site. Then in early 1945, I left the RAF to give birth to our son, Ray. After he was born, Ray and I went down to Brixham and lived in a fisherman's cottage so that we could be close to Ken and be much more of a family. He was eventually demobbed in early 1946.

I spent more than four years in the RAF during the war and had a wonderful time. Despite all the sadness, the hardship, the rationing, the danger and the worry, I wouldn't have missed a day of it for the world.

A picture of innocence: Mary at about 5 years old.

Mary and bicycle.

[l-r] A friend, Mary, Ken, Ida & Harry.

Mary, Mary [Bryant] & Joan, 1943.

Ken's faithful No115 Squadron Wellington bomber.

Ken's No 214 Squadron B17 crew. Ken and Paddy More are back row on the right and between them is 'The Man in the Bowler Hat'.

Edna Taylor.

Edna with pet Scottie dog.

Chapter Ten
Edna Taylor

> *"Gracious Lord, oh bomb the Germans. Spare their women for Thy Sake,*
> *And if that is not too easy we will pardon Thy Mistake.*
> *But, Gracious Lord, what'er shall be, don't let anyone bomb me."*
>
> From 'In Westminster Abbey'. *John Betjeman*

I grew up in Old Fletton in Cambridgeshire, just outside Peterborough. My father had his own hairdressing business, and so it was probably fairly natural that my brother would work for Dad. I had been born on 20th July 1921 and when I left school in 1935, I too started to train as a hairdresser and joined the family business.

Times were very hard in the 1930s. The great depression, which had started with the Wall Street crash in America in 1929, had spread around the world bringing trade to a virtual standstill. It was all very like the banking crisis which started in 2007 and which we are going through now. No matter how the experts may try to dress it up, the causes have been much the same now as they were then; greed by those who were already very rich but not satisfied with the great wealth that they had, and of course once more it is left to the ordinary people of the world to try to put the wheel back on the wagon.

To see us through the 1930s, at least we had a business which attracted repeat customers, simply because their hair kept growing and so needed cutting again. Of course, those families who had no spare money and needed every penny to buy food cut their own hair, but for the people who were lucky enough to have a job and needed to be smart, they had the spare money to have their hair cut and so we stayed in business.

By 1938 we knew that war with Germany was coming again. My dad was a Special Constable and so took a particularly keen interest in the daily news broadcasts as each day drew us closer to the start of the conflict.

Important though a good haircut was, it was not a reserved occupation, and so just after my nineteenth birthday in July 1940 my call-up papers arrived and I volunteered for the Peterborough Fire Service. We were issued with two types of uniform, the serge one with a forage cap for daily work and the gabardine one with a peak cap for best.

By this time, my brother Donald had already been called up into the army and had gone out to the Far East, to Singapore. When he first joined the Cambridge Regiment he went to the Bury St. Edmunds barracks, where the recruitment sergeant recognised Don's surname, Poole; it turned out that he had been Dad's RSM in the Great War. Later, after Singapore fell, we believed that Don had been taken prisoner by the Japanese, but we didn't hear from him or have any other news about him for some time. Meanwhile, my mother had become a fire watcher and with Dad being a Special, our whole family was involved in the war and with the bombing. However, it had its advantages for Dad, anyway, because when he was on duty as a Special, he would call in to the fire station where I was based for a cup of tea; like all policemen, he had his regular tea stops.

At this time every town of a reasonable size had its own fire service, usually staffed by volunteers, although the bigger towns and cities had paid firemen. Consequently, there were over 16,000 different fire brigades throughout Britain and co-ordination between neighbouring services in the event of a large fire was a bit haphazard at the best of times; in wartime, with sustained bombing, it was hopeless, but amalgamation into a single national service was still more than twelve months away.

I started my service in Peterborough and then moved to Whittlesey, first for training and then working in the main control room as a wireless telephony [W/T] operator. We worked seven days at a time on a twenty-four-hour shift. Of course, I wasn't on the go all that time but was on call for the whole duty period, so when it was quiet I would try to get some sleep on one of the camp beds that were provided. However, that wasn't quite as good as it might sound because I caught impetigo from one of them and wasn't able to work until it cleared up. Also we had to do stirrup pump training and drill which was great fun and somehow we always managed to make sure that everyone got wet.

Nevertheless, when the call-out bell sounded it was all go at top speed. If I was in bed, I would just pull my uniform trousers and jacket on over my pyjamas, grab my steel helmet and run to the switchboard to take the calls. The call-out meant that a raid was starting and we would be inundated with telephone calls from all over Cambridgeshire. As the bombing started I simply put my helmet on over my curlers and pulled the strap down tightly under my chin; there was no time to fiddle with curlers, hair and make-up. If the call-out was for our station and I was in the control room, I would lean across and press the button, and each of the six-man crews would come sliding down the pole, jump into the fire engines, even as some of them were still pulling their jackets on, and drive out into the street with one of the crew on each appliance ringing the bell by hand as they went.

Besides the bell, appliances were fitted with two hoses on reels attached over the back wheels. One was a fifty-foot rubber-lined hose which allowed the water to pass through it very quickly and was much easier for the crews to control. The other one they carried was a seventy-five-foot hose which was made from a very coarse canvas and had a narrower pipe. This had the effect of holding the water, which was under great pressure, back in the pipe with the consequence that controlling it was much more difficult and took a lot of strength and sapped the energy of the crews when using it for long periods.

Often I could hear the bombs falling very close to the fire station but I had to stay at my post in the control room to take the calls and pass the messages on. There were no shortwave radios in those days so we used messengers to carry information to the crews who were out fire fighting. These were young lads of sixteen to eighteen, or at least they were supposed to be, but some of them had obviously lied about their age to get into the service as a messenger. I think that for every one person who tried to dodge being called up, there must have been twenty who lied about their ages to get in and do something towards the war effort.

When I moved from Peterborough to Whittlesey, I would cycle the fifteen miles each way for duty, whatever the weather; I had no choice, there was no public transport to rely on which coincided with my shifts. But then, most people cycled and I thought nothing of it. However, one day as I pedalled along, not long having left home I came around a corner and bumped into our local postman, almost literally. He smiled at me and said, "Ah, Edna, I have something for you that will make you happy."

And he had. I could have cried with joy; it was a postcard from my brother in a prison of war camp to tell us that he was fine and uninjured. I was so happy that I turned my bicycle round and pedalled all the way back home to show the card to my mother.

When I rushed in through the door at home, she could tell by my face that whatever it was that had brought me back, it was good news, and when I showed her the card from Donald I think she became ten years younger in as many seconds. I couldn't stay, though, I still had to get to Whittlesey in time for roll-call, but I think my legs were super-charged that day and I made it in time. I was still so full of Donald's news that I disrupted the roll-call to show everyone the card which I had brought with me. This was the very first card to arrive in East Anglia from a Japanese POW camp, which is why everyone was so keen to see it, because many of them knew of others who had been captured in the Far East and could now expect some news too.

Sunday the 29th December 1940 was the one-hundred-and-fourteenth night of the London Blitz and on this night the enemy attacked the financial and commercial square mile of the City with a concentration of bombing even greater than Rotterdam on 10th May, Coventry on 14th November or Manchester only a week earlier. On that Sunday night, the City was relatively deserted, with some of the businesses not intending to open again until after the New Year; and therein lay the reason for much of the devastation which followed. After nearly four months of continuous bombing, the City had become accustomed to the East End and the docks being the target for most attacks and so few businesses had left fire watchers guarding their buildings.

During that one night, the Luftwaffe dropped 100,000 bombs and incendiaries on the City, starting a fire of unequalled scale anywhere; even the firestorm of Dresden in 1945, although causing more deaths, was not of the same magnitude. The attack on London that last weekend of 1940 was very carefully planned by the German High Command to create a firestorm and cause maximum damage. More than 1,500 separate fires raged across the City and its surrounds in petrol stations, timber yards, warehouses and chemical plants as well as in homes and offices. Walls crashed down blocking the streets, all too often killing the firemen who were fighting the blaze and caught by the collapse. The heat, the smoke, the noise were overpowering and all the time the bombs were falling around these men.

From the 7th September until the end of the year, over 25,000 men from fire brigades across the south-east and Home Counties were drawn in to help the London Fire Brigade, with crews starting what would be weeks of fifteen-hour shifts. Had the lessons of Rotterdam been learned, much of the damage to the City area could have been avoided or mitigated, but we hadn't taken heed of the Dutch experience. There was no proper chain of command, no proper assessment of water resources or maps showing the route of the Thames and the location of canals, pools, mains and so on. That, added to the businesses which had left no caretakers, fire watchers or key holders, meant that too many fires burned freely for hours and, just as in Coventry, the fires lit the sky to act as a beacon for later waves of bombers.

But this was just another battle in the constant war which was being waged between Britain's fire brigades and the Luftwaffe; a war which ultimately the firefighters, whom Winston Churchill described as 'those heroes with grimy faces', won. It also swept away any lingering animosity between the regular fire services and the Auxiliary Fire Service, the AFS. Then, on 18th August 1941, the National Fire Service came into being, drawing together into one service the more than 16,000 separate brigades from all over the country.

During this time, I still kept up my hairdressing skills by helping my dad when he went to the nearby Newells' munitions factory to cut the men's hair. During their break periods, the men would come and take a seat waiting for us on a first come, first served basis. The long shifts in the factories meant that many men couldn't get to Dad's barber shop during the day, so Dad brought the barber shop, and me, to them.

When I was off duty, together with some of my friends, I would go to the dances that were held in the local village halls or sometimes a hotel. It was nearly all live music in those days with a dance band playing, and if not then the wireless set would be tuned in to the BBC, which on a Saturday night would have a programme of dance music. After 1942 when the Americans arrived in Britain, the BBC broadcast concerts given by the Glenn Miller and Artie Shaw bands amongst many others. Most of the time, there were only soft drinks available for us because beer was always in short supply. Some of the pubs only sold half pints whilst others only opened three or maybe four days out of the seven, particularly in the early years of the war.

If we were on call but there was a dance not too far away, we would take the fire engine to the dance, complete with crew and sometimes they would let me drive it, although I had to put wooden blocks on the pedals because my legs weren't long enough to reach them otherwise. One night, coming back from a dance through the blackout, I got hold of the cord and gave the bell a good ringing coming along the lanes. It was great fun. Of course, if anything like driving the fire engine or taking it to a dance happened today there would be a national scandal, but then, despite the war, I think we had a lot more fun than people do today. Life was for living because it might end very suddenly at any moment. Things are so safe and cosy today and everybody is much better off but people don't seem to be very happy; there is so little sparkle around.

There were a lot of airfields around Cambridgeshire, both RAF and American, and we were always being invited to dances on these stations. I got to know quite a lot of the aircrew chaps, but all too often, as the months rolled on and each dance came and went, one by one these brave young men, so full of life, would be missing, shot down and, more often than not, killed; gone from my life forever. It was very sad because they were so young; I suppose we all were; that is why I say we had so much fun because life could be very short, and for so many it was.

After a time at Whittlesey I was moved to the Water Department at Cambridgeshire headquarters because they thought it suited my surname, which was Poole. We were in a big house where a brick control room had been built in the garden for our use. It was rather pleasant there because during my lunch break, after I had eaten, I would cycle to King's College and listen to the choir practising. In Water, we started to implement the lessons from Rotterdam which we should have learned before the City of London Blitz on 29th December 1940: to know where all the water resources were in a given area, how to access them and what the potential of each was. Rivers, pools, canals, streams, wells, mains and even flooded bomb craters were all identified so that we would know which was nearest to the fire and which was most suitable to use. Whenever there was a major fire, which was very often in wartime, we would set up a mobile control room so that we could co-ordinate the crews in drawing water from the various sources.

I then moved on to St. Albans and afterwards to Watford, but while I was there I caught a bad dose of influenza, which ultimately led to the end of my fire service career and my return to the family hairdressing business.

Whilst my brother Don was a POW in Changi prison camp, he met up with a chap from the Suffolks called Horace Taylor, who was also a hairdresser. They became good friends and between them, they cut all the prisoners' hair in the camp whilst in captivity. When Don arrived back home on VJ Day, 15th August 1945, I couldn't believe how thin he had become. The POWs had come to Peterborough on a special train from London, having been flown to Rangoon and then brought by ship the long way, round the Cape of Good Hope. There were some terrible sights amongst those lads; many were without one or more limbs and all of them were so thin and drawn. I think that the authorities brought them back the long way via the Cape rather than the shorter route through the Suez Canal to allow more time for the men to put some weight on and receive further medical attention on the ships, so that we wouldn't see just how emaciated they had become and how badly treated they had been. They had been virtually starved whilst in Changi and the other camps and over time, of course, we began to learn of the atrocities which the Japanese had carried out on Allied prisoners, including torture, executions and beatings. Both Don and Horace had worked on the Burma railway, and whether prisoners were suffering from beriberi, malaria or a myriad of other sicknesses and ailments, it made no difference, they had to go on working. The Japanese had stripped them all of their uniforms at the outset and instead they wore what was known as a 'Japnappy', a kind of native cloth thong.

When Horace had arrived at his local station near Billericay in Essex, there was not even a taxi to take him home and he had to walk. One day, Don had arranged to meet up with Horace, and had suggested to him that he might like to meet me, so I just tagged along with Don to Selfridge's in Oxford Street where they had arranged to meet, and that is how Horace and I were introduced. We started to see each other on a regular basis as the two men often met up. One thing led to another and we were married on 25th March 1946 at Old Fletton church, with my brother as Horace's best man, of course. By coincidence, the nephew of the vicar who married us had been a POW in the Far East as well.

Horace worked in his father's hairdressing business in Canning Town in London and we lived there in Hermit Road after we were married. However, Canning Town had taken a terrible battering during the war and the council were busy pulling down what was left of it, so we moved out to Hornchurch and started our own hairdresser's business. We moved several times over the years with the business, from Hornchurch to Watlington in Oxfordshire, then back to Cambridgeshire at Chatteris, followed by Towcester and finally retiring to Bideford and then to Whitchurch in Shropshire.

One lovely occasion in the 1950s we often laughed about was when Horace and I were still in London with our daughter Pamela, who was only a little girl at the time. We were travelling on the underground and Horace saw a man who he recognised as someone he had been a POW with in Changi. They chatted away for the rest of the journey until the other man got off the train. As he walked away down the platform, Pamela piped up in a shrill voice for everyone in the compartment to hear, "Mummy, was that man in prison with Daddy?"

It's true what they say; never work with children or animals.

Edna & Horace Taylor.

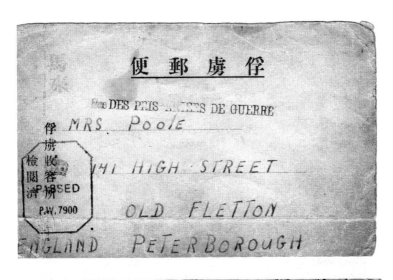

便郵虜俘

DES PRIS....ES DE GUERRE

俘 MRS. Poole

141 HIGH STREET

OLD FLETTON

ENGLAND PETERBOROUGH

PASSED
P.W.7900

5824942   PRIVATE   POOLE

MY DEAR MOTHER   IT IS SO NICE TO
BE ABLE TO WRITE TO YOU AGAIN PLEASE
DONT WORRY AS I AM PERFECLY FIT
AND WELL   STAN JIM AND SID ALSO
WE ARE BEING FED AND TREATED
VERY WELL   I HOPE YOU ARE ALL
WELL AT HOME I AM ALWAYS THINKING
OF YOU   HOPE TO SEE YOU ALL SOON
YOUR LOVING SON

DON

The postcard from Changi prison camp.

Hilda Buchanan

Chapter Eleven
Hilda Buchanan

> *"Where lies the land to which yon ship must go? Fresh as a lark mounting at break of day festively she puts forth in trim array; is she for tropic suns or polar snow?"*
>
> From 'Outward Bound'. *William Wordsworth*

Life for me began on the cold, damp, dismal, overcast day that was 5th April 1926 at Salford in Lancashire, now part of the Greater Manchester conurbation. I was born at home, the third of four girls; Ethel, Annie, me and later, Elsie.

Home was the local shop and off-licence run by my mother that stood at the corner of Victor Street and School Street, opposite St. Clement's School, which was the origin of one of these street names, but I have no idea who Victor was. In one of those strange coincidences of real life, long after the Second World War was over, my daughter Helen, who became a head teacher, started her career at St. Clement's School.

In traditional corner-shop fashion, there were two windows to our shop, one facing each street. In one of these windows, mother displayed various sweets, including the popular Cadbury's ½d chocolate bars which were wrapped in silver and purple foil, and one of my earliest memories is of climbing into the window and breaking these little bars so that they could not be sold and I would have to eat them. I also remember my mother's scolding when she found out what I had done.

I had arrived in Salford a month before the beginning of the General Strike of 1926, which heralded the start of some twelve years of economic decline culminating in the great depression years of the 1930s. For most people living in the cities of the north of England money had always been tight, but as the depression years progressed, so it became even tighter, and simply surviving was a daily preoccupation. My parents did sell some bottled beer and some spirits too, but most of the alcohol sales were in the form of 'loose beer'. Customers would bring an empty jug of any size from home, or more often send one their many children with it, and father would go down into the cellar and fill the jug with foaming beer from the large barrels we kept down there. In time, I realised that when the older children were sent for the beer, many of the jugs arrived at their destination containing less beer than had been put into it in the cellar, which is why it was usually the younger children who were sent out with the jug.

It was always a lovely sight when the beer was delivered from the brewery. I would wait to hear the two great Shire horses pulling the dray up the street with a steady, rhythmic clop, clop, ti-clop as their iron shoes clacked and sparked on the granite cobble sets of the road surface. I would run outside to watch them gradually growing bigger as they got nearer until at last they stopped outside the shop and towered above me, their harnesses jangling and their coats steaming from their labours. One of the draymen, who both seemed nearly as big as their horses, would put a nosebag with a few oats in it over the head of each horse whilst the other dropped a huge straw-filled sack onto the pavement for the barrels to fall onto as the men heaved them off the dray. Then, lifting the trap door in the pavement outside the shop, they would put two ropes around each barrel and slowly lower them down the ramp into the cellar one at a time. A pint of suitable refreshment awaited the completion of their efforts. It's a good job that there was no breathalyser in those days because the draymen had a drink with each of their deliveries and even though they were great big men, they must have been well over the limit at the end of each day.

When I was very small I remember that we had a black mongrel dog called Nigger, who died long before the war came. At that time there was a formal colour known as Nigger Brown, an almost-black shade of brown, and because our dog was black, he got the name. The most famous dog with the same name, of course, belonged to Wing Commander Guy Gibson, and was so sadly killed by a motor car on 15th May

1943, the day before the Dam Busters' raid. He is buried just inside the main gates at RAF Scampton in Lincolnshire. It was a very popular name for black dogs in those days and was used without any of the racial connotations which were brought to Britain by the white American GIs from 1942 onwards.

My father, Harold White, was a highly skilled man; he was a turner, which was a trade within engineering, but as the 1930s rolled on and the depression deepened, not only across Britain but across the world, business dwindled, order books emptied and workers in so many industries were made redundant: my father was amongst them. The little corner shop was our lifeline and from it we eked out a living, even though most of the families around us owed my mother money from having things on 'tick'. On 20th January 1936, King George V died and the Prince of Wales became Edward VIII, only to abdicate on 11th December so that he could marry the American, Mrs Wallace Simpson. When he did so, he became the first English monarch in over five hundred years to abdicate; not since Richard II on 29th September 1399 had a reigning monarch left the throne.

In so many ways, 1936 was what today would be called a tipping year. It was the year in which, amongst many other things, London's Crystal Palace burned down, the Eleventh Olympic Games were held in Berlin, the Spanish Civil War started, the Spitfire made its maiden flight, future Prime Minister Major Clement Atlee became leader of the Labour Party, two hundred unemployed workers from Jarrow marched three hundred miles to London to ask Stanley Baldwin for help and the Nazis held the largest and most dramatic of their rallies in Nuremberg.

However, as a ten-year-old girl, of much greater importance to me than all these things was that during 1936 my beloved father became very ill and died shortly afterwards from septicaemia, at only forty-six. He had cut himself and the wound became sceptic causing blood poisoning. In the days before antibiotics such a tragedy was not uncommon, particularly amongst men who worked with tools. Mother was devastated and was now left with four girls to bring up on her own with a widow's pension of ten shillings a week.

My mother, whose name was Sarah Ellen Dean before she married my father, was a wonderful woman. Although she suffered from poor health for most of her life, as did so many people in those days, particularly in the north, she worked desperately hard at all kinds of jobs just to put food in our mouths. We had an elderly neighbour who would look after my younger sister and me whilst Mother was out at work.

My very first school was Sussex Street School; I then moved to Grecian Street, which I attended until I was eleven, before moving to Pendleton High School. Two years later, in 1939, the war started and the following year, together with my younger sister Elsie, I was evacuated to Accrington. It had originally been the intention to send me to my aunt and uncle who lived in Canada, but when U-48, the most successful U-boat of the war, sank the *City of Benares* on 17th September 1940, with the loss of most of the children on board, the government put a stop to all further evacuations across the Atlantic.

So it was that I said goodbye to my mother at school and went with the teachers and other children to Salford railway station to catch the train for Accrington, each of us with a small brown suitcase containing all our worldly possessions, and with our buff-coloured luggage labels tied to our coat buttonholes, we began the first adventure of our young lives. I was heart-broken to be leaving my mother and my home, though.

Also evacuated to Accrington with me was my friend Faye Montague, who was a young Jewish girl. The two of us were taken in by the widow of a local doctor. She lived in a large, old Victorian house that smelled musty. I suppose that, like the rest of us, she was finding things a bit hard especially now that the war had started and rationing had been introduced. She did, though, have a maid, who, as soon as we arrived, took away our bread and cheese which was wrapped in brown paper bags. Faye and I had to share a bed, but at least it kept us a bit warmer on the cold winter nights.

My little sister Elsie was billeted with another family who lived about half a mile away from where I was. Their daughter was older than Faye and me but still lived at home with the family and she took a great liking to Elsie. She was a seamstress and, even though there was clothing rationing, she made Elsie some lovely dresses to wear out of odd pieces of material. Because Elsie was little, it didn't take a lot of material to make a dress for her and so the daughter could easily make a dress from a piece of material that would have otherwise been too small for many other items.

During my stay at Accrington, we put on a concert for the locals and called it "The Evacuees Review". However, after about three months the evacuee billeting officer came to assess us and because our gym teacher at Pendleton taught dance and I wanted to be a ballerina, I returned home, just in time for the Christmas blitz. On the nights of $22^{nd}/23^{rd}$ December and $23^{rd}/24^{th}$ December 1940, the Luftwaffe visited Manchester and dropped around 450 tons of high explosives and nearly two thousand incendiaries on the city. Six hundred and eighty-four people died in those two nights just before Christmas and another 2,364 were injured.

My mother's sister Ethel lived with their stepmother, and as the bombers approached the city for a second time in as many nights, the air-raid sirens started to wail their warning of the impending attack. Because the bombing had been so heavy the night before, Aunt Ethel suggested to Grandma Dean that they should go to the big communal shelter at the end of the street. It was bitterly cold outside and my grandmother, getting ready to go up to bed, was warm and comfortable. She said she was too old to turn out on that winter's night into the frosted streets and huddle on a bench or the floor in a crowded, stinking air-raid shelter, where there was no privacy or proper sanitation, and told Ethel that she was going to stay in her own home.

After the pounding the city had taken the previous night, my aunt was not going to give up easily and eventually her stepmother gave in. Gathering up her coat, pillow, blanket and handbag, all the while grumbling and chuntering bitterly about Hitler, Germans, bombs and the cold, she followed Ethel as they made their way to the shelter, which was by then almost full. As Grandma Dean had predicted, the night was uncomfortable, the shelter was crowded and the air smelt foul. Sleep was impossible with the constant noise. Bombs falling close by screamed their high-pitched wailing as they neared the earth, followed by shattering explosions which vibrated the walls of the shelter and brought the dust from the ceiling falling in a trickling mist to hang in the air, slowly coating everyone and drying their throats. It was a terrifying night for them all.

Finally, early on the morning of Christmas Eve the raid ended and the ARP wardens worked their way around the public shelters to let people know that it was now safe to go home. There were no 'All clear' sirens to sound because, as with Coventry six weeks earlier, after two nights of concentrated bombing, most of the gas, electricity and water supplies across the city had been destroyed, along with the telephone cables.

Aunt Ethel and Grandma Dean collected their few belongings and, with Grandma still grumbling about the misery of the night, joined the throng of people shuffling along the shelter passageway to the door. The air outside was cold and damp, holding in the stench of cordite, burning timber, and death. In the half-light of the dawn, the sky was still a mass of orange flames from the fires in the city centre just a few streets away. My aunt and grandmother began to slowly pick their way through the debris which seemed to be everywhere. Collapsed buildings, broken bricks, tiles, roof timbers and a million shards of glass lay in their path. Slowly and carefully, they struggled towards their house, but the closer to it they got, the greater the damage was to the buildings that they were passing.

After picking their way over the heaps of rubble strewn across the street, they finally stood in front of their house, or where their house had once been. Now there was just a great twisted heap of bricks and timber; it had received a direct hit and, but for my aunt's persistence that they should go to the shelter, they would have been added to the death toll. They had lost everything, but they were alive.

My mother, three sisters and I had spent the two nights of the Christmas blitz in the Anderson shelter in our front garden. It had been a terrifying experience for us, too. Although the shelter was dug into the ground and covered with soil, we had felt the ground tremble with every explosion and the noise was deafening. The bombs screamed down at us and seemed to be falling so close that we were sure that sooner or later one of them was going to fall on top of the Anderson and kill us all. We could hear the bells on the fire appliances and the ambulances as the crews tried to get around the city to where the bombs were falling, to where the incendiaries were starting hundreds of fires, to where people were lying trapped, dying and bleeding in the shattered rubble of their homes.

I could hear the sound of the anti-aircraft guns firing and the German aircraft passing overhead, but there was nothing that we could do except sit in that little shelter and pray that we would survive. Helpless and vulnerable though we were, there was nowhere else to go, nothing else to do. The five of us tried to keep cheerful and my mother was wonderful, as always. My sisters and I were frightened, but it must have been appalling for Mother, because she had the added burden of the responsibility for us; how she must have longed for my father.

The night of 23rd/24th December was the worst because the bombing came so much closer to us. I think that the Germans had learned from Coventry that there was no point in keeping on bombing the same ground when there was nothing left standing, and they started to move out into the inner-city residential areas on the second night. When we struggled out of our shelter as the growing daylight announced the arrival of Christmas Eve, like my aunt and grandmother, we could see the sky bright with the fires burning around the city. There was wreckage from people's houses all across the road; most of our own windows had been blown out, and inside the carpets, furniture, everything was covered in soot from where the vibrations of the exploding bombs had cleared the chimneys.

It was inevitable that, having been bombed out, Aunt Ethel and Grandma Dean would come and live with us. There were now seven women all in one household; it made for a lot of fun and a lot of talking.

The following year I was evacuated again, this time to the Worthington family in Lancaster, where only six years earlier, on 15th September 1935, Dr Buck Ruxton had murdered his wife Isabella during an argument brought upon by another of his fits of jealousy. Their maid, Mary Jane Rogerson, had unfortunately witnessed the argument between her employers and had been transfixed with horror as she saw the doctor strangle his wife. Her fate was sealed; he coldly walked across the room and strangled her, too. He disposed of their dismembered bodies in the Scottish Borders, but as is so often the case, by a series of mistakes and happenstances, he was caught, brought to trial and convicted. He was hanged at Strangeways prison, Manchester, on 12th May 1936. Even as a teenager, I was acutely aware of this case, which had captured the imagination of the public, especially in Lancashire.

After another three more months of being an evacuee I had once more had enough. I was studying hard for my School Certificate and so I packed all my books into my suitcase and set off to go home. I had no idea how I was going to get from Lancaster to Salford, but I set off anyway, struggling to carry my suitcase full of books. After a short while I stopped for a rest and a woman came up to me and asked me where I was going with my heavy case.

"Salford," I told her.

"Goodness me," she replied, and put my suitcase in her pram along with the baby and took me to the bus station. I was home in time for tea.

It was very difficult to study at home with all the noise of my sisters, aunt and grandmother around me, but one day a friend of my parents, whom I had always known as Uncle Tom, said that he knew a good place for me study where I would not be interrupted, and told me to go with him. I had no idea where he was taking me but he knew exactly what he had in mind and took me straight to Salford Police Station, where he was a superintendent. After that, every day I would go to the police station and study for my Certificate in the peace and quiet of a room there. After all, no-one was going to interrupt the superintendent's niece to ask her what she was doing in the police station. When the examinations came round, I passed my Certificate with good grades, especially in mathematics and German, which would influence my later career in the WRNS.

Also whilst at school during this time, I was a member of the Women's Junior Air Corps. However, when I left school, I joined the Ministry of Health for a while and then in April 1944, at eighteen, I volunteered for the WRNS. I had wanted to join the Women's Land Army for the fresh air and better food after years of living in a city on the meagre rations which we got. There was certainly no obesity in the war years. In the event, the Land Army was closed to me and I was told that I could either go into a munitions factory or join one of the Services and so, despite being in the WJAC, I joined the WRNS. It was whilst in the WRNS that I picked up the nickname 'Slim', which has stuck with me even to this day.

Finally the day came when I was to leave home: it was 8th May 1944, exactly one year before VE Day. I said goodbye to my mother and youngest sister, Elsie, who was still at home, and caught the bus to Manchester Piccadilly for the mainline train to London. At Mill Hill I did my two weeks' initial training, which included a medical examination, taking my oath of allegiance to the King and being kitted out with my uniform. We then moved on to Earl's Court, where we were billeted at Barkston Gardens.

I had really wanted to be a driver in the WRNS, but because my time studying at the police station had led to a credit in mathematics, I was sent on a radio mechanics' course. These courses were very thorough and had a typical Services logic to them. Everybody and anybody could get sent to one of any number of similar courses if they expressed an interest. However, to be of value, personnel had to be very good at whatever it was they were being trained for, and so at the end of every week there was an examination. To remain on the course and progress, a pass was essential. Failure meant leaving the course; it was as simple as that and resulted in only the best completing the course and obtaining the trade qualification.

When we finished our training each day, we would catch the underground and go into London despite the V1 flying bombs. Whilst we were making our way to the various clubs, Londoners were once more returning to the habit of bedding down in the underground stations for the night to avoid the V1s, just as they had done in the early years of the war during the Blitz. At this time the V1s were coming in day and night, and during the daytime we would see them coming in across Streatham Common. As long as the engine kept going until they were past you, everything was all right. It was when the engine stopped that you had to take cover. There was about seven seconds between the engine cutting out and the bomb hitting the ground, so we had to be very quick at finding cover; it didn't take long to get used to the idea of subconsciously looking for places to dive into if need be.

Service personnel had free entry into all the Forces Clubs but as WRNS we got in free almost anywhere. One favourite haunt was Rainbow Corner, the American Red Cross Club at 23, Shaftsbury Avenue near Piccadilly Circus. It opened its doors on 11th November 1942 and they remained open, twenty-four hours a day, until 9th January 1946. It was a very respectable club, run by the Red Cross as a home from home for American servicemen, and, as well as thousands of GIs, it played host to some very well-known people, including Generals Dwight

Eisenhower and Theodore Roosevelt, Captain James Stewart, the song writer Irving Berlin and actor George Raft. Glenn Miller made his Eagle Broadcasts from there and on one very special occasion, Artie Shaw's Navy Band played the club. Another talent who entertained the troops at Rainbow Corner on several occasions was the young Petula Clark, destined to become one of Britain's biggest singing stars of the 1950s and 60s.

Fred Astaire's sister, Lady Charles Cavendish, also helped out at the Club throughout the war. The GIs were very generous and we could easily pick up free tickets for the latest shows which the theatres were once more putting on. When war broke out, and particularly when the London Blitz started, the clubs, cinemas and theatres in the capital were ordered to close, although most stayed open. There was one notable exception to this order: the Café de Paris on Coventry Street. It was the most glamorous of all London's nightclubs, considered to be the safest as it was situated four floors below Leicester Square and was officially permitted to remain open. Royalty, the famous and the well-heeled all gathered here to put some glitz into the Blitz, to dine and dance the night away to some of the best-known bands of the day, almost oblivious to the bombing going on above their heads. However, after the start of the war it was also a frequent haunt of service men and women.

The lavish interior of the nightclub was reminiscent of the ballroom on the Titanic, and on the evening of 8th March 1941 it came to a similar end, also caused by a tragic and unforeseen twist of fate. During the air raid that night, two bombs fell on the West End and found their way straight down the club's ventilation shaft. They exploded in a blinding blue flash in the centre of the dance floor. Somewhere between thirty-four and eighty people died in the club that night including band leader Ken 'Snakehips' Johnson, along with most of his musicians.

Nevertheless, even amongst all this death and destruction there was a moment of humour when one diner, badly injured and being carried out on a stretcher past a crowd of on-lookers, quipped, "At least I won't have to pay for dinner tonight." Others who were not injured simply made their way to other clubs to continue with their night's entertainment. In war, life and death is seen very differently than in peacetime.

By the time I arrived at Earl's Court, the Café de Paris had been rebuilt, but was now part of Lord Nuffield's Centre, which although on Wardour Street, was actually next door underground. After the destruction of the club, one of the remaining interior walls was taken down and the two premises joined into one. Lord Nuffield had great concern for British service men and women and wanted them to enjoy the best of London life whilst on leave without breaking the bank in the process. He set up his centre along much the same lines as the Red Cross ran Rainbow Corner for the Americans. Thus, the Café de Paris became a Forces Club and we enjoyed many evenings dancing the night away to the bands of the day.

Often at weekends, however, we would queue up to get into the Queensbury All-Services Club at the London Casino on Old Compton Street. I saw Glenn Miller and his American Band of the Supreme Allied Command play there twice, on Sunday 30th July and Saturday 2nd September. In between these two concerts, in August 1944, he was promoted from a captain to major but I don't think that it had anything to do with me dancing to his music.

We had a lot of fun at these clubs and especially at the Queensbury, which, in the two years up to September 1944, had hosted more than 1.6 million men and women of the Armed Services. All the big stars of the day were there at one time or another, including the RAF Dance Band, The Squadronnaires. The performances were part of the Variety Bandbox series and were broadcast to the troops by the SHAEF (Supreme Headquarters Allied Expeditionary Force) broadcasting service. However, the end of the radio broadcast was not the end of the entertainment for those of us in the club because the music and dancing just carried on for the rest of the evening. Saturdays were the best nights as we didn't have to get up so early on Sunday morning and there were no classes. These were simply wonderful times to have been young and we lived life to the full, because with the V1s falling every day and night, we never knew where the next one would explode and whether it would have our names on it.

My training was going well and I excelled at the practical side in the workshop, no doubt inheriting my skills from my dad, but I was not very good at the theory. Inevitably the day came when I failed the weekly exam and, after five months at Earl's Court, I left the radio mechanics' course.

I was very quickly posted to New College, Finchley, for re-mustering and whilst there was selected for SDX, Special Duties Executive; it was all very 'hush-hush' and nobody knew what they were going to be doing. Also around this time the V2 rockets started to land on London. These were even more frightening than the V1s because they were proper rockets which literally descended on the city from out of the blue. There was no give-away engine noise to track their progress across the south-east and, whereas our fastest Spitfires and Tempests could catch the V1s and shoot them down, as many did, there was nothing that could be done about the V2s once they were sent on their way. The only defence we had was in the hands of RAF Bomber Command and our ground troops being able to destroy the launch sites.

My next posting from Finchley was to the secret code-breaking centre at Bletchley Park and for my time there I was billeted at Woburn Abbey. There were plenty of different people and trades at Woburn, but WRNS had their own quarters as there were about five hundred of us, including a fairly liberal sprinkling of the aristocracy such as the Honourable Jane Dalrymple-Hey and the daughter of the Marquis of Queensbury, who owned the All Forces Club where just a few weeks previously I had danced to the music of Glenn Miller and his band.

In addition to the Manor House, the extensive grounds were filled with huts, each one numbered, which is where the secret code-breaking work was carried out. The grounds were magnificent and particularly the beautiful magnolia trees by the lake. There really cannot have been a more splendid setting in which to work, especially in wartime.

The first thing we had to do before starting at Bletchley Park was to sign the Official Secrets Act. We usually worked from 16.00 to midnight, midnight to 08.00 and 08.00 to 16.00, travelling by Service bus from Woburn Abbey each day for our different watches, with thirty-six hours off between watch rotas. The washing facilities at Woburn included great big baths and when they were in use and full of Wrens, there was always a great deal of laughter and fun.

One day, a sailor who was around forty, came right into the bathroom where I was bathing and had a good look at me. I sank as low into the water as I could whilst he continued looking at me, then after a few moments, he calmly said, "Oh sorry, I didn't know you were in here." He then just as calmly walked out, followed by a string of suitable comments, but it was harmless enough and I wasn't at all bothered.

Bletchley Park, also known as Station X, was located about 50 miles north-west of London and the secret code-breaking team of mathematicians was led by Alan Turing. At the start of the war, there were, comparatively speaking, only a handful of people working there, but by the time I arrived, there were thousands working around the clock.

Station X covered a very large area and people tended to work in small isolated groups, and because the level of security and secrecy was so high you could meet people socially and not know that they too worked there. One couple who both worked at Station X but in different sections took this to its extreme; they met, fell in love, married and then only some years after the war was over did they find out that they had both worked at Bletchley Park. The Official Secrets Act has a long reach.

The importance of the work which we did at Bletchley Park was pivotal to the Allied success because the Germans never realised that their Enigma and Lorenz codes had been broken. Consequently, they continued to send the vital messages that we were able to intercept, decode and act upon. Mostly they used the Enigma code machine although the Kriegsmarine, the German navy, added two more drums to their versions which made the work for our people much more difficult. The German army High Command, however, used the Lorenz machine which was a different code altogether and worked on teleprinter punched tape.

Unsurprisingly, the German machines were extremely good; among the best in the world and, had they been used properly, the job of the code breakers would have been much harder. However, as is so often the case, human error opened the door and sloppy practices by the German operators helped us considerably, but that is not to understate the immense task which faced the teams, nor the magnitude of their successes.

Brigadier John Tiltman and Bill Tutte, a distinguished Cambridge graduate, began to exploit the mistakes made by the German operators to discover how the Lorenz machine worked. By 1942, the code could be broken, but the work was painstakingly slow, so much so that very often by the time the message had been decoded the information was so far out of date as to be of little or no value.

What was needed was a quicker way to find the Lorenz machine settings and the famous mathematician Max Newman devised the Colossus to do the job. Colossus was the very first electronic computer in the world and at its simplest level, worked with two tapes on reels, one containing the message to be decoded and the other with the possible Lorenz machine settings. By running the two tapes simultaneously and through a process of elimination, the settings could be found and another machine known as Tunny would then decode the message. The great advantage of Colossus was its speed, and messages could be decoded within hours and acted upon.

My job at Bletchley was as part of the team working with the Colossus in Hut 7. Part of what I did was to repair the tapes that ran between the great reels if they broke, which they often did, by using Scotch tape. I then had to punch holes in the tape repairs in the correct places to keep the sequence going and then restart the reels. We also had to watch over the Colossus very carefully to ensure that the valves, which were its life-blood and which hummed gently all the time that it was running, did not over-heat and bring everything to a standstill.

The social life at that time was tremendous fun. Because there were so many American airbases nearby and five hundred Wrens at Bletchley, whenever there was a dance or a party at one of these bases, which seemed to be most of the time, they would send some trucks across for us. Those of us not on duty would climb up into the transport, which always seemed to have a handful of Americans already in the back, and bounce our way to whichever base was hosting the entertainment. I must say, we were always treated very well by our American hosts and brought back to Bletchley safely after another enjoyable evening.

When the end of the war finally came, we received the news first at Station X, because we decoded the German messages carrying the orders and information to their commanders in the field. The news spread like wildfire, long before the official announcement, so we were given railway passes and two days' leave to go and enjoy it. Where else was there to go from Bletchley Park but London? Together with my friend Joyce, I dashed off and we arrived in the city early on the morning of VE Day, Tuesday 8th May 1945, exactly one year after I had left home to join the Wrens. It was a beautiful day and the streets were already thronging with people. Together with the other Wrens who had come from Bletchley, I went across to Trafalgar Square so that we could listen to Winston Churchill broadcast to the nation and declare an end to the war in Europe.

As the hours ticked by, more and more people arrived. I was so excited; everyone was. There were girls doing strip-tease dances in the road; there were drunken men walking on parapets of buildings to show off; there were people climbing onto buses and lorries and up trees. We walked around arm-in-arm, danced and sang 'Knees up Mother Brown', 'Roll out the Barrel', and all the songs like that; the licensing laws had been relaxed and the pubs were open all day. However, like everything else in the war, beer, although not rationed, was in short supply and soon ran out. But it didn't matter; we had waited six years for this day and we were intoxicated with the excitement and knowledge that the war, in Europe at least, was over and we were going to enjoy it with or without beer.

It wasn't long before I found myself on the very top step of Nelson's Column with a bunch of navy lads, waving a Union flag, singing and cheering. The whole scene was captured by the newsreels and shown again fifty years later on the 50th anniversary; sure enough, there I was, still waving my flag and singing on the top step. I also appeared on the front of the *Morning Post*, the *Daily Telegraph* and some of the other newspapers, standing there as part of the crowd on Nelson's Column. I hope my mother didn't see them. So many people had cameras, both private and for the papers and newsreels.

After a while we made our way across to Buckingham Palace to hear the King make his speech. There were thousands of people there, all along Pall Mall and around the front of the Palace, on the Victoria monument and even hanging off the lamp posts. When the King had finished speaking, along with a few thousand other people, I shouted, "We want George. We want George," and so on.

Eventually he came back out onto the balcony together with the Queen and the two princesses.

What a wonderful day it was; there has been nothing to compare with it before or since. The atmosphere was simply boiling over with excitement and fun and relief. As a nation we had won, and as individuals we had survived. When I returned to Trafalgar Square many years later with my husband and looked at the height of those steps on Nelson's Column, I have no idea how I got up there. I suppose I was a lot younger then and no doubt had a helping hand or two from some of those matelots.

The celebrations went on all night and a crowd of us made our way to St James' Park, where there was a massive bonfire. We sat around talking, drinking a little, eating a little, but most of all, just savouring the great victory we had all won. Nevertheless, through all the enjoyment, it did not escape me that I had had a very good war and enjoyed myself immensely having so much fun that it almost seemed wrong, but I had been very lucky. I had not lost any family members, although my aunt and grandmother did have a narrow escape, and I didn't know anyone then who had been killed. Tragedy, however, was waiting down the road, because my brother-in-law, who had served for seven years throughout the war with a Scottish regiment, was drowned in Austria whilst with the forces of occupation not long after VE Day.

My war was not typical of everyone's. The cost to so many families had been the terrible heartache from the death of a loved one, or sometimes several family members. Other families had been ripped apart by injury, by long periods overseas or as a prisoner of war. Wives at home had found comfort in the bed of someone else; husbands overseas had found comfort with a nurse, a Wren or the daughter of a French family. The old adage of 'up with the lark, to bed with the Wren,' was certainly true in some cases. The job of rebuilding whole families and family relationships had to start all over again. Men came home to children they had not seen since infancy, a stranger to their own children, others faced immense difficulty trying to readjust to peace and civilian life; and for some there was simply nothing left to rebuild.

And then there was Japan. We were celebrating victory in Europe, but the war was still raging in the Pacific, and that is where everyone's attention now turned. After two days of partying, dancing and enjoying myself, it was time to get back to Bletchley Park and the work we did there. At five o'clock in the early morning I caught the underground to Euston Station and then changed to the surface train, arriving back at Bletchley Park just in time to freshen up, get a meal and be on duty for 09.00. We were still at war and this was still the navy.

Those forces, mainly the RAF and Royal Navy, who were not involved in repatriating troops and prisoners of war in Europe, were building the Tiger Force and preparing to move out to the Far East to fight the Japanese. I had already volunteered to go overseas and now that peace had returned to Europe, it wasn't long before I set sail on a troopship, bound for I knew not where. We left Liverpool and sailed down the Irish Sea into the Western Approaches and across the Bay of Biscay. For the last five years this had been the hunting ground of the U-boats, a treacherous journey for Allied sailors, and it had claimed the lives of so many, especially from the Merchant Navy, but now I strolled around the deck enjoying the early summer sunshine and the fresh salt air. I was a Wren and was at last on board a ship at sea, even if only en route to my next land-based posting.

We called in to Gibraltar for fresh supplies of food and water, and left a few personnel there, then on through the Mediterranean, past Sicily, and Malta, which had received the George Cross in 1941, Crete and Cyprus to Port Said and the Suez Canal. We docked at Suez for more fresh water before sailing down the Red Sea into the Gulf of Aden and then across the Indian Ocean. There was not a great deal to do on board and by the time we got halfway along the Mediterranean, the view of great expanses of water on both sides of the ship had long since lost its novelty value. What we needed was a revue and so the Wrens and a few of the sailors set about putting one together. I took my part as Carmen Miranda. The whole show was a great success. We finally arrived in Colombo, the capital of Ceylon, as it was called then, some three weeks after having left Liverpool.

Since leaving Gibraltar, it had become increasingly hot on board the ship, but it was a great deal hotter once we went ashore. We had been kitted out with all-white cotton tropical uniforms in Gibraltar and they were certainly cooler than our navy-blue serge ones and lovely to wear. The base in Colombo was home to three thousand servicemen and five hundred Wrens and our jobs here were much the same as they had been at Bletchley Park, code breaking. We were part of the Tiger Force and were preparing to fight the Japanese on every little island all the way back to the steps of the Emperor's palace.

In the event, ironically with the help of captured German scientists, the war in the Pacific was brought to a shattering conclusion with the dropping of the two atomic bombs on Hiroshima and Nagasaki on 6th and 9th August: that week a new world order began. Six days later, the Japanese surrendered and the war was finally over. VJ Day, August 15th, was another immensely proud day for me as we paraded along the Galle Face in Colombo in front of Lord Louis Mountbatten, who took the salute, General Slim and Lord Gort, VC. It was party time once more as we celebrated the final victory of the war, but, just as in Europe, there were horrors to come when the extent of the appalling and inhuman treatment of Allied prisoners of war by the Japanese was discovered.

These were the last great days of the British Empire and there were still British bases around the globe to be serviced, and it was the Royal Navy and Merchant Navy which had the task of transporting the troops and their supplies to and from these bases. Once the Japanese had surrendered, the priority was to bring the POWs home and then the Forces who had been in the Far East for a long time, many of them not having seen their homes and families for several years. The ships of the Merchant Navy which had survived the war plied the seas from Singapore and Rangoon to Glasgow and Liverpool via

Gibraltar, bringing troops home and then going back again transporting others out to take their place. Of these ships, perhaps the best known was the SS *Orduna*, which plied this route full of service men and women and their families until the winter of 1949.

In the meantime, we enjoyed a wonderful social life in this colonial outpost and Wrens were always in great demand for the countless parties and dances which were held at the various tea plantations. I have some lovely memories of my time in Ceylon, but it was also tainted with deep sadness; whilst we were there, my great friend Margaret Moxley died from polio. I had been in the sick bay with her and so was quarantined for two weeks; however, I was allowed to attend her funeral, which was held with full naval ceremony.

Peace had removed the threat from this part of the world and code-breaking teams were not needed here any longer so, like all good things, my posting came to an end, and in January 1946 I once more boarded a troopship to start the long voyage back to Great Britain. I was very sorry to leave Ceylon because I had enjoyed myself so much whilst there. I missed it even more when the ship arrived back to Glasgow's Gourock docks on the Clyde in the freezing cold and driving rain of mid-winter. We then spent the next eighteen hours with nothing more than two packs of sandwiches each, sitting in a rather tired compartment on a train which was as cold as charity, as it meandered unendingly south towards Chatham Barracks. The company was good but even our repartee wore a bit thin as tiredness overtook us and, through the carriage windows, we were reminded of what six years of war had done to the towns and cities along our journey.

I re-mustered at Reading and whilst waiting for my next posting, we did another revue. In the days before television, DVDs and computer games we made our own entertainment and putting on revues was a very popular form of bringing some fun and laughter to stations.

My next posting was to Eastney Marine Barracks at Portsmouth where I became a marine Wren, and then it was on to Ilfracombe, where I was part of the team carrying out the clerical pay duties. It was all a bit dull after the excitement of Station X and Ceylon, but I knew that my demob was coming soon. However, before that happened I took part in the victory parade in London on 8th June 1946; then my great adventure was all over, it was time to return to civilian life. So, clutching the £13 demob money which I had been given I went shopping in Barnstable, where I bought a black barathea suit and yellow shoes, hat and handbag to go with it. I can still remember that outfit and I looked very smart in it too.

My intention upon leaving the navy was to emigrate to Canada to live with my aunt and uncle there, but a man got in the way. I had met Keith long before I joined the WRNS. One night, my friend Audrey and I were pushing our bicycles home and whilst walking past Salford's Hope Hospital we bumped into her great heartthrob and his friend Keith, who were also pushing their bicycles. Keith and I hit it off and he walked me home. We became good friends and he would telephone from wherever he was and sing the song, "If you like me, like I like you".

We started to write to each other and carried on doing so after I joined the WRNS. I had written to him after VE Day, telling him everything that I had been doing and hoping that he'd had a good time too, as I was sure he would have, but now that we had both been demobbed we started to see each other on a more serious basis. I returned to work for the Ministry of Health and passed my Civil Service exams. However, Keith's father was a head teacher and persuaded me to join the profession, so I entered teacher training college and Keith went to Durham University to read commerce. He was a born salesman.

After I had finished my training and Keith had graduated, on a bright and chilly 8th April 1950 we married at St. Anne's Church, Brindle Heath in Salford. I taught until Ian, the first of our three children, was born. The twins Helen and Kate followed; once again Hope Hospital was pivotal to my life as all our children were born there. In 1956 my mother died at the age of sixty-three. Her life had been so hard even without the war, but she had loved her four daughters dearly and brought us all up well. The love she had for us was returned, not only by us but also by her four sons-in-law. Her death left a big hole in our lives.

In 1959 we left Salford to take over the post office and shop in the village of Wincle just outside Macclesfield. Wincle stands on the river Dane near Danebridge and together they form one of the prettiest parts along the river where it separates Cheshire from Staffordshire. It was a lovely place to live and we had seven very happy years there before moving into Macclesfield so that I could return to teaching and Keith could become a manufacturer's agent. In 1977 we moved to Buxton and then to Congleton before returning to Macclesfield for our retirement. My dear Keith died in 2001 but he left me with treasured memories and a wonderful family; in addition to Ian, Helen and Kate, I have seven grandchildren and one great-granddaughter.

I have led a very happy and interesting life; I have been to places, met people and done things that as a child I could never have dreamed were possible. War is a terrible thing and I would not wish another one, but for me, the years of the Second World War were some of the best and most exciting of my life. I know I was very lucky and I feel truly blessed with everything that has come my way.

Hilda, next to her mother, with sisters and father.

Hilda, Keith and children Ian, Helen & Kate.

Centre: Hilda in Station X days

*Top right & bottom left: Hilda's programmes
from the Glenn Miller performances.*

Hilda's friend Margaret Moxley in Ceylon.

An image from the wonderful days in Ceylon.

More images from the wonderful days in Ceylon.

Pier Nuke

Chapter Twelve
Pier Nuke, MiD [The Baron]

> "*When can their glory fade? O the wild charge they made! All the world wonder'd. Honour the charge they made! Honour the Light Brigade, Noble six hundred!*"
>
> From 'The Charge of The Light Brigade'. *Alfred, Lord Tennyson*

Author's introduction

Lieutenant-General Frederick Browning, Commander of the British 1st Airborne Corps, pondered upon the map on the wall. Standing beside him, Field Marshal Bernard Law Montgomery had just outlined his latest plan to open the invasion route into Germany, to be code-named Operation Market-Garden. It was to be a daring dash by British armour along sixty-four miles of a narrow road through Holland, and the capture by British and American paratroopers of five major river and canal crossings including the vast bridges at Grave, Nijmegen and Arnhem, the latter giving direct access to Germany. For the plan to succeed, all the many bridges along the route had to be seized intact and the road, often no more than a single track, kept open. Montgomery, however, anticipated little or no resistance from a German army in full retreat. General Browning, though, was uneasy; he could see the enormity of the task being asked of his airborne troops.

Tapping his finger on the map at Arnhem, the most northerly point in the plan, he asked, "How long will it take the armour to reach us?"

"Two days," clipped Montgomery.

Without taking his eyes off the map, Browning hesitated, then replied slowly, "We can hold it for four; but sir, I think we might be going a bridge too far."

In the late summer of 1944, as the Allies stood poised along the western border of Germany, there was amongst the British and American senior commanders a strong desire to use their highly trained airborne troops to spearhead a break-out and open the way to Berlin, thus ending the war. There was also a deep and not very healthy rivalry between Montgomery, who led the British forces on the northern route, and General George Patton, who led the American forces on the southern route, to be the first to break out and reach Berlin before the Russians, who were advancing from the east.

After the destruction of Caen, the German forces retreated at an unprecedented rate in the face of the superior strength of the Allied armies and air forces. As the troops under Montgomery's and Patton's commands each broke out of Normandy, the Germans retreated faster than the Allies could advance across France and Belgium. By the time the German army passed through Holland to regain the Fatherland, it was little short of an outright rout; a confused rabble of soldiers, Luftwaffe airmen and civilians riding on vehicles, carts, bicycles, indeed anything that moved, but mostly stumbling along on foot, desperate to keep ahead of the advancing armies.

However, the unprecedented speed of the German retreat caused the Allies considerable logistical difficulties with their supply lines; difficulties which increased exponentially with each day of the advance. Still only able to come ashore through Normandy, the Allies could not get the necessary supplies of fuel, food, ammunition and equipment to Montgomery's front line on the northern route and to Patton's front line on the southern route fast enough and it became no longer possible to supply both commanders at the rate each needed to push through to Germany. By the time the British reached Antwerp, the supply line had been stretched beyond capacity and Montgomery's advance had stalled. Patton's advance to the Saar further south had suffered the same fate. General Eisenhower, the Allied Supreme Commander, could no longer supply both his advancing armies simultaneously; something had to give.

It was not only a logistical matter of the great length of the supply line, the ground troops were tired and needed to rest, and their equipment needed repair, facts not lost on Eisenhower. However, unknown to anyone at the end of August, this enforced stall of the advance, although welcomed by the Allied troops, was to have a major impact upon the outcome of Market-Garden. It threw a lifeline to the German commander, Field Marshal Gerd von Rundstedt, providing him with the opportunity to stem the flow of his retreating forces and to re-group them into fighting units.

Eisenhower wanted this period of rest and re-supply for his troops so that he could capture a Channel port, shorten his supply lines and make an advance on Germany across a broad front. Montgomery and Patton both wanted to push forward and be the first to break through, but to do so it would be necessary to deny the other his essential supplies. There had been several plans during that summer to use airborne troops on a modest scale but for various reasons they had all been cancelled. Montgomery felt that the northern route into the heart of the German Ruhr was the way to go, but Eisenhower still wanted a broad front. Nevertheless, there was political pressure on Eisenhower from both the Americans and the British to use their airborne forces, and Montgomery seized the moment by devising Operation Market-Garden, which would utilise three-and-a-half divisions of airborne troops, 35,000 men, and in that way open up the northern route to Germany under his command, out-flanking Patton as well as the German armies.

In short, the plan was for Major-General Maxwell Taylor's American 101st Airborne Division, the 'Screaming Eagles', to land on three drop zones north of Eindhoven, to take the various bridges in a fifteen-mile section between Eindhoven and Veghel, including the vital crossing over the Wilhelmina Canal at Son. The American 82nd Airborne Division led by

Brigadier-General James M Gavin, at thirty-seven the youngest Brigadier-General in the United States army, was to land on five drop zones near Nijmegen. Their orders were to capture the massive bridges at Grave and Nijmegen over the rivers Maas and Waal. They were also to protect and hold their landing grounds on the Groesbeek Heights, which adjoined the Reichwald Forest and marked the border between Holland and Germany. Later drops which would bring in reinforcements, armour and supplies for the 82nd would need to use these landing grounds. This was also the area where General Browning, the overall commander in the field, would need to establish his headquarters.

The glittering prize in Montgomery's plan, though, was the road bridge over the Lower Rhine at Arnhem. This was the most difficult and most dangerous part, and the task of capturing and securing this great three-span bridge was given to Major-General Robert 'Roy' Urquhart's 1st Airborne Division supported by the 1st Polish Parachute Brigade led by Major-General Stanislaw Sosabowski. Without the capture of the road bridge at Arnhem, the operation would fail.

But in their haste to get to Germany, the Allied commanders in the field and in London made a catastrophic mistake which would ultimately cost them success. Eisenhower's supplies had to come ashore at the Normandy beaches since the Germans still controlled all the Channel ports. The British, however, had captured the port of Antwerp but did not control the waterway from the port to the North Sea. As a result of the British presence in Antwerp, General Gustav van Zangen's 15th German army was cut off in the area to the west, caught between the British forces and the cold waters of the North Sea. At SHAEF [Supreme Headquarters Allied Expeditionary Force] in London and in the field, all commanders were so focused on finding a way into Germany that they missed the opportunity to close the only escape route open to van Zangen's men.

In one of the greatest miscalculations of the war in Europe, no-one capitalised upon the outstanding success of Major-General George Roberts' 11th Armoured Division in reaching Antwerp and capturing the massive port before the Germans could destroy it. A handful of tanks and eighteen more miles of unopposed advance would have sealed the two-mile-wide isthmus and prevented the German 15th Army from slipping out through Walcheren Island and the single road across South Beveland. As it was, 65,000 men, together with their 225 guns, 750 trucks and 1,000 horses, escaped to enter the battle along the vital sixty-four-mile corridor of Dutch towns, villages and countryside to Arnhem. Their presence in the field was to prove as fatal to the Allied success in the operation as was the random choice by Field Marshal Model, the commander of German Army Group B, of the area around the sleepy town of Arnhem in which to rest Bittrich's battle-weary *Panzer* troops.

Operation Market-Garden, like so many plans in so many wars before it, was designed to end the fighting by Christmas. It was scheduled to start at 10.30 on the morning of Sunday 17th September 1944 and would be the largest airborne operation ever seen before or since. In all, 35,000 men, 2,500 gliders, 1,000 Douglas Commercial C-47 Skytrain aircraft, better known as Dakotas since the C-47 was the military version of the ubiquitous civilian DC-3, together with Stirling and Halifax bombers acting as troop transporters and tugs, and 1,500 fighters including Spitfires, rocket-firing Typhoons and American Thunderbolts for protection, would take off in waves from airfields in England, fly over the Channel to Belgium, then turn for Holland. Briefing his senior commanders, General Browning told them that the object of the operation was *"to lay a carpet of airborne troops down over which our ground forces can pass."*

However, his Intelligence Officer, Major Brian Urquhart [no relation to General Urquhart], was deeply troubled by the light-hearted optimism which pervaded the senior officers' thinking. The prevailing view was that Allied troops would be faced largely by old men and young boys, the bulk of the fighting force having retreated behind the German frontier. Brian Urquhart, highly intelligent and perceptive, feared that would not be the case. From analysis of Dutch underground reports, he knew that the rout of the German forces which had occurred at the beginning of September had slowed and then halted. He believed that these forces were being strengthened, and he had learned that Field Marshal Model had his headquarters at Oosterbeek, a village just outside Arnhem. He also believed Dutch reports that SS *Panzer* troops were in Arnhem.

At the beginning of September, Lieutenant-General Wilhelm Bittrich, Commander of the élite veteran II SS *Panzer* Corps, knew that his battered troops needed rest. They had fought all the way back from Normandy and had suffered heavy casualties. Bittrich raised the matter with Model, who, at about the same time that General Browning was doing the same with Montgomery, looked at the map of Holland and pointed to Arnhem, sixty-four miles behind the front line, as the place they should withdraw to for refitting and rest, because to him *"it was a peaceful sector where nothing was happening."* On 4th September, the 9th and 10th SS *Panzer* divisions reached Arnhem and fanned out north, south and east of the town. Camouflaged and bivouacked, these tough, veteran, battle-hardened troops rested, unaware of what awaited them.

At General Browning's briefing, the young Major Urquhart was so worried about the lack of regard which the High Command had for the intelligence reports he offered that he had the temerity to ask whether the 'carpet' of airborne troops was to consist of live troops or dead ones. Realising the depth of his Intelligence Officer's concerns, Browning approved a request to the RAF to send a low-level photographic reconnaissance sweep over the Arnhem area. But Major Urquhart wasn't the only one who was worried about the reports of armour in the Arnhem area; Lieutenant-General Walter Smith, Eisenhower's Chief of Staff, was also so concerned about the intelligence reports from the Dutch underground that he flew to Brussels to tell Montgomery that the 'lost' SS *Panzer* divisions from Normandy had turned up at Arnhem and that the Market-Garden plans might need revision. Montgomery would not hear of such a proposal and, blinded by his desperation to beat Patton to Berlin, insisted that Market-Garden would 'go all right as set.'

Back in England, Major Urquhart had received the photographs taken by the Spitfire pilot from RAF Benson; from hundreds of photographs taken of the Market-Garden area during the previous 72 hours, the major held five in his hand, five photographs which showed German tanks sitting almost on top of the landing grounds to be used by the British 1st Airborne Division. Distraught at the evidence, he hurried to General Browning, who saw him immediately. After studying the photographs, the General, already uneasy with his own doubts expressed to Montgomery at the outset but by now caught up in the driving optimism of the plan, hesitantly observed, "I wouldn't trouble myself about these if I were you. They're probably not serviceable at any rate."

Despite the major's further protests, Browning was not prepared to entertain a re-evaluation of the operation and he was dismissed. Urquhart had been no more successful than General Smith had been with Montgomery. Exhausted from over-work, but also wracked with foreboding that the intelligence information he had given was being ignored, on 16th September he was visited by the corps medical officer and told to go home. It was clear that no-one was going to let him spoil the 'party' at this stage; he was given enforced sick leave and his request to be allowed to go to Holland with the rest of the corps, despite the disaster that he was sure awaited them, was refused.

The following day, his namesake, Major-General Roy Urquhart, took 10,005 British airborne troops into Arnhem; only 2,163 would return. One of them was eighteen-year-old Trooper Pier Nuke, who would be Mentioned in Dispatches for his courage and actions whilst under fire; this is his story.

I was born at Chatham Barracks Hospital on 15th April 1926, the youngest of three boys. My father, whose trade was a cabinet maker, was the Regimental Sergeant Major at the Barracks, having served on the Western Front all through the Great War. When conflict with Germany came again in 1939, Dad was still serving. By 1944, he had been commissioned, reached the rank of captain and, though really a little long in the tooth for front-line fighting, was part of the D-Day landings on the Normandy beaches, arriving there on D+3, 9th June. Dad fought through the long battle for Caen and then on across Europe until Germany was once more finally defeated. There weren't too many father and son combinations fighting in the same theatre of war at this time, but later that summer when I parachuted into Arnhem, although I had no idea where my father was, I joined him in the European theatre.

Retaining the rank of captain, Dad finally left the army in the early 1950s after forty-eight years' service and went to work for the Forestry Commission in Hampshire, where for many years my parents lived in one of its cottages, which had been a coach house on the estate during the 19th century, at Lyndhurst, just outside Southampton. However, in his later years after my mother had passed away, Dad relinquished his commission and retired to the Royal Hospital as a Chelsea Pensioner, where he lived for four years before he died at the age of ninety-three after a very full life by anyone's standards.

My surname dates right back to around the time of the Norman Conquest when my family were barons and very wealthy landowners, but sadly no longer so, with our own coat of arms. On active service we were known by a code name and because of my family background I was called The Baron.

Military service for me began in 1943 when I was called up and joined the Royal Engineers. My first posting was to the camp just outside the small town of Clitheroe in Lancashire, close to the border with Yorkshire. In the summer of 1944, just after D-Day, a request went out asking for volunteers to join the Parachute Regiment. Paratroopers were paid an extra 2/6d per day [12½p today]. I volunteered, was sent to York for a medical examination and then posted to Ringway aerodrome in Manchester for training.

Each day started at 05.00 hours and followed the same pattern to get us to a level of supreme fitness. I could never have imagined how glad I would be of that training in the next few weeks. First, dressed in singlet and shorts, came a session of PT exercises, followed by a five-mile run then a five-mile walk in full combat kit. Another part of our training to get us really fit was to be able to run for a hundred yards whilst carrying another man on our backs, fireman's-lift style. Then, when we were able to do that we had to run two hundred yards whilst carrying a man on our backs. This part of the training was not just about being fit, though; it was also about making sure that we could save our wounded comrades and run to shelter with them. When we were fit, we started our parachute training.

First, we were taught how to roll over when landing on the ground. In addition to our own weight, we would be carrying some of our kit, in particular our weapons and ammunition. Then came the worst part of the training; the basket jumps. The basket, in which there were about six of us, was winched up underneath a barrage balloon to a height of around eight hundred feet and then one at a time we would jump out through a hole in the floor. There was nothing to be done but drop out, scream and pray to God that the parachute would open. The first jump was terrifying, but since we had to do eight basket jumps in order to move on to jumping from an aircraft, they just had to be done. By now it was early September.

Practice jumps from aircraft followed and these gave us confidence in the line and the parachute, but ultimately my life, like everyone else's, hung on the thin thread of the skill of the person who had packed the parachute. With eight basket jumps and four from aircraft successfully completed, I received my parachute wings.

After little more than three weeks of this training we were moved to RAF Cottesmore in Rutland. When we arrived, there were aircraft everywhere, hundreds of gliders, Dakotas and Halifax bombers, and when we asked what was going on, we were told that it was a big exercise as part of our continued training. No-one told us that it was going to be on-the-job training. Unusually, there were Military Police all over the airfield and no-one was allowed to leave the base that evening, which made us think that something out of the ordinary was about to happen. Later I understood that maintaining secrecy about the operation was of utmost importance and might help to save our lives. With so many troops involved and the need to organise everything in just a few days, detailed briefing of everyone was just not practical. On reflection, I'm not sure that a briefing before we took off would have helped anyway, since it could not have prepared us for what we were to experience.

The next day, an orange sun lifted lazily into a bright clear blue sky and teased the layered wisps of early-morning mist which, reluctant to leave, cloaked the ground and played between the aircraft in a soundless game of shrouds. The cool still air held the promise of a warm breathless early-autumn day, when the countryside flaunted its bounty of trees laden with fruit and hedgerows bounding narrow lanes and intimate fields burdened with a harvest of nuts and berries and hips. It truly was a day of Keats' mists and mellow fruitfulness; but not for me, because today was also Sunday 17th September 1944, the day which marked the beginning of one of the greatest land battles in British military history.

We were up early that day, had breakfast and then put on our full combat kit and paratrooper helmet. I was issued with fifteen rounds of ammunition, a pack of 'hard tack' biscuits, told to fill my water bottle and then join the line of waiting paratroopers. There were thousands of men on the airfield, all slowly moving forward in a steady line to the waiting aircraft and gliders. Our group was directed to one of the dozens of khaki-coloured Dakotas which were parked in row upon row at the side of the runway, part of Brigadier Hicks' Air Landing Brigade.

There were twenty-two of us in all, our officer, Lieutenant Simmonds, a sergeant, two corporals and eighteen troopers. When it came time to jump out of the aircraft, the red holding light which would come on as we neared the drop zone would go out and a green light would come on. That would be the signal to go and we would leave the aircraft in numbers. The officer would jump first and the rest of us would follow as directed by the jump master, who was part of the aircraft crew. I was to jump number five and so was one of the last to get into the Dakota. We clambered into the aircraft and sat in seats down each side facing one another and waited. I think we all knew that this was different, but we had had no official briefing, still being told that this was just a big exercise.

Around about 09.30 on that Sunday morning, the peace and quiet of the Rutland and Lincolnshire countryside was shaken as hundreds of aircraft engines simultaneously came to life. We heard them starting up across Cottesmore airfield and then the two engines of our own C-47 fired, first one side and then the other. The side door was still open and the noise from outside was thunderous. At 09.45, on twenty-four different airfields across southern Britain, aircraft slowly began to move. A few minutes later, the note of our Dakota engines changed, the jump master closed the rear door and we eased forward, turned, held for a moment then started down the runway. Sitting near to the rear of the aircraft, I felt the tail come up and heard the increasing noise of the tyres on the ground and of the engines as she raced towards take-off speed, then it was just the engines; we were up and slowly climbing. Line after line of aircraft steadily left the ground behind and headed out for the gathering point over the town of March.

On other airfields in Gloucestershire and Oxfordshire, troop carriers, tugs and gliders were doing the same; as tug aircraft moved forward, so the coils of tow-lines started to run out until, with a gentle jerk, the glider attached to the other end inched forwards; another jerk and the wheels started to roll. The largest airborne armada in the history of the world had begun.

By coincidence, this particular Sunday had been designated as a national Sunday of thanksgiving for our deliverance in the Battle of Britain and the churches across southern England, as elsewhere, were full. As this great armada took to the air and gathered into mile upon mile of close-formation aircraft, three columns wide, the noise on the ground was overpowering, totally enveloping. For those hymn-singing congregations at the church services, the growing deep reverberation from the engines of hundreds of approaching aircraft filled the naves and chancels until it became a deafening crescendo. No longer able to resist temptation and increasingly unable to hear the organ anyway, at first in twos and threes, then in a steady trickle, the worshippers left their pews and slipped outside to wonder at the spectacle as line upon line of aircraft roared by barely two thousand feet above their heads. Soon whole congregations had poured out of churches across the south to gaze skyward at the seemingly endless stream of aircraft that took half an hour to pass over them. It was a momentous sight to behold and one that nobody in Britain would ever see again.

Two hours later, one German officer stood marvelling in envy and awe at the same sight. Colonel-General Kurt Student, the founder of Germany's parachute forces and commander of the German 1st Parachute Army, could not believe what he was seeing from the balcony of his cottage near Vught. Later, he was to admit that he and his chief of staff, Colonel Reinhardt, 'simply stared, stunned like fools' as wave upon wave of troop transport aircraft, tugs and gliders flew overhead. Turning to Reinhardt, he had said, *"Oh, if ever I had such means at my disposal. Just once, to have as many planes as this!"*

Presently, we crossed the Suffolk coast at Aldeburgh and Lt. Simmonds stood up to brief us.

"Well, chaps, now that we are over the coast and well on our way, I can tell you where we are going and what we are going to do. As you may have guessed by now, this is not a training exercise but the real thing. We are part of the largest airborne assault ever mounted. We are going to Arnhem in Holland to seize the bridge over the Rhine. We will need to hold the bridge for about four days until XXX Corps get there and relieve us. The American 101st and 82nd Divisions are going to capture the bridges to the south at Eindhoven and Nijmegen, but we get the prize, the bridge at Arnhem.

"Unfortunately, we won't be able to jump very close to the bridge. The drop zones are about seven or eight miles away. Still, the Intelligence chaps do not expect the opposition to be up to much, mainly old men and young boys, but for all that, I don't think that this will be a push-over. Anyway, we'll find out when we get there, so be ready for anything."

He then went on to tell us what our specific role was to be and finished by asking if there were any questions.

"Yes, sir," asked one of the lads, "why are the drop zones so far away? Won't we lose the advantage of surprise?"

"Well, the operation planners thought that it would be better if we landed on solid ground rather than in the flooded polders or amongst the spires and buildings of the town. It's the best we can do, I'm afraid, chaps, and we'll just have to get on with it."

For a while the Dakota droned on across the sky, part of a group of about thirty aircraft in our serial heading for the drop zone. Sitting with my heavy kitbag on my lap, I remember thinking again what a lovely day it was and that the trip so far had been just like a training exercise. I did hope that the bombers which had been over the night before and those that had been out that morning had done a good job and demolished whatever German armour might have been waiting for us. My kitbag contained my webbing, ammunition, digging tool, field dressings and all my other combat kit. My knife, in its sheath, was strapped to my leg and the kitbag and Sten gun were attached to my belt by a long cord and the idea was that I would lower them to the ground during my descent. It was a good theory to reduce the impact upon landing of the great weight we carried; however, some lads lost their grip on their bags as they jumped causing the cord to snap, so losing everything as the bags smashed into the ground.

Suddenly we were all wide awake; some anti-aircraft and small arms fire started to come up at us as we crossed the Belgian coast. Fortunately, it didn't last long; there wasn't a lot of it and our fighter escort of rocket-firing Typhoons peeled away to attack the gun positions, taking them out. Then, just before 13.30 hours, the red light on the aircraft bulkhead lit up and the jump master ordered us to 'Stand up and hook on'. It was almost time to go. I stood up and connected the strap inside the aircraft to my parachute ring, tested the line and then called out in my turn that I was properly hooked on. Anxiously, I waited for the green light to show. I could feel my heart beating inside my chest as the adrenalin started to pump through my veins. Would the aircraft be hit before we got out? Would my parachute open? What was waiting for me out there? Would I survive?

The jump master pushed the rear hatch of the Dakota open and, standing in the doorway with the wind flapping in his battle smock, Lt. Simmonds turned to us and shouted above the roar of the engines, "Good luck, everyone. See you all on the ground."

Then the green lit up and the jump master called out, "Number one, jump; number two; number three; number four;" the corporal in front of me disappeared and I moved into the gale at the open doorway ready to go. "Number five", a pat on the shoulder and at fifteen hundred feet I jumped into a 120-mile-an-hour slipstream. Instantly, the line jerked hard to open my parachute, forcing the air out of my lungs with a grunt and I slipped underneath the tail of the Dakota, grimly hanging on to my kitbag as the wind tearing at my face and body tried to rip it from my arms. For what seemed an eternity, but actually only a few seconds, I tumbled through the air until I felt the jolt as the canopy of my parachute fully opened and billowed above me.

I lowered my kitbag on the cord and freed my arms to hold onto the canopy lines ready for my approach. We were the first aircraft in our group and, looking down to the land of Renkum Heath, near Wolfheze, now a thousand feet below, I could see the ground covered with the gliders which had landed twenty minutes or so before us. The pathfinders had marked the drop zone for the gliders with orange and crimson strips and a thin trail of blue marker smoke continued to slowly curl up towards me. I was coming down into the zone but off to the right a little, near to some woods, and I hoped that I wouldn't get pushed too close to them. Landing in trees is not good; but drifting down, everything seemed so calm with only the wind whistling in my ears and the roar of the following Dakotas passing overhead. I looked around me and as far as I could see there were hundreds upon hundreds of white parachutes drifting towards the ground like snowflakes in a winter storm whilst dozens of brightly coloured red, yellow and brown canopies supporting guns, ammunition and equipment tumbled down amongst us.

But now the heath was rushing up to meet me and I tried to pick out the exact spot where I would land, hoping that there would be no hidden rocks as I didn't know exactly what to expect. Then my kitbag hit the ground and with a thump. I followed a second later, rolled over, stood up and released my parachute harness. The ground was hard, but apart from a couple of bruises I knew I was down safely.

The first task was to ensure that my Sten gun was ready to fire, then get the kit out and attach the webbing, ammunition, water bottle, shovel and so on to me and fill my pockets with field dressings. That done, I looked around for Lieutenant Simmonds and the rest of my platoon. We had all made the drop zone in one piece and our next job was to dig slit trenches around the perimeter of the heath to protect the landing area for the gliders that were following us in over the next day or so. Within half an hour, we heard the drone of the tugs and could see more glider trains approaching. At about a thousand feet and a couple of miles away, the gliders started to cast off from the tugs and made their approach to the landing area.

Some came in really well and landed safely, but as the heath filled up others struggled for space, whilst still more came in too fast or collided with other gliders. The air on the heath was full of noise; aircraft overhead, men shouting orders on the ground, the grinding, splintering sounds of wooden gliders crashing and breaking up and the unbearable screams of the men trapped inside, already injured and dying. I was glad that I had come in by parachute. As men tumbled out of the gliders that had landed safely, they set about unbolting the tail sections and pulling out the howitzers, ammunition trailers, jeeps and whatever else they had brought with them. Nevertheless, a lot of much-needed men and kit were lost both on the flight to Holland and in these shattered landings.

The 1st, 2nd and 3rd battalions moved out from the drop zones on different routes towards the bridge. Lieutenant-Colonel John Frost led the 2nd battalion along the lower road on the northern bank of the Rhine. His was the only battalion that was to reach the bridge; although over the next few days, small groups of men, in no more than twos and threes at a time, did manage to fight their way through to join him, no substantial support was able to get through to Colonel Frost.

As Royal Engineers in Brigadier Hicks' Air Landing Brigade, part of our job was to help with getting the jeeps and armour out of the gliders and to secure the landing zones for the gliders coming in with the second and third lifts over the following two days. We had quickly dug in our defensive positions around the perimeter of the landing areas right at the edge of the woods which bounded the heath, but what we didn't know was that we had landed almost right on top of not only the *Panzer* Grenadier Training and Reserve Battalion, but also the 9th and 10th SS *Panzer* divisions. Having been taken completely by surprise, the Germans were very quick to react and at about 16.30, not long after the main forces from the three battalions had left the drop zones to march to the bridge, the sound of gun fire reached us and it was not very far away.

At first we heard small-arms fire, machine guns and mortars, but then, to our horror, the unmistakable roar of heavy artillery reached us. It meant only one thing; tanks. We were lightly armed paratroopers and no match for heavy armour, especially so since it wasn't supposed to be there. As the evening light began to fade and darkness fell, the battle reached us. At this stage it was mainly machine-gun fire and mortars which were directed at us and it came in short bursts from different points in the woods just a few hundred feet away. Crouching in my slit trench I could hear the bullets whiz and whine as they passed by, uncomfortably close. We had been sent out from England with very little ammunition, but earlier in the afternoon, fortunately, we had taken the opportunity to substantially increase our supplies from the dead and seriously injured in the gliders which had crashed on landing. We were going to need it now.

It was very dark out on the heath, but in the woods it was pitch black and it was impossible to see anything in there at all. Nevertheless, they seemed to be full of Germans and it felt as if they were all firing at me. I carefully raised my head above the level of the slit trench so that I could see where the shooting was coming from. Against the blackness, I could see the little spurts of white light from the gun barrels and took aim at one of them. Gently I squeezed the trigger of my Sten gun and felt it kick in my hands as two or three rounds sped towards their target in the inky black of the woods. Quickly, I ducked again as the return fire threaded through the wood, sending lethal splinters from the tree trunks flying into the air, and thudded into the ground in front and behind the trench.

It was like that nearly all night; we had no chance of sleep and had nothing to eat but a few biscuits and a drink of water. At one point, the Germans set fire to part of the woods to try to burn us out. However, a company of our lads managed to slip round behind them and drive them into their own fires and next morning the news began to filter back to us that one of our units had killed a German general on the road at Wolfheze. It turned out to be General Kussin, the Arnhem commander. It all pointed to how bitter the fighting for that bridge would be over the next few days.

We had been told to expect the second lift bringing in Brigadier Hackett's 4th Parachute Brigade and much-needed reinforcements of men and supplies to arrive at 10.00 on Monday morning. However, it did not appear. This made a bad situation even worse for us because the Germans had by now realised that it was the bridge that we were after and they were starting to use the *Panzer* tanks to cut us off from it. If they turned those tanks onto the landing zones, they would easily push us off and the 4th Brigade would get cut to shreds as it tried to land. It was vital that we held on, but it was becoming more difficult as each hour passed. We didn't know it at the time, but whereas the weather was bright and clear with us in Holland, it was a typically foggy morning in England and the aircraft could not take off.

By mid-morning wide stretches of the heath were burning. Mortars had exploded in some of the Horsa, Waco and Hamilcar gliders, setting them on fire, fires which were making the heath a blazing mass of flame into which the next lift would be dropping. Time and again, the Germans swept the area with deadly machine-gun fire, keeping up the pressure on us. As we had done for most of the night, we fixed bayonets and charged them to push them back into the woods, sometimes with hand-to-hand fighting; above all, we had to keep control of the drop zones. There was smoke everywhere and all morning Luftwaffe fighters had come in and strafed the heath.

The noise of the battle seemed constant; exploding mortar shells, the stutter of machine guns, the crack of rifle fire, the screams of men injured on both sides. Everywhere we were under attack. Snipers had managed to get into some of the empty gliders and were able to shoot anyone who moved on the heath. We went about setting on fire as many of these wrecks as we could to deny the snipers a hiding place; but they were in the trees around the edges of the wood as well and much harder to get at. There must have been about a hundred gliders burning across the heath throughout the morning's fighting. Then at last, around 14.00 we heard the steady drone of aircraft; the 4th Brigade was here. I looked up and could see hundreds of aircraft approaching from the south, and everywhere around them were the tiny dots of the accompanying fighters forming a blanket screen against the Luftwaffe, which was why we hadn't been strafed during the last hour.

Back in the cover of my slit trench, I strained my eyes at the approaching force and could see the gliders dipping below the tails of the tugs and making for the landing zone. But it was very different from the day before. These gliders were coming into a full-scale battle. The heath was littered with wrecked and abandoned gliders from Sunday's drop, many of which were now on fire, others still occupied by snipers. Most of the pilots seemed to be aiming for the middle of the zone, but it was already too crowded, and as the heath filled up, the casualty rate escalated along with the struggle for landing space. Crash followed crash as gliders came in too fast or collided with others in the diminishing clear heath land.

Nevertheless, through the smoke and unrelenting machine-gun fire, these very courageous pilots brought their gliders in and, despite the appearance of devastation on the heath, they were for the most part successful; however, as the lads poured out of them, they were caught by the enemy's machine guns and mortar fire. The Germans had also brought up mobile anti-aircraft guns. The noise was terrible now as a deafening barrage was put up against the low-flying tugs and gliders. I saw two combinations shot down like this, flames steaming out from the aircraft as they hurtled towards the ground dragging their gliders with them.

Then the Dakotas came over and the paratroopers started to jump into this cauldron of death. We were doing everything we could to cover them and in the end, incredibly, most seemed to get down in one piece, although I did see several hit by tracer fire as they helplessly floated earthwards. Once on the ground, the troopers had to run for their lives to gain some cover, often covering just a few yards at a time. The snipers were picking them off as they struggled out of their parachute harnesses or tried to gather their weapons. It was chaotic. Between the snipers, the machine guns and the blazing heath land, it is astonishing that anyone made it through safely.

All this time, we were firing back at the German positions, which we now knew were occupied by battle-hardened SS troops. The noise had become even worse and was overpowering. The whole heath was filled with the sound of explosions, heavy artillery fire, the chattering stutter of machine guns, the grinding crunches of gliders colliding and the sharp cracking of their timber frames snapping like matchwood; and yet above all this terrible noise I could still hear the screams of the young men trapped inside them. One had crashed very close to where we were and we could hear the agonised cries of the injured men who were still inside. We had pushed the Germans who were close to our positions back into the woods for the time being but they were still close enough to be able to shoot at our lads as they parachuted in, and the snipers were deadly.

Three medics arrived in our trench and spoke to our sergeant, saying that they were going into the glider closest to us to help the injured in there and that they could do with some help.

"Right, four volunteers to come with me to the Horsa," the sergeant asked. Before I knew what was happening, I had volunteered for the job.

The rest of the platoon gave us covering fire as we ran across the open ground of the heath to the twisted and broken shell of the Horsa. Many of the troopers inside were already dead but a lot more were injured and needed to be got out and behind the glider for shelter, such as it was, to receive treatment. Some of them had horrific injuries, with arms and legs having been torn off; others had dreadful head injuries and others still had their stomachs ripped open from the heavy equipment inside the glider, which had been thrown about in the crash landing, like toys in a box. They were in a hell of a state, shouting and screaming in unimaginable pain for someone to come and help them.

There was blood everywhere. The men were covered in it, the floor was covered in it, the sides were covered in it; I had never seen so much blood before. I couldn't believe that it was possible for there to be so much. Trying not to slip on the wet floor or tread on anyone, I carefully worked my way through the bodies and the injured to help the medics identify who needed attention and who was obviously dead, even to the untrained eye. One lad had been decapitated by a box of ammunition which had broken loose and been thrown through the air on impact; another must have died in terrible pain as I found him with his abdomen slit from side to side and his intestines lying over the floor around him. I found another lad, no older than myself, whose leg was broken. I gave him a shot of morphine and carried him out of the glider. In the open, the air was full of smoke from the burning heath land, but it was giving us a little cover. I laid him gently onto the ground and told him that the medic would be with him soon and then went back into the Horsa to find some more survivors.

One of our blokes was being violently sick through a gaping hole in the fuselage, but despite the stench of blood, intestines, smoke and cordite inside the confined space of the Horsa, strangely I didn't feel sick at all at these sights, I think I was simply numb at the appalling scene, and all the time we were in there, the Germans were shooting at us, whether deliberately or just generally, but either way, bullets were zinging through the shell of the flimsy broken fuselage or ploughing into the ground with a dull thud as we worked away at our humanitarian task.

I had never seen anyone dead before and yet here I was, just turned eighteen, surrounded by bodies, helping to carry wounded men out of a glider over their dead comrades. Once we were sure that all the wounded were out, we set about lifting the bodies of the dead troopers out onto the heath. At least most of them would be identified now and get a decent burial later. We collected up as much ammunition, medical supplies, food and water as we could and ran back to our trenches. It took four such trips to the Horsa to recover all the supplies that we needed, and all this time, the enemy were firing at us, they never let up; I was sure that I would be hit before I got to cover each time, but in the end we all made it safely back even though the Germans were desperate to stop us getting the ammunition and supplies.

Whilst all this was happening, another glider came in and crashed nearby. The two pilots had been wounded by ack-ack on the way in. They had done remarkably well to get down at all. I saw four lads stumble out, that was all, and then a sniper in the trees shot one of them as he struggled to his feet. Some more of the men from my company ran across to the Horsa and pulled the two pilots out and then they opened fire up into the trees with their Sten guns around where they thought the sniper was; a moment later there was a clatter amongst the branches as a rifle crashed to the ground, followed by the lifeless body of an SS soldier as he tumbled into view, suspended from his safety rope, slowly swinging like a discarded puppet.

Not long after this, the enemy seemed to withdraw from around the perimeter and we were ordered to move out and make our way through the woods and fields towards the bridge. Tired, cold and hungry, we set off, and then it began to rain. As it got dark we dug in and tried to get some shelter. We didn't have any protective clothing, only groundsheets, and as the rain cascaded down all night long, it soaked everything. There was no sleep that night as the woods were full of Germans and they would shoot at anything that moved; they had more ammunition than we did.

At first light we started to move towards Arnhem. There were twelve of us in my own group and we carefully threaded our way through the woods beside the road that led to the town. It wasn't long before we came across the signs of the fighting the day before; British and German soldiers lay dead throughout the woods, sometimes a solitary body, at other times there would be several together. Whenever we could we replenished our ammunition and field dressings from our dead comrades, but no-one had any food and we were very short of water, despite all the rain the night before.

The bullets split the bark of the tree above my head; instantly I dropped flat to the ground, trying to see where the shots had come from. One of the others in the group saw the machine-gun position up ahead and we gave him cover as he edged around the trees until he was close enough to throw a grenade into the middle of it. With a resounding thump, the grenade exploded, killing one of the crew and injuring the other two; we quickly charged forward and shot them. We had no facilities to take prisoners and, quite honestly, we didn't feel like doing so. Throughout the battle, whilst instances of chivalry were recorded, no quarter was given by either side, and we had seen too many wounded British soldiers shot by Waffen SS infantry and snipers to be feeling very charitable.

Taking great care, all day we edged forward until we got close to Oosterbeek, where we were joined by another outfit. There were mainly British forces in this area, but snipers were still a real problem and the further towards the bridge we pushed, the more contact with the enemy there was. We were little more than three miles from the bridge now but were pinned down. The Germans knew that Colonel Frost's 2nd Battalion was running out of ammunition and would have to surrender if not relieved. They had plenty of weapons and ammunition; all their own and most of ours which had been dropped by the supply aircraft. Once they had overrun the drop zones we became starved of supplies and were now really struggling, so we dug in for a third night. According to the plan, XXX Corps were due to be here by now, but there was no sign of them and hope that they would get to us in time was fading. During the night, we got orders from General Urquhart that we were to stay where we were and create a defensive position around Oosterbeek.

The Dutch civilians were incredibly brave. On our way to the bridge we came across a farm; the sergeant sent a couple of lads ahead to see if the occupants were friendly. Like so many of their countrymen, they took the worst of the wounded into their homes, and hid others. Even General Urquhart was hidden in one family's attic for several hours. Many of the houses had holes in the walls, covered up with furniture, and they would pass trapped soldiers and the walking wounded through these holes into the care of others to prevent the Germans from capturing them and to give them the chance to get back to their own lines. They would guide them to the Rhine and then, well, it was up to the individual what they were able to make of their chance for escape.

During the dark, we made more of our positions around Oosterbeek; there were hundreds of us in small groups scattered amongst the woods and meadows around the village, all the way down to the Rhine. We were in a small pocket and then, as the daylight broke on Wednesday morning, they attacked us time and again. I had arrived in what the Germans would soon come to call *Der Hexenkessel*, the witches' cauldron, because from now until the end of the battle, the fighting in this small area around Oosterbeek remained so intense, ferocious and unrelenting.

I was tired, dirty, unshaven, hungry and thirsty; we had had no sleep or proper food since leaving England. The fighting never let up long enough and it was about to get worse. We had defended our improved slit trenches all day but during the late afternoon, the enemy had managed to get too close and we were in danger of having hand grenades lobbed at us.

"Fix bayonets, lads," came the order from the sergeant, and then we were up and charging at the Germans, firing as we ran and yelling our war cry "Whoa Mohammed" at the tops of our voices. It's surprising the impact this can have on an enemy soldier, and, Waffen SS or not, they retreated very rapidly and didn't come that close again for the rest of the day. But the machine guns, mortar bombs and the snipers never let up; they were at us all the time.

I was slightly to the west of Oosterbeek and being constantly shelled; there seemed to be no let-up in it. The German tanks and heavy armour were gradually squeezing us from three sides. Mortars and shelling had reduced this quiet pretty little village to a wasteland; virtually every house had been badly damaged, many had been completely destroyed, and the bodies of dead soldiers and civilians lay everywhere.

As Thursday morning 21st September dawned, we had news that XXX Corps tanks were within range. This gave a huge boost to our morale and then the first salvos came whistling over our heads, exploding amongst the Germans just a few hundred yards away, giving them a terrible fright. The British heavy armour kept up the barrage for what seemed like hours, and then, in the late afternoon, the enemy fire was no longer coming at us; the long-awaited Polish reinforcements had arrived, and just like the drop on Monday, they parachuted into the middle of a raging battle. Their drop zone was across the river from ourselves, on the south side at Driel and they took the full force of the German fire as they floated helplessly down to the ground.

All through that long afternoon we fought to hold every inch of ground, hoping that the Poles would be able to get across those four hundred yards of the Rhine to reach us on the northern bank. But as the day wore on, the prospect seemed increasingly bleak. On Friday morning, the weather was miserable and damp. Already cold and desperately tired, it did nothing to lift our spirits, and then I heard the squeaking, clanking rattle that betrayed the approach of a tank. A few moments later, a Tiger tank appeared coming along a woodland track towards us. We did not have a Piat anti-tank weapon and could do nothing to stop it, so we had to pull back and let it pass. We were squeezed a little more.

We knew by now that the 2nd Battalion on the bridge, despite the desperate house-to-house fighting, must have run out of ammunition and been forced to surrender, with a prison camp awaiting them. For me, time had lost all meaning; the whole battle just seemed to extend into one long struggle for survival. Inch by inch, tree by tree, the Germans pushed us further back into Oosterbeek and towards the Rhine. I remember someone saying that it was Sunday. We had been here a week. It was the eighth day of the battle and yet I had no impression of the passing days. What we feared most was being completely wiped out; our ammunition was now desperately low and we could not last much longer. Almost everyone had been wounded and their once clean field dressings were now, like our uniforms, dirty, blood-stained and ripped. Troopers crouched in slit trenches, dug-outs and gun pits waiting for the next attack, saving precious ammunition until we had a target to shoot at.

All morning and into the afternoon, the sounds of fighting echoed around the woods; the metallic chattering of machine guns, the crump explosions of mortars, the deep rumble of diesel engines giving away the presence of tanks and self-propelled guns, the sharp crack of rifle shot and the agonised screams of injured men. Then at 15.00, silence. The guns had stopped. It felt strange after eight days of continual battering noise. The medical officers of the two sides had negotiated a truce to evacuate the severely wounded, German and British alike, although it was an uneasy truce at first as the occasional shot echoed through the woods.

We used the time to strengthen our position and, most importantly, to collect some fresh ammunition. We had long since run out of field dressings and there was nothing that could be done but tighten the knots on the already blood-soaked bandages. Those of us who were not seriously wounded stayed where we were whilst the seriously injured were carried out. I was so thirsty. I had had nothing to eat or drink all day. My few biscuits were long gone, eaten, now there was nothing; but more than anything, I so wanted a drink of cool clean water.

At the stroke of 17.00, the carnage started again exactly where it had stopped; in a matter of moments the ceasefire faded as if it had been nothing more than a pause for breath. The shells came in again, followed by machine-gun fire. The Germans had done the same as we had during the ceasefire, consolidated their positions and carefully identified ours.

Further down the line from where I was, the few Poles who had managed to get across the river during the nights since their drop had some old scores to settle and they took no prisoners; I was very glad that we were on the same side.

Late on Sunday evening, the enemy began to push hard at our positions on the western perimeter of the pocket. Still desperately short of ammunition, we were opposed by forces that had plentiful weapons and ammunition, much of it British. At one time, earlier in the battle, I had thought that each time I raised my head above the rim of the slit trench, I might get it blown off; I hated the snipers. Now I was too weary to even think about it, I was totally focused upon survival and that meant making sure we were not overrun.

In the half-light of the dusk, made darker and brought on earlier by those autumn leaves that were left on the trees, I peered hard to see any movement. Just a glimpse was all I needed, and there it was. I felt my Sten gun vibrate in my hands, the others beside me joined in. Three of the young men I had seen through the trees sagged at the knees and fell to the ground. The others, however many, faded away. Shortly afterwards, our slit trench was being shelled with mortars. To stay meant certain death; they had our range and we had to move again. Carefully crawling across the woodland floor, returning fire and keeping behind the trees as we went, we withdrew. The pocket had shrunk again; we had been squeezed a little tighter.

During the night, I could hear heavy fighting taking place down by the river. Heavy German machine-gun fire and hand grenades were being answered by Bren guns and British grenades, but if we lost our foothold on the river bank, we were trapped and our fate sealed, it would be death or a prison camp; there could be no escape.

Monday morning, 24th September dawned once more wet and miserable. The clattering of tank tracks and the deep roar of their engines seemed even louder now, ever closer. From over the river, the guns of XXX Corps continued with the bombardment of the German positions, supporting what was left of our own artillery. Without that barrage we would have been crushed days ago, but even so, the odds were too great and during the day we struggled hard to hold our position, by now almost inside the wrecked village of Oosterbeek. Throughout the day their troops pressed hard in attack after attack, but we held them back; and all the time the rain got heavier.

At around 19.00 on that soaking wet Monday night, we got word that we were pulling out. At first I couldn't take it in. I had never given a thought to withdrawing; I thought that we would stay until we ran out of ammunition or men. The medics, radio operators and those too badly injured to make the river crossing would stay behind to provide covering fire and to give the impression that we were continuing to fight on.

The evacuation would start in two hours, but as Royal Engineers, we would be responsible for marking the route through the woods down to the river bank, part of it with white tape for the troopers to follow. Behind us, the glider pilots would act as guides taking the men along this route to where the boats would be waiting to ferry them across to the southern bank, although in the event many men had to swim the river under fire in order to escape.

I carefully withdrew from the battle front and, with the others, followed the sergeant to the point where we met up again with Lieutenant Simmonds. The teeming rain, which had already soaked every inch of my battered uniform and paratrooper's smock, now ran down my back and legs, washing the blood from my dressings into my boots.

The British 1st Airborne Division, or what was left of it, together with 160 Poles and 75 Dorsets of the 43rd Wessex Infantry Division which had managed to get across the river to reinforce us, were now confined to a small thumb-shaped pocket, the base of which was barely 650 yards of river bank; but it was our back door out of *Der Hexenkessel*.

Silence was the key to this evacuation. We were forbidden to tell anyone what we were doing. If the Germans found out that we were withdrawing, they would rush the lightly defended perimeters and annihilate us. With our boots wrapped in any sort of cloth that we could find to deaden the sound of our footsteps, we worked in total silence, marking the route and at the same time watching out for the many German patrols which constantly tested the perimeter defences.

Finally, just before 21.00, suddenly totally exhausted, drained of every drop of energy, cold, hungry, thirsty, my last job done, I found myself at the water's edge of the River Rhine, where I was greeted silently by a Canadian engineer, part of the team that had brought the precious few boats available across the river under the noses of the Germans, to take us back. Then at the stroke of 21.00, a massive barrage started again from XXX Corps' guns, bombarding different parts of the German positions on the northern bank. As soon as it started, the Canadian told me to get into the nearest boat. I hadn't realised as I had stood on the bank for those few moments that troopers were already queuing up behind me and all along the water's edge. In no time the small boat was full, the motor running and, with the Canadian engineer steering, we set off to cross the four hundred yards of open water that had been the grave of so many brave troops who had tried to reach us over the last few days.

The little canvas craft seemed so small and fragile as it doggedly ploughed against the heavy river current in the driving rain. Leaving the dark shadows of the bank behind, we came out into the light cast over the water by the fires and exploding shells which XXX Corps were bombarding the enemy positions with on the three sides of the collapsing pocket. At any moment the German gunners might see us and rake the boat with machine-gun bullets. The passing of time had long since lost any sense of scale and I have no idea how long the crossing took, but presently I felt the canvas bottom beneath my feet bump and scrape on the muddy southern bank at Driel. Almost too tired to move, I clumsily clambered out and was helped by unseen hands up the slippery slope and on to the high embankment.

I turned and looked back to where the incessant noise of battle still raged and where the sky from Oosterbeek to Arnhem was lit by the orange glow of a hundred fires. It seemed that with each new exploding shell, the sky was wrenched open again like a wound from which bright flashes of light poured into the ground, just as the blood of enemies and civilians alike had freely poured over the last nine days. Standing there, I could hardly believe that I was still alive, that I had come through it all, that I had survived *Der Hexenkessel*.

"Come on, lads, keep moving. Watch your step. There's a cup of tea waiting for you at the reception centre."

The formless voice came to me out of the darkness and I felt a tap on my shoulder; it was time to go and I lurched unsteadily down the steps and joined the line of bedraggled but immensely proud troopers making their way to the reception centre, where I had my first cup of tea since breakfast on 17th September. It wasn't supposed to have been like this, we had been told that we would be in Arnhem for four days; we were there for nine.

At the centre, Lt. Simmonds turned up together with our sergeant and a few of the other sappers I had jumped with. Throughout the hours of darkness, I was moved down the line and away from the bloody carnage in which I had lived for those nine terrible days and nights. Presently our little group came into Nijmegen and in the daylight, we were escorted by the American 82nd Airborne over the hard-fought-for captured bridge. From there we were moved further south until we reached Eindhoven when we met up with the Screaming Eagles, the American 101st Airborne, who, despite their own struggle to capture their bridges, could not believe the hellish state that we were in. Most of us were unshaved, unwashed, soaking wet, and with eyes that were red raw and sunken from the fatigue of nine days and nights without proper sleep; but we still marched with our heads high.

We bivouacked with the 82nd and they gave us some proper food, as only the Americans can. Then those of us who could tried to get some sleep, but it was much harder than I had expected; there were too many images keeping me company. The next day, the Screaming Eagles gave us breakfast and they put us into some trucks which sped us south and out of Holland. I was on my way home.

I arrived back in England with a group of other paratroopers and was given transport to Chatham Barracks. Although by now we had had the chance to get properly cleaned up and shaved, we were still only dressed in the kit that we had come out of the battle with, which was dirty, torn and blood-stained.

Arriving at Chatham, we were greeted by the RSM with, "Who the hell are you lot?"

We stood to attention and the corporal said, "1st Airborne Division returning from Arnhem, sir."

"My God, we thought you blokes were all dead. At ease."

It quickly became obvious that they didn't know what to do with us to start with, and so in true army style, they gave us some money, fresh uniforms and sent us home on leave and out of the way for a week until someone decided what to do with us. At the end of that leave, most of which I spent either sleeping or having a couple of beers, I was sent to a holding camp to await my next posting. I knew that I was being sent somewhere hot by the number of injections that I was given; sure enough, I was destined for India and then the Burmese jungle.

My eldest brother, Maurice, had been killed by a mine at Tobruk in 1941, but my other brother, Roy, was already out in Burma serving with the Chindits. On one occasion, after some very intense fighting, his unit had to withdraw from their positions, but his mate had been badly wounded. Roy lifted him on to his back and carried him through the jungle and across a shallow river. Leaving him behind to fall into the hands of the Japanese was not something he would have considered doing, even though carrying his pal slowed Roy down. All the time that they were pulling back, they were under constant fire, especially when crossing the river.

Eventually, having reached safety, Roy laid his friend down, only to find that he was dead, killed by a bullet in the back; a bullet which would otherwise have killed my brother. Nevertheless, there is no escaping the likelihood that someone deliberately shot a wounded man being carried to safety. It was a far cry from the several instances of British and German soldiers dressing each other's wounds in the midst of the Arnhem battle field.

So, in late 1944 we set out by ship from Liverpool bound for India, sailing past Gibraltar into the Mediterranean, through the Suez Canal and across the Arabian Sea to Bombay. I was with what was known as 'the oil and water' platoon and our job was to dig wells for water and lay the pipes to carry it to central points around the various camps. Inevitably we were moved around a great deal from camp to camp. We had a team of bricklayers with us, who would line the wells once we had dug them out and reached the water table. In addition to this water being piped, it was also run into five-gallon drums and then parachuted to our troops who were still fighting in the jungle.

It was whilst I was in India that I learned that I had been Mentioned in Dispatches for my actions on the heath at Arnhem and for helping with the wounded from the glider whilst under constant enemy fire. I had not given any thought to what I had done that day but I was, and remain, immensely proud to be able to wear the bronze oak-leaves emblem on my medal ribbon.

After a short time in India with the oil and water platoon I was posted on to Rangoon in Burma. Having shared the European theatre of war with my father, I was now about to share the Far East theatre with Roy. My job here was as part of the team that supplied the jungle troops. We used the good old ubiquitous Dakota most of the time, but there were also some modified Lancasters. These carried a much larger payload and were altered to have rear doors out of which we could push the supplies. Sometimes on these trips I would look back out of the doorway and see the line of parachutes floating down to the jungle beneath us and remember the sight of all those parachutes around me as I had floated towards Arnhem. It already seemed so long ago.

One of the great problems we had was that the fighting on the ground was a very fast-moving action as our troops inexorably pushed the Japanese out of the country, and from the air all we could see was jungle. Our lads had no permanent camp down there and so we would try to find a clearing amongst all those trees and swamps that the parachutes could land in, with the pilot also having to allow for the drift of the wind and the direction of the fighting, trying to ensure that the Japanese did not get to the supplies; but inevitably on occasions they did.

Flying in a flight of three aircraft at a time, we would repeat these drop missions as often as we were asked to do so by the ground troops through radio messages and bring to them whatever it was that was needed most, ammunition, food, water, or medical supplies. All the materials were packed into nets or containers and then dropped under the parachutes, but of course the Japanese could hear the aircraft approaching and would try to get to the clearings first and take the supplies. It took us about two hours' flying time to get to where the supplies were needed and often by then the fighting had moved on and so had the troops.

It all made me realise how difficult it had been for the RAF crews bringing our supplies into Arnhem and also I knew how desperately important it was for the lads on the ground to get the drops. Because the Germans had overrun our drop zones, not only couldn't we access our supplies but the Germans had ours as well as their own. We ran so low on everything that eventually the outcome at Arnhem became inevitable; I did everything I could do to make sure that the same thing didn't happen here.

Our ground and air forces gradually pushed the Japanese out of Burma, but it was the atomic bombs on Hiroshima and Nagasaki which finally brought an end to the war. Whatever the view about using those atomic weapons, there is no doubt that they saved the lives of thousands of Allied troops who would otherwise have had to fight on every little island, all the way to Japan, and then effect yet another invasion. The war could have dragged on for many more months, possibly years.

I know only too well what it is like to fight against a determined enemy, and the Japanese were not only determined but fanatical too, which made them particularly dangerous. As it was, we had to carry out the drops of supplies to our ground troops all the way right up to VJ Day, 15th August 1945, and for a short time afterwards too.

The war may have been over, but there was no relief for the Royal Engineers, and in late 1945 I was posted to the newest war zone: Palestine. I would be there for two years, until just before the last British troops left and Israel declared independence. The Jews who came to Palestine after World War Two were not welcomed by the Arabs and during the time that I was there, a great deal of terrorist activity took place. It seems that not a great deal has changed in the intervening years.

I was posted to Haifa, but our base was out of the town, up in the orange groves where we lived in tents. The terrorists would place home-made bombs, IEDs in today's language, in the many tunnels which ran under the roads and each morning it was the responsibility of the Royal Engineers to inspect every one of these tunnels together with the drains and other likely hiding places.

When moving around Haifa, we stayed on the trucks. The Palestinian police were British volunteers and were very unpopular with the locals. However, they helped us a great deal and showed us the places to watch out for. Despite the nice weather, it was not a good time to be at the eastern end of the Mediterranean Sea.

In late 1947 I was posted to Germany, to Hameln of Pied Piper fame. At the conclusion of the Nuremberg war trials, eleven Nazi leaders were sentenced to death by hanging; afterwards I was part of the team which dismantled the gallows.

The Bailey bridge system, that wonderful British invention which the American 101st Airborne Division had made such good use of at the Son crossing over the Wilhelmina Canal on the road to Arnhem, was my next job. It was for me to issue the bridge pontoons, the part which floats across the water and carries the roadway, to the different regiments who were practising the building techniques under the watchful eyes of the Royal Engineers.

After Haifa, Hameln was a great relief. We lived in the Bridging Camp; there were only six of us in the unit; an officer, an RSM, a sergeant, a corporal and two sappers. During the day we carried out our proper duties, but we had no parades to bother us, and in the evening we were free to go out into the town and do whatever we wanted to so long as we did not break the German law. We certainly had a few good nights and, for the first time in my army career, nobody was trying to shoot me every day.

In 1948, I was made up to corporal and posted back to the Mediterranean, but this time to the western end, to Gibraltar, which was very good. The border between Gibraltar and Spain was still closed as this particular piece of very valuable British territory was hotly disputed between the two countries. Spain had remained neutral during the war, but had been a safe haven for much German naval and covert activity, but Gibraltar had proved to be an invaluable Royal Navy, RAF and military base for Britain; we were not about to give it up.

Nevertheless, Spain was not off limits to troops as long as they had the necessary visa and as Orderly Corporal, I had the very enviable job of issuing the visas to those who wished to cross over into Spain for a few hours; I was a popular chap.

My time in Gibraltar was very happy; it was a good posting all round. There was proper beer on sale in the pubs, the locals spoke English, the weather was generally very good and I was being paid more than I was during the war. My great friends here were Duggie Farmer, Jimmy Smith and Jim Corby and we spent most of our leisure time together. I remember one of our pastimes was that whenever a Royal Navy ship arrived in the harbour, we would row out to it.

All good things come to an end, and in 1951 I was posted back to Hameln to help finish off the post-war clearing up operation and more Bridging Camp work. One of the many things which struck me about the futility of war whilst I was in Hameln was that whenever we needed supplies, we would go with the German troops in their trucks into Hanover. We had a really good relationship with these troops and often went out drinking with them. They were not so different from us, just young lads in the army. How sad that they had been ordered to try to kill me at Arnhem and I them!

By 1954, I had been in for eleven years and my army service was coming to an end. On returning to Britain, I was promoted to sergeant and along with Jim, Duggie and Jimmy was sent to a holding camp. Gradually as demob progressed, blokes drifted away in twos and threes, and in 1955 it was eventually my turn to enter Civvy Street, a place I had no knowledge of. We all went our separate ways, although I did always keep in touch with Duggie right up until the time he died.

My twelve years in the Royal Engineers were at different times the most exciting, terrifying, interesting, varied and rewarding of my life. After Arnhem and *Der Hexenkessel*, I have valued every day because I could so very easily have for ever stayed in that quiet Dutch town, that *"peaceful sector where nothing was happening"*.

Author's conclusion

Whether Arnhem was indeed a bridge too far, and if so why, will be debated for a long time to come. However, there can be little doubt that there were four major impediments which beset the Allied forces and the British 1st Airborne Division in particular, without which the battle would almost certainly have had a different outcome, the war in Europe would have ended sooner and many lives would have been saved.

The first was the catastrophic failure of British commanders to close off the escape route of van Zangen's 15th Army, allowing 65,000 men and their guns to come into the line. The second was the almost total failure of the British radio communications, both ground to ground and ground to air, resulting in a lack of cohesion and co-ordination during the battle and, critically, a lack of air support to attack the German armour positions. The third was the unfortunate and wholly unforeseeable decision of Field Marshal Model to choose Arnhem as the place for Bittrich's 9th and 10th SS *Panzer* Divisions to rest and refit. The final impediment was the weather. Fog in Britain and Belgium delayed reinforcements reaching General Urquhart, in particular General Sosabowski's

1st Polish Parachute Brigade, and prevented fighter air cover getting off the ground, although the radio communications debacle would have significantly reduced their effectiveness in any event. Overlaying all these factors was the speed and determination with which the German forces under the command of Field Marshal Gerd von Rundstedt, having been caught totally unprepared, responded to Market-Garden, though undoubtedly they were helped by the capture of a complete set of the British plans.

Following the war, Montgomery would point in his memoirs to the fact that 90% of the operation had been a success, and he remained resolute.

> *"In my, prejudiced, view, if the operation had been properly backed from its inception, and given the aircraft, ground forces, and administrative resources necessary for the job, it would have succeeded in spite of my mistakes, or the adverse weather or the presence of the 2nd SS Panzer Corps in the Arnhem area. I remain MARKET-GARDEN's unrepentant advocate."*

> Field Marshal Sir Bernard Law Montgomery,
> *Memoirs. Montgomery of Alamein*, p. 267

After the battle, the Germans evacuated the entire Arnhem area. In the six months from 17th September 1944 until 14th April 1945 when Canadian troops finally liberated the town, some 10,000 Dutch civilians had died, mostly from starvation and cold in the bitter winter which followed Market-Garden and ultimately led to Operation Manna, in which during late April and early May 1945 some of RAF Bomber Command's heavily laden Lancasters flew over Holland and dropped not bombs but food parcels to the starving population.

The Dutch took a more pragmatic view of Operation Market-Garden, expressed by Bernhard, Prince of The Netherlands to Cornelius Ryan in an interview for the book, *'A Bridge Too Far'*,

"My country can never again afford the luxury of another Montgomery success."

Notwithstanding Montgomery's view, in the final analysis, without the bridge at Arnhem giving access to Germany, the operation failed. How many additional resources would have been needed and at what point they would have inevitably overwhelmed the defending troops is a matter of conjecture. The Allies went with what they had and what they had amounted to the greatest airborne invasion in history. Whatever the failings, whatever the reasons, what can never be denied is the immense courage of the young men of the 'Red Devils', who gave their all and then some more, to try to achieve the success of Montgomery's plan.

In terms of the personal commitment of the men who went to Arnhem, it was one of the greatest battles in British military history. The unqualified admiration of their German opponents was expressed by the veteran warrior Lt-General Wilhelm Bittrich in a conversation he had with Field Marshal Model during the battle: *"In all my years as a soldier, I have never seen men fight so hard."* However, in terms of military planning and command, it was an unmitigated disaster which achieved little, if anything of any value and yet cost the lives of more Allied troops than during the whole of the first twenty-four hours of D-Day, 6th June 1944.

Perhaps there were too many mistakes at the planning stage, perhaps there was too much optimism amongst the commanders, perhaps there was too little importance given to the intelligence reports, or perhaps, as General Browning had feared at the outset, Arnhem was simply a bridge too far.

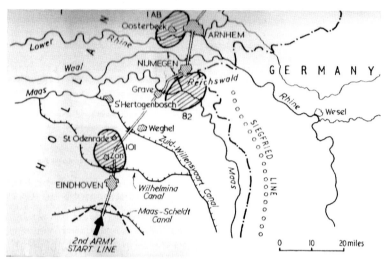

Overall map of Operation Market-Garden.

In the Dakota waiting to go [note the kitbags with cords].

Hitler with some of his élite troops.

1ˢᵗ Polish Parachute Brigade dropping onto waiting German troops.

Fighting in the woods around Arnhem.

The mighty bridge at Arnhem today.

Memorial to British, Polish & Dutch who fought at Oosterbeek.

The author in conversation with Pier at the National Memorial Arboretum.

The Author

Born to Army officer parents at Gibraltar Military Hospital in 1949, Kenneth Ballantyne was educated at schools across Europe, Scotland and England. His father, a career soldier with the Royal Artillery, had served throughout the Second World War, as had his mother, who trained as a nurse at the outbreak of war and then joined the FANY, the First Aid Nursing Yeomanry.

Part of Kenneth's early years were spent living and playing amongst the bomb craters left in the German Ruhr by RAF Bomber Command. At seven, his parents took him and his brother Iain to the Reichswald Forest War Cemetery to educate them both about the true price that had been paid for their lives and freedom, an experience which became an indelible memory for him.

After several years as a police officer, Kenneth graduated and then practised law as a solicitor before retiring to combine his love of writing with his interest in the personal experiences of those who fought the Second World War, an interest which had grown out of that visit to the Reichswald Forest War Cemetery. A member of the Shropshire Aircrew Association, the Bomber Command Association, No50/61 Squadrons Association and No210 [Flying Boat] Squadron Association, he now spends much of his time collecting and recording the true stories and experiences of the men and women who served on the Home Front and in the Armed Services during the war as an important historical project for an enduring legacy.

By giving talks about his books to community groups across the country, Kenneth and his wife Elaine raise money to support several charities, including the Severn Hospice in Shropshire, the Eden Valley Hospice in Cumbria, and the Bomber Command Memorial Fund. He established his own publishing business in 2005 in order to put his first book into print, and other titles have followed.

Bibliography

A Bridge Too Far, Cornelius Ryan [1999 Wordsworth Military Library]

Another Dawn Another Dusk; Kenneth Ballantyne [2009 Laundry Cottage Books]

Britain Since the 1930s; Mandy Barrow

It Never Snows in September; Robert Kershaw

Land Girl: the Manual of The Women's Land Army 1941; WE Shewell-Cooper [2011 Amberley Publishing Plc]

The Home Front; Maureen Hill

The Women's Timber Corps; Rosalind Elder [2009]

U-boat.net